MONEY GAMES

MONEY GAMES

**Profiting from
the Convergence of
Sports and
Entertainment**

David M. Carter

STANFORD BUSINESS BOOKS

An Imprint of Stanford University Press

Stanford University Press
Stanford, California

© 2011 by the Board of Trustees of
the Leland Stanford Junior University

Library of Congress Cataloging-in-Publication Data

Carter, David M.
 Money games : profiting from the convergence of sports and
entertainment / David M. Carter.
  p. cm.
 Includes bibliographical references and index.
 ISBN 978-0-8047-5955-7 (cloth : alk. paper)
 1. Sports—Economic aspects. 2. Sports—Economic aspects—
United States. 3. Sports—Social aspects. 4. Sports—Social aspects—
United States. I. Title.
GV716.C363 2011
306.4'83—dc22

                                        2010012010

Printed in the United States of America on acid-free, archival-
quality paper

Typeset at Stanford University Press in Helvetica and 10/14 Minion

Special discounts for bulk quantities of Stanford Business Books
are available to corporations, professional associations, and other
organizations. For details and discount information, contact the special
sales department of Stanford University Press. Tel: (650) 736-1782, Fax:
(650) 736-1784

CONTENTS

Acknowledgments   ix

Introduction   1

Part I: At-Home Convergence   13

1   Television Content   19
2   Video Gaming   45
3   Athlete Branding   68

Part II: Away-from-Home Convergence   93

4   The Internet   99
5   Mobile Technology   125
6   Gambling   147

Part III: At-Venue Convergence   173

7   Sports-Anchored Development   179
8   Venue Technology   204
9   Corporate Marketing   229

Notes   255
Index   277

ACKNOWLEDGMENTS

What began as an exploratory phone call with Stanford University Press in 2007 became one of the most rewarding projects I have ever been associated with, one that substantially contributed to my understanding of the industry I have been involved in for more than twenty years. A dynamic and rapidly changing sports industry made analyzing the convergence of sports and entertainment a daunting task, especially given how our team decided to approach this first-of-its kind research. As indicated below, the enormous breadth and depth of support from those integral to the book's publication three years later served as great validation of our topic and approach to comprehensively covering it. It also served as a constant reminder of the responsibility we had taken on behalf of the sports business industry.

The Sports Business Institute was fortunate to have this endeavor quickly and consistently supported by student researchers. The three-year research process was shepherded by project leads Courtney Brunious, Todd Jacobs, and Phil Wallace, each of whom worked tirelessly to ensure the project was on time and maintained relevancy. I strongly believe they pushed me more than I motivated them. Supporting this group was a battery of students who served as project contributors, researching and analyzing myriad elements of the project, specifically Antranig Balian, Raul Campos, Arturo Castro, Grant Geisen, Dan Graham, Anne Meurs, Ari Shandling, Jonathan Waxman, and Shane Wilson.

It would not have been possible to deploy these students and provide them with the resources required to complete this research absent our funding partners, each of which contributed in ways beyond simply underwriting the project. Instrumental in making this book a reality were Gary Cypres, the founder and CEO of the Sports Museum of Los Angeles; Ernst & Young LLC; Korn Ferry International; Rossetti; Tickets.com; and Yahoo! Sports.

Sports Business Institute advisory board members also materially supported our efforts by serving as sounding boards, making introductions on our behalf to industry executives, reviewing our progress, suggesting courses of action, and serving as interviewees. In addition to Gary Cypres, the Sports Business Institute advisory board members are Fred Claire, Anita DeFrantz, Mitch Dorger, Jim Ellis, Dick Glover, Ed Goren, Bob Graziano, Shawn Hunter, Jeff Moorad, Arte Moreno, Dave Morgan, John Nendick, Ed Roski, Alan Rothenberg, Kathy Schloessman, Jeff Shell, Bill Shumard, and David Simon. Warranting a special acknowledgment is Jim Warsaw, who, as a board member, served as cheerleader, mentor, and close friend throughout. His passing in 2009 had a profound impact on me, and he will be dearly missed by all of us who so regularly sought his counsel and welcomed his sense of humor.

Perhaps the most amazing development witnessed throughout this process was the extent to which the sports business industry at large stepped up and supported our efforts. None of us attached to this project would have ever envisioned so many executives pledging their time and resources to this project; time and resources offered without hesitation. In fact, beyond members of the Sports Business Institute's board, dozens of industry executives made themselves available for personal interviews, offering unparalleled levels of insight, guidance, and support. Without their individual and collective contributions, this research would have been fundamentally lacking. We wish to personally thank Ray Baker, Mike Bidwill, George Bodenheimer, Bob Bowman, JP Brocket, David Campbell, Terry Denson, Frank Fahrenkopf, Brian Farrell, Frank and Lorenzo Fertitta, David Hill, Jack Hill, Robert Hollander, Terry Jicinsky, Perrin Kaplan, Will Kassoy, Blake Krikorian, Tim Leiweke, Sandy Montag, Peter Moore, David Neal, Jeffrey Pollack, Ken Potrock, Ron Ricci, Matt Rossetti, Michael Sepso, Adam Silver, John Skipper, Michael Tchao, Malcolm Thorpe, Larry Witherspoon, and David Yu.

Numerous others helped facilitate the research and made our lives much easier along the way, most notably Linda Barnes, Michael Bass, Pete Dropick, John Drum, Robert Fusco, Gary Hourihan, Tracy Hughes, Rex Kovacevich, Dennis Kuhl, Chris LaPlaca, Rich Levin, Ekta Mangal, Gareth Morgan, Jeff O'Brien, Aaron Pempel, Laurel Prieb, Andy Reif, John Semcken, Bill Simon, Nicola Shocket, Alex Vergara, and Dan Wu.

From USC, the input from Shantanu Dutta, Tony Jennison, and Courtney Surls proved vital. So too did that from the pros at Stanford University Press, especially Margo Beth Crouppen, John Feneron, David Horne, and Jessica Walsh.

Finally, as is always the case, such massive undertakings cannot be successfully completed without substantial family support. My wife, Vickie, and our daughter, Paige, were supportive throughout—as they always seem to be of my professional endeavors.

MONEY GAMES

INTRODUCTION

Sports and entertainment have been converging since the dawn of capitalism, if not before—businesspeople were just slow to notice and identify the monetizing opportunities this trend offered, although they are now making up for lost time. *Convergence* can be defined as "the process of coming together, or the state of having come together, toward a common point." "Common points" can vary, depending on which forces have been converging and what the goals and expectations of such converging entities are, but in the case of the convergence of sports and entertainment, the "common points" or, perhaps more accurately, the desired outcomes, are to build brands and generate revenue and, by extension, increase value for myriad stakeholders in the process. While the story of this convergence can be told from multiple vantage points, this book tackles it from a "sports-moving-into-entertainment" perspective.

Historically, the convergence of sports and entertainment has been relatively contained, primarily taking place in and around sports venues. Today such convergence, like the rest of business, is borderless—both literally and figuratively. Though consumers continue to experience the entertainment aspects of this merging while enjoying sports on location, they increasingly experience it as they relax in the comfort of their own homes watching sports on TV. When traveling for work or pleasure they check their laptops for streaming content of their favorite teams, and while at the office or running errands they frequently check their smartphones for scores and statistics.

The convergence of sports and entertainment is pervasive, and it continues to create business challenges while simultaneously providing significant opportunities for those hoping to make money from it. Although it is often easy to confuse savvy cross-promotion or other tactical marketing initiatives—such as cross-branding—with convergence, the former tends to be less symbiotic and, more often than not, represents short-term, opportunistic marketing and business development. By comparison, convergence typically includes an "experiential" element, providing fans a multidimensional marketing experience in the process.

To gain an even better understanding of what convergence is and how it has evolved and differentiated itself, it is useful to highlight critical milestones that have led to the current era of convergence—an era defined and reinforced by rapid advances in technology, the advent of multifaceted marketing strategies, and mixed-use or themed real estate development.

IN THE BEGINNING: BREAD AND CIRCUS, COLUMBIA VERSUS PRINCETON, AND IMG

About two thousand years ago Roman poet and satirist Juvenal, who routinely denounced what he viewed as the corruption and extravagance associated with the privileged classes in Rome, noted that most Romans seemed content with what he termed their "bread and circuses."[1] To him, "bread and circuses" suggested that rather than express interest in other, more vital and cerebral public interests, especially the arts and other cultural undertakings, Romans were happy to distract themselves with sports and entertainment, particularly chariot racing and gladiator fighting. Events were advertised and promoted, avid fans supported their favorite individual gladiators, gambling on event outcomes was commonplace, and vendors sold special souvenir glass cups and flasks embossed with the names of the most popular gladiators—activities bearing a striking resemblance to today's "game day" experience.

The convergence of sports and entertainment is not a recent phenomenon, but advances in business and technology have dramatically transformed it since the days of Juvenal. In terms of technology, a watershed moment occurred about two thousand years later. Playing in the first-ever televised sporting event in 1939, the baseball teams from Columbia and Princeton universities found themselves at the forefront of media-related convergence.[2] Even though the broadcast elements were limited due to the use of a single camera, one focused along the third-base line, and the broadcast was picked up by only about four hundred sets, this signaled the beginning of a technological movement that continues today—a movement that has captivated advertisers and sponsors, as well as fans, more than seventy years later.

Even then, the power of sports as content was not lost on the networks, which were actually manufacturing and selling their own televisions. Broadcasters, whose goal it was to increase consumer adoption of the television, believed sports would be the compelling hook to drive demand and, shortly thereafter, provide advertisers a platform to reach customers. While not entirely attributable to televised sports, the number of television sets in use by 1950 surpassed ten million—a dramatic increase from just two years earlier when a mere 190,000 sets were in use.[3]

In the years that followed, television broadcasts enabled fans from coast to coast to root for (and against) athletes such as Major League Baseball legend Joe DiMaggio and eventual heavyweight champion Cassius Clay, as the era of personal branding—and the ability to monetize it through endorsements—began in earnest.

More quickly than his competitors, Mark McCormack recognized the inherent value of athletes as both content and pitchmen. While representing and managing such golf icons as Arnold Palmer, Gary Player, and Jack Nicklaus, McCormack launched what would become the sports business industry's first vertically integrated sports management firm, International Management Group (IMG), in 1960. By 1963, McCormack's IMG had become the world's first international agency engaged in the representation of athletes and entertainers because he accurately believed that the popularity and marketability of athletes could transcend borders, cultures, language, and even sports itself. IMG's clients endorsed a wide range of products and did so while touring the globe to participate in exhibitions and tournaments. McCormack regularly made his athletes and entertainers available for corporate hospitality events, further cementing important bonds with corporate America. The company's broadcast division, Trans World International (TWI), established in the 1960s to film a handful of golf events, remains among the world's largest independent television sports production companies and rights distributors. IMG also owns, operates, and represents many major sports properties, including Wimbledon, as well as other sporting events around the world, several sports academies, and even a fashion division that manages and represents top international models. McCormack's approach to positioning his athletes as personal brands and leveraging their notoriety through IMG's stable of holdings could not have come at a more opportune time, as he was at the forefront of a marketing platform that would fundamentally accelerate athlete marketing: the televising of sports in primetime.

ON THE AIR: MONDAY NIGHT FOOTBALL
AND ESPN RESHAPE SPORTS

In what was believed by many to be a risky move, the National Football League (NFL) and American Broadcasting Company (ABC) began shifting one televised football game per week from Sunday afternoon into primetime. The first *Monday Night Football* game aired on September 21, 1970, a bold move that forever changed the television landscape. Appreciating the differences between Sunday afternoon and Monday night viewing audiences, those behind the launch of *Monday Night Football*, NFL commissioner Pete Rozelle and ABC Sports's Roone Arledge, recognized that reaching and, more important, holding onto a broad family audience required a blend of sports and entertainment. By increasing the number and location of cameras used; perfecting the use of storytelling while simultaneously teaching casual fans about the nuances of the sport; providing on-air talent that included Howard Cosell, Frank Gifford, and Don Meredith; and inviting dignitaries and entertainers including Vice President Spiro Agnew, Beatle John Lennon, and Kermit the Frog into the broadcast booth, *Monday Night Football* became one of the most successful shows of all time. *Monday Night Football* ultimately became the second-longest-running primetime show on American broadcast network television (behind *60 Minutes*), and its visionaries were recognized for their contribution to blending sports into entertainment when, in 1999, *The Sporting News* named Rozelle the most powerful person in sports during the twentieth century; he was followed by Arledge at number three.

Perhaps as notable as the building of *Monday Night Football*, the development of the Entertainment and Sports Programming Network (ESPN) was a significant milestone. It was launched on September 7, 1979, and the first program to air on the cable network founded by Scott and Bill Rasmussen was *SportsCenter*, which remains ESPN's flagship program. Beginning with a modest household penetration of 1.5 million homes, and since growing to about 99 million homes, ESPN not only changed how we watched sports but also fundamentally changed how we consume sports, due to its wide range of content and distribution channels.[4] ESPN transformed sports the way MTV forever changed the music industry in 1981 and CNN redefined the news business a year earlier. ESPN has become a lifestyle brand to a generation nicknamed the "Highlight Generation," a reference to *SportsCenter*'s programming format. The cable network continues to put the "E" in ESPN with its original programming, notably movies and made-for-television events, including its award show, the ESPY's; branded sporting competitions, particularly the X-Games; and even themed ESPN Zone restaurants. ESPN measurably contributed to advertisers' ability to reach what had historically been an evasive demographic, young men, and reinforced its ability to do so when, in 2002, it became the first network to hold simultaneously the broadcasting rights of all four major sports leagues. (It bears mentioning that following thirty-six years on ABC, *Monday Night Football* has been televised by ESPN since 2006).

The rapid and consequential evolution of sports on television, highlighted by *Monday Night Football* and ESPN, helped cultivate corporate America's interest in using sports as a vehicle to sell goods and services.

BROUGHT TO YOU BY CORPORATE AMERICA: THE 1984 SUMMER OLYMPICS AND SUPER BOWL ADS

While *Monday Night Football* and ESPN helped cultivate corporate America's interest in sports marketing, the 1984 Summer Olympics in Los Angeles secured it. Following a failed ballot measure that would have helped underwrite the Games using public subsidies, Los Angeles Olympic Organizing Committee president Peter Ueberroth was required to finance the Games through private sources. Ueberroth successfully communicated with corporate America regarding the marketing and business development benefits that would come with linking corporate brands to this unparalleled global sports and entertainment event. As a result, forty-three companies became official sponsors, sixty-four secured the rights to become official Olympic suppliers of goods and services, and licenses were granted to an additional sixty-five companies and organizations. Most of those sponsoring the Games were large, multinational corporations, including Coca-Cola, McDonald's, and Fuji, that received exclusive marketing rights, as well as the right to use Olympic symbols in their advertisements. In addition to being the first privately financed Olympic Games, those held in Los Angeles were also the first to turn a profit for the host city. The unprecedented profit, $215 million—much of which was attributable to Ueberroth's sports marketing acumen—resulted in his being named *Time* magazine's Man of the Year.[5]

The success of the 1984 Games triggered an increase in the cost of doing business with the International Olympic Committee, especially in the areas of sponsorship and broadcast rights. These games also set the stage for the modern era of sports marketing, one in which every league, event, and team—at virtually all levels of competition—seems to be sponsored.

In addition to sponsorship taking hold in the 1980s, so too did advertising during major sporting events. A must-see sporting event that has generated half of the top-twenty-rated TV shows of all time, the Super Bowl, continues to be a source of pride and competition for companies buying advertising time during the game.[6] Coca Cola's 1979 "Have a Coke & a Smile" commercial featuring the Pittsburgh Steelers' "Mean" Joe Greene was followed five years later with what is considered by many to be the most important single television advertisement of all time: Apple Computer's Orwellian "1984" commercial, which introduced the Macintosh computer.

Prior to these advertisements, corporate America had been using the Super Bowl as a marquee platform to reach large audiences, but it may very well have been these two ads that most materially contributed to the Super Bowl becoming a mass entertainment experience for fans and advertisers alike. In the years that followed, advertisers began allocating substantial resources to their Super Bowl ads to ensure they resonated with a viewing audience that had become increasingly interested in watching the ads and debating their effectiveness. In 1989 USA Today created the "Super Bowl Ad Meter" in an effort to gauge consumers' opinions about Super Bowl ads. With this data, USA Today essentially developed a new competition for Super Bowl Sunday, one in which corporate America eagerly participates.

Corporate marketers, such as Pepsi, integrated celebrities and entertainers, notably Michael J. Fox (1987), Ray Charles (1991), Cindy Crawford (1992, 1995), Brittney Spears (2002), and Jackie Chan (2006) into their Super Bowl commercials in attempts to increase awareness and sell more soda. Others continued to rely on a combination of humor, such as Anheuser Busch's series of Bud Bowl ads of the late 1980s and 1990s, and vivid imagery, such as the same company's famed Clydesdales, to reinforce their brands' attributes.

Emerging technologies and the trend toward user-generated content enabled corporate America to extend the marketing reach of its Super Bowl ads by actually placing the fan at the core of the marketing message. Frito-Lay and Chevrolet were among advertisers that aired commercials written and submitted by fans, thereby taking the convergence of sports, entertainment, and business to a new level. Super Bowl advertisers, regardless of their methods or messages, spend handsomely to be a part of the game, with the cost for a single thirty-second spot commanding approximately $3 million, a seventy-five-fold increase since 1967's Super Bowl I.[7]

Of import, marketing and business development opportunities have not been limited to *real* sports, taking place at *real* venues, but regularly include the use of technology.

TECHNOLOGY CHANGES EVERYTHING:
MADDEN AND FANTASY SPORTS

Video games entered the home market as early as the 1970s and created a new entertainment format for sports-craved consumers in the process. However, none have had the impact of Electronic Arts's (EA's) signature sports video game, John Madden Football. Debuting in 1989, it has become North America's best-selling sports video game of all time, selling approximately eighty five million copies and generating about $3 billion in revenue.[8]

Despite the fact that the game play was basic by today's standards, and that the initial game launched with only sixteen of the NFL's twenty eight teams included, it was more the timing of the game's release that altered the video game business. While other products released during the Atari, Nintendo, and PlayStation eras contributed to the emergence of video games as a legitimate art form, it was the Madden franchise that elevated video games beyond "toy" status. By attracting and largely maintaining its loyal following, even as this following matured beyond the traditional video game demographic, Madden Football has secured its place in pop culture, alongside movies, television, and music.

Not only have domestic sales of the game in the United States surpassed the multi-billion dollar mark but the Madden game has spawned numerous other opportunities for EA, including being among the first to successfully integrate a music soundtrack into the game, one record producers clamor to be associated with given the typically elusive target demographic that plays Madden Football. Companion events, such as the Madden Challenge, whereby thousands of participants compete in a global tournament, and the Madden Bowl, in which current NFL players compete against one another during Super Bowl weekend, have enabled the brand to further elevate its status by taking advantage of the melding of sports and entertainment.

Like the Madden video game franchise, the Internet boom of the late 1990s forever changed the way fans consumed and played sports. In addition to delivering more timely news, information, and statistics to rabid fans, the Internet also provided the ultimate framework for sports junkies to participate in sports, given the Internet's ability to efficiently aggregate what was once a modest, low-revenue undertaking: fantasy sports leagues.

In fantasy sports leagues, participants select players from real professional sports leagues and then accumulate points on the basis of the actual statistical performances of their hand-picked players. Websites that host fantasy sports leagues generate revenue from subscriptions and advertising, as do other publishers who sell research and statistical information and content to participants. From their humble beginning in the early 1980s, the once-dubbed Rotisserie Leagues, named after the New York restaurant La Rotisserie Francaise, in which its creators regularly met, grew dramatically in popularity because of the ease of use and scalability brought about by online technologies.

Among the early online entrants was sportsline.com, which in 1998 purchased the rights to commissioner.com, one of the original fantasy websites. To many, this transaction marked the beginning of what was destined to become the fantasy sports phenomena; one that quickly became the thriving, multibillion dollar industry we have today.

With a user demographic consisting of young males willing to pay several hundred dollars a year to participate, fantasy sports quickly drew the attention of major advertisers and sponsors. It also sparked enormous interest from professional sports leagues, which viewed fantasy sports as an opportunity to extend their brands and build viewer interest.

With estimates suggesting that as many as twenty-seven million American adults play fantasy sports, major television networks, including ESPN, have created television programming (including pay-per-view events) and website content specifically targeting these online players and their desire for the latest player information.[9] Consumers are delighted that information about, and the ability to participate in, fantasy sports is now everywhere. But this is not so much the case with employers, who remain concerned about the lost productivity brought about by employees checking their fantasy league statistics during work hours.

The aforementioned examples of convergence incorporate multiple business tenets, and each has provided the impetus from which big business has recognized a compelling opening to establish and build shareholder value. Industry stakeholders are poised and compelled to continue building on this opportunity, as described in the next sections.

WHY ANALYZE CONVERGENCE?

The array of companies, organizations, and individuals affected by the increasingly rapid pace of convergence provides a dynamic backdrop from which to examine established and emerging best business practices. Sports business industry stakeholders affected by—and hoping to profit from—this combination include, but are not limited to, financiers in the investment banking and private equity fields; developers of commercial, retail, and residential real estate; media and technology professionals focusing on enhanced content distribution; corporate marketers desiring to leverage sports to sell products and services; and sports management executives who oversee leagues, events, venues, and athletes.

Each of these professionals recognizes that none of their businesses operate in a standalone fashion anymore but rather are intertwined with multiple business disciplines, often those well beyond their own core competencies. While they strive to supply what they believe to be sought-after sports entertainment, it is in fact consumer preferences and associated demand that are driving a substantial portion of convergence. Stakeholders also acknowledge the incremental shareholder value to be gained by optimizing convergence as it relates to their primary businesses, provided they take evolving consumer wants and needs into account. This is especially the case in an era when doing so routinely requires constructing strategic alliances with partners once considered to be operating unrelated businesses. Properly structured, the strategic alliances brought about by this evolution enable partners to monetize sports becoming entertainment. Finally, because the sports business industry recognizes that this merging will continue unabated, a comprehensive analysis is warranted.

All of these reasons have contributed to the overwhelming show of support provided to this research by prominent industry participants. Not only has their outpouring of support reinforced the timeliness and relevance of *Money Games: Profiting from the Convergence of Sports and Entertainment*, but it also helped frame how such an analysis of convergence should be undertaken.

TACKLING CONVERGENCE

Tackling a topic as expansive as the convergence of sports and entertainment and, more precisely, how industry stakeholders monetize it, is made even more challenging when factoring in the speed with which this phenomenon continues to evolve. All-encompassing, convenient, and linear discussions are all but impossible to frame. So too are analyses that focus on how convergence is delivered to consumers, as these rapidly become unwieldy. Accordingly, *Money Games* describes how stakeholders from the sports and entertainment industries have monetized convergence by presenting and analyzing the interconnected—and ongoing—evolution of the two industries from the consumer's perspective. That is, the focus will be on consumer touchpoints—specifically how and where consumers experience or are otherwise affected by, or exposed to, convergence.

Realizing that fans now have the opportunity to consume sports when and where they choose, and to exercise great discretion in determining precisely what they are willing to consume, it was determined by our research team that identifying the primary locales where these activities occur made sense. Further, by focusing on these locales separately, it is possible to partition distinct areas to examine while simultaneously minimizing the potential for overlap yet highlighting the symmetry between and among the topics analyzed. Therefore, the book has been divided into three sections:

Part 1: At-Home Convergence
Part 2: Away-from-Home Convergence
Part 3: At-Venue Convergence

Each part includes a brief introduction intended to "set the table" for the subsequent chapters within that section. Chapters within each part begin with a case study that immediately distinguishes the subject matter at hand. Case studies are followed by brief histories of the topic, as well as discussions of two prominent examples of convergence. Following these examples, an analysis is provided describing the key takeaways. Finally, each chapter features a Q&A with an industry patriarch who shares his perspective on the convergence of sports and entertainment and how it is having an impact on his approach to business.

Prior to a description of each part's content, four goals associated with this research undertaking should be highlighted. First, it was necessary to analyze a representative cross-section of topics in order to reinforce the extent to which convergence has had an impact on all facets of the sports industry. Next, it was mandatory to include both domestic and international examples of convergence, especially given worldwide interest in sports. Third, it was essential to include a diversity of impacted stakeholders. Finally, and given the considerable industry relationships enjoyed by the USC Marshall Sports Business Institute (SBI), which conducts research, undertakes consulting projects, and hosts special events, it was deemed worthwhile by our research team to include input and analysis gained from three dozen first-person interviews of senior sports industry executives, conducted by SBI representatives. With this as a backdrop, the following paragraphs describe the important elements of each part.

Part 1: At-Home Convergence

Traditional forms of media have been forced to evolve with the advent of new media platforms. Sports is the most unique driver of all new media platforms and has, more so than any other form of entertainment, truly blended with traditional media entertainment. The creation of on-demand programming, digital video recording, and Internet services has provided today's consumers with numerous ways to experience sports in the comfort of their own homes. Sports are now consumed around the clock and, notably, fans are utilizing multiple platforms simultaneously (that is, using their computers to check scores and statistics while watching a game on their high-definition televisions).

The means by which sports leagues, teams, and individual athletes are marketed to home-bound fans is also continuing to evolve to reflect consumers' ever-changing consumption patterns. Marketers actively search for ways to communicate directly with these at-home core target audiences. So too do athletes who wish to differentiate themselves by taking advantage of the wide array of home entertainment platforms to establish or extend their brands and generate additional endorsement dollars.

Part 2: Away-from-Home Convergence

Consumer acceptance of wireless Internet and mobile technology in the form of cellular phones, handheld devices, and consumer electronics has resulted in a rapidly growing platform upon which sports and entertainment are accessed in increasing amounts. Sports properties and media rights holders are now able to control content distribution and unlock incremental revenue by reaching fan bases and consumer groups directly. Brands, sports properties, media outlets, and electronics manufacturers that succeed in driving innovation and meeting burgeoning consumer demand in these areas will add market, mind share, or both. First movers in this space thus far have been brands and sports properties that have harnessed the power of digital content and information distribution. Mobile devices and other content delivery systems will continue to evolve and will support increased gaming and interactive functionality, simultaneously meeting consumer demand while building shareholder value.

Part 3: At-Venue Convergence

Due to their lack of revenue-generating capabilities, multisport, standalone athletic facilities and venues have become obsolete. To keep pace with expanding consumer entertainment expectations, and the revenue emanating from these expectations, sports leagues, franchises, properties, and sponsors are focused on establishing unique, experiential marketing programs through the development of sports and entertainment-themed facilities and venues. Providing stakeholders, especially retail, commercial, and residential real estate developers and corporate sponsors extensive and tactical branding opportunities that target captive audiences in and around venues will be vital to long-term financial success.

With the book's structure outlined and convergence now defined as it applies to sports and entertainment, including a historical backdrop and a description of its relevance in today's business environment, it's time to get started by considering "at-home" convergence.

Part I

AT-HOME CONVERGENCE

"At-home" convergence, the most prevalent form of sports and entertainment convergence throughout most of the 1900s, continues to have an enormous impact on consumers' lives. Centered on home-based activities, this form of convergence has become widespread, its growth accelerating in large part due to technological innovations that have blurred the line between sports and entertainment.

For much of the twentieth century, sports consumption tended to be a one-dimensional experience, largely limited to at-venue experiences or the reading of a newspaper's account of a prior day's game. However, steady innovation in at-home entertainment has nearly eliminated the gap between the consumption of sports and the consumption of entertainment to the point where the focal point of almost every American home is its "entertainment center."

Not only are sports available at all hours of the day, it is not uncommon for a sports fan to simultaneously access sports using multiple platforms. A Chicago Cubs fan can now watch his team play live on cable television while concurrently checking his fantasy baseball statistics and listening to streaming, web-based sports commentary—all without leaving the comfort of his family room. It is these same consumers, for whom sports are a powerful and unique driver of content, whose utilization preferences substantially contributed to the evolution of convergence.

This "at-home" convergence, particularly as it relates to the evolution of TV content and video gaming, has greatly expanded the ways in which fans effortlessly consume sports programming. It has also ushered in a new era of personal branding, enabling athletes to monetize their brands through the marketing of goods and services.

In examining how at-home convergence has evolved within American households, it is useful to recall a few critical milestones that shaped the current era of this form of convergence. The beginning of the modern-day association with public radio broadcasts as a form of entertainment may be most notably linked to Orson Welles's radio broadcast adaptation of H. G. Wells's classic 1898 novel *The War of the Worlds* on October 30, 1938. However, sports radio as entertainment in the American household dates back nearly two decades earlier.

Westinghouse engineer Frank Conrad built the first non-experimental licensed radio station, KDKA, in Pittsburgh, Pennsylvania. Shortly thereafter, KDKA broadcasted a blow-by-blow account of the 1920 Johnny Ray versus Johnny Dundee prize fight. In July of the following year, RCA station WJY cemented the entertainment relationship between sports and broadcast radio with the airing of the high-profile bout between Jack Dempsey and Georges Carpentier.

The first electronic medium to enter the home, radio became a major outlet for family entertainment, with an increasing number of sports broadcasts helping to pave the way. Radio broadcasts allowed people, particularly those in rural America, the opportunity to follow their favorite athlete or team without the complications of travel or additional expense.

Although many sports leagues initially viewed radio as a threat to in-person attendance at games, it became apparent by the early 1930s that radio would serve as a vehicle to promote event attendance rather than cannibalize it. Significantly, radio also provided advertisers and sponsors the opportunity to connect with their core target markets.[1] This compelling connection, which remains today and features technologically advanced media distribution channels, enabled sports leagues and teams to generate much-needed incremental revenue.

The appearance of networked and high-power stations such as NBC in 1926 expanded regional audiences and established national ones. This increasing radio penetration helped to broaden, diversify, and expand sports' fan base and allowed families across the country to gather together to listen to such feats as Babe Ruth's record-setting 1927 season, during which he hit sixty home runs. By the end of the 1930s, and due in large part to their entertainment value, home radio sets had become mainstays in American homes.

As enticing as radio had become to sports fans, there was no way it could continue to compete in the long term following the famous phrase spoken by RCA president David Sarnoff at the 1939 World's Fair. When Sarnoff confidently stated, "And now we add radio sight to sound," he ushered in a media revolution that accelerated the convergence of sports and entertainment, and forever changed how Americans lived their lives.[2]

As mentioned in the Introduction, the 1939 baseball game between Columbia and Princeton universities was indeed a watershed moment for convergence. This event, when coupled with the steady adoption of the television set into the American household during the 1950s had a huge subsequent impact on the popularity of sports. Television networks, sponsors, and advertisers were quick to realize the power of sports content to attract and keep viewers. In an effort to captivate these growing audiences, networks created dedicated sports programming focused on showcasing multiple sports. NBC, for example, premiered the first network sports broadcast show, *The Gillette Cavalcade of Sports*, in 1944.

With the success of this programming format, the sports variety show became a fixture among primetime network offerings, as evidenced by ABC's signature program, *Wide World of Sports*. *Wide World of Sports* "spanned the globe" from 1961 to 1997 in an effort to acquaint its growing audience with such diverse sports as rodeo, jai-alai, surfing, and badminton, as well as traditional Olympic sports including figure skating, skiing, gymnastics, and track and field.

Aside from sports variety show programming, the evolution in network coverage of some of America's greatest games and events helped popularize sports on television. For example, NBC's national telecast of the 1958 Baltimore Colts overtime victory over the New York Giants in the National Football League title game, often referred to as "The Greatest Game Ever Played," helped propel professional football and captured the collective attention of the nation.

Further, in October of 1974, live television coverage of the heavyweight championship bout between Muhammad Ali and George Foreman, dubbed "The Rumble in the Jungle" because it took place in Kinshasa, Zaire, attracted an enormous American television audience. This legendary fight was staged at 3:00 A.M. local time to allow for its broadcast during the day on American television. Because it was broadcast in a more American-friendly time slot, Ali was able to continue building his personal brand while the sport of boxing enjoyed a boost to its global notoriety.

The beginnings of televised sports convergence with entertainment were directly related to network television, but this continued unabated in the 1980s due to the rapid growth of cable television, particularly via networks such as ESPN, WTBS, and HBO. The ability of cable sports networks to provide continuous, around-the-clock coverage of sports delivered a much-needed fix to hardcore sports fans.

Another industry that took shape and rapidly innovated during the 1980s was the at-home video gaming industry, which, until the mid-1980s, was dominated by console and arcade system maker Atari. Atari, which grew during the 1970s and will be discussed in more detail in Chapter 2, was instrumental in bringing video gaming to the masses.

The popularity of this new form of at-home entertainment, one complemented by the growing personal computer gaming market, fueled the launch of the Nintendo NES console in 1985 and was the platform for such sports video games as *Tecmo Bowl* and *Mike Tyson's Punch-Out*. While the competition among console makers Nintendo, Sega, and others continued throughout the 1980s and early 1990s, the success of the early sports video games paved the way for video game publishers, especially Electronic Arts (EA), to secure a niche within the video game publishing industry by focusing on sports games.

Much of EA's early success can be attributed to its strategy of platform-agnostic development and the creation of strong multiyear sports franchises, including *Madden Football* and *NBA Live*, both of which were firmly established by the mid-1990s. Significantly, EA was the first publisher to release annual updates of its popular video game franchises such as *Madden Football*, *FIFA*, *NHL*, *NBA Elite* (formerly known as *NBA Live*), and *Tiger Woods*. Offering updated player rosters and small graphical and game-play enhancements enabled EA to secure a market leadership position in sports video gaming, and annual sales of these games remained high.

Although more extensively covered in Part II, which addresses "away-from-home" convergence, the Internet has proven to be integrally connected to many areas of at-home convergence. With its arrival, the demand for extensive, wall-to-wall coverage and consumption of sports reached beyond mere television broadcasts as content distributors began leveraging the Internet to provide new levels of interactivity. With the inception of ESPN.com in 1995 (then known as ESPNet.SportsZone.com) and Yahoo! Sports in 1997, the latest sports information was at every fan's fingertips. Not unlike the early radio broadcasts of sports in the 1920s, these websites allowed sports fans the opportunity to follow their favorite athlete or team from afar in a more timely fashion. Although not as interactive and user-friendly as today's sports websites, sites such as ESPN.com and CBSsportsline.com, which already boasted strong brand names given their affiliation to televised sports programming, these sites captivated fans by providing content that made them visit their sites on a regular basis.

The delivery of sports news, information, and statistics in "real time" on the Internet continued its rapid expansion throughout the decade. This has created substantial revenue-producing opportunities for a wide range of industry stakeholders, especially sports leagues, their sponsors, and content developers.

Opportunities to experience at-home convergence increased exponentially over the past decade. The addition of viewer-friendly broadcast elements, increased accessibility of a growing number of cable television channels, the Internet, and new and improved consumer electronics all enhanced the sports viewing experience.

Not only are fans interested in taking advantage of such enhancements and services, they are in large part responsible for them because their evolving consumption patterns mandate that the industry stakeholders producing these goods and services quench their demand for technological innovation. As is the case with all forms of convergence, the stakeholders in the at-home category include the owners of sports properties, the developers and distributors of content, and the athletes who play the games, as well as marketers hoping to sell myriad products and services to fans. Accordingly, we will be discussing the areas and developments affecting these stakeholders as they navigate at-home convergence.

Part I considers how established and emerging stakeholders are attempting to monetize at-home convergence. In Chapter 1 we will study television's evolution by focusing on how changes in sports-related programming and related technology have played, and will continue to play, a role in taking at-home convergence to new levels while striving to meet ever-changing consumption patterns. Chronicled in this chapter will be the impact of the Beijing Olympics, ESPN's *College GameDay*, and the Ultimate Fighting Championship (UFC). Laced throughout the chapter will be observations from leading industry executives David Neal—EVP, NBC Olympics; John Skipper—then EVP, content, ESPN; Frank and Lorenzo Fertitta—founders of Zuffa, LLC, which owns UFC; and David Hill—Chairman, Fox Sports.

Video gaming is evaluated in great detail in Chapter 2, with a distinct focus on the evolution of consoles and peripherals, as well as on how interest in video gaming was successfully captured to establish and build video game franchises and professional video gaming leagues. Specifically, the chapter will include analyses of how Nintendo, THQ, and Major League Gaming (MLG) parlayed their keen understanding of the marketplace to build thriving enterprises. As in each chapter, additional insight is provided from those who have shaped the industry, in this case Perrin Kaplan—(former) VP, Marketing and Corporate Affairs, Nintendo; Brian Farrell—CEO, THQ; Michael Sepso—co-founder, MLG; and Peter Moore—President, EA SPORTS.

Finally, in Chapter 3 we describe recent developments in the area of athlete branding. Few stakeholders have as much to gain by this type of convergence as superstar athletes. Examples looked at in this chapter are David Beckham, Tony Hawk, and Yao Ming, three marketing icons who have developed and extended their personal brands on a global basis, warranting an analysis of their efforts. This athlete branding discussion and analysis is complemented by first-person observations shared by Shawn Hunter—(former) President, AEG Sports, now President, CEO, and Investor-Operator, Chivas USA; Will Kassoy— then SVP, Global Brand Management, Activision; Adam Silver—Deputy Commissioner, NBA; and Sandy Montag, SCVP, IMG Sports & Entertainment.

1   TELEVISION CONTENT

NBC AND THE BEIJING OLYMPICS

As on many Saturday nights in Manhattan, The Gin Mill is packed. Although not necessarily known as a sports bar, the place is transformed into one on the evening of August 16, 2008. Patrons' attention is riveted to numerous high-definition televisions, not because of a Yankees-Red Sox game but rather in anticipation of watching forty-one-year-old Dara Torres swim the 50 meter freestyle at the 2008 Beijing Olympics.

The close race has everyone captivated, but there is collective disappointment as Torres wins the silver medal, finishing .01 seconds behind Germany's Britta Steffen. Not long thereafter, patrons again put down their drinks and watch the women's 4 x 100 meter medley relay with anticipation. Three minutes and fifty-three seconds of nonstop swimming action later, there is again collective disappointment as the team of Torres, Natalie Coughlin, Christine Magnuson, and Rebecca Soni place second to Australia.

Despite the crowd's demonstrated interest, the evening's main event has yet to occur. Then, at approximately 11:00 P.M., the U.S. men's 4 x 100 meter medley relay team of Aaron Perisol, Brendan Hansen, Michael Phelps, and Jason Lezak steps toward the pool. The previous night, more than sixty-six million people had watched Phelps win his dramatic seventh gold medal of these Games, barely edging Serb Milorad Cavic in the 100 meter butterfly.[1] With the victory Phelps had tied the legendary Mark Spitz by winning seven gold medals at one Olympic Games, and was about to compete for an unprecedented eighth gold medal in Beijing. All eyes at The Gin Mill were focused on the pool at the Water Cube.

"Alright, we're going to turn off the music and turn on the commentary so that we can all watch the swimming," a voice says over the bar's loudspeaker—an exceptionally rare respite from the pulsating music normally heard.

Everyone listens to the commentary of Dan Hicks and Rowdy Gaines on the NBC telecast, which is being broadcast live, a half a world away. The race begins and Peirsol gives the U.S. a strong start in the backstroke. Then Hansen takes over on the breaststroke, but he falls behind Japan's Kosuke Kitajima. Phelps dives into the pool and pulls the U.S. ahead on an incredible butterfly sprint. Lezak then finishes with a strong freestyle swim that gives the U.S. the gold medal in a world record time of 3:29.34.

Overflowing with national pride, the patrons at The Gin Mill shout, "U-S-A! U-S-A!" Just two miles south, a large crowd at Times Square erupts with cheers that echo throughout the entire city. And back at The Gin Mill, a TV in the corner shows thousands of fans staying forty-five minutes after the conclusion of a Baltimore Ravens preseason football game at M&T Bank Stadium to watch their local hero, Phelps, swim for the record gold.

More than seventy million people watched at least some portion of the Olympic broadcast on NBC that Saturday night, an evening generally known for modest TV ratings.[2]

Olympic Games on Television

The first televised Olympics in the United States were the 1960 Winter Games in Squaw Valley, California, anchored by Walter Cronkite on CBS. Later that year, CBS aired the 1960 Summer Games in Rome. Since communications satellites were not yet available, CBS had to produce and edit the coverage in Italy, then fly it back to a New York studio, where the events would be described by a young and relatively unknown broadcaster named Jim McKay. Eventually, McKay would move to ABC, where he would become the face of Olympic coverage for much of the next two decades.

Following NBC's airing of the 1964 Summer Games in Tokyo, most of the Olympics for the next twenty years were broadcast on ABC, as network executive Roone Arledge had decided to use the event as a cornerstone of the network's sports coverage.

ABC had developed a strong competency in covering international sporting events through its television program *ABC's Wide World of Sports*, which started in 1961. The program aired a wide variety of sporting events from around the globe, many of which were unfamiliar to American sports fans. Still, *Wide World of Sports* proved to be a ratings hit, and it successfully introduced Americans to many periodically held or unique sports, such as gymnastics and logging.

Arledge took advantage of ABC's competencies in international sports coverage to produce high-quality Olympic broadcasts. He believed the Olympics attracted more than just hardcore sports fans, and undertook measures to appeal to more casual fans, including women. Olympic coverage included numerous personal profiles, introducing athletes and their unique stories to the American public. Olympic broadcasts were also a nice change of pace from the typical football-baseball-basketball-dominated sports airwaves. Americans could watch some of the best athletes in the world in track and field, or they could see the grace and composure exhibited in diving or archery.

But the Olympic Games were about more than sports. They were routinely affected by global political strife such as the Cold War, and provided a platform for terrorists to make political statements such as the kidnapping of eleven Israeli athletes at the 1972 Summer Olympic Games in Munich, which resulted in their massacre. Significantly, such events also had an impact on the legacy and broadcast elements of the Games.

NBC Becomes America's Olympic Network

By paying $300 million, NBC won the rights to broadcast the 1988 Olympic Games in Seoul, and have aired the Summer Games in the United States ever since.[3] In 1989, Dick Ebersol became the head of NBC Sports and, like his former mentor, Arledge, sought to make the Olympics a signature part of the network's brand.

Like all Olympic broadcasting networks, NBC faced numerous challenges in covering the Games, many of which were linked to the impact of showing events on a tape-delay basis in the U.S. In addition, the Olympic Games continued to expand their sports offerings, forcing NBC to make difficult decisions about which events to air, and when.

In 1992, NBC paid $401 million for the rights to the Barcelona Olympics.[4] To help defray some of its costs, and to show as many events as possible, NBC partnered with Cablevision to create the "Olympic Triplecast." For a fee of $95–$175, the Triplecast, which consisted of three pay-per-view stations, enabled viewers to watch many events live. Unfortunately for NBC, the Triplecast turned out to be a failure, as few people were willing to pay subscription fees to watch broadcasts that were at odd hours of the day for most Americans. NBC and Cablevision lost almost $100 million on the joint venture.[5] However, all was not lost for NBC. The primetime ratings for the Barcelona Games were very strong; the

Games earned an average of 17.1 and a 33 share according to Nielsen data. Of significance, these Games were anchored by Bob Costas, who began to establish himself as the new face of televised Olympics.

NBC enjoyed even greater ratings success with the 1996 Atlanta Summer Games, as 209 million Americans tuned in at some point during the network's seventeen days of coverage.[6] Buoyed by the strong ratings in Atlanta and Barcelona, Ebersol in 1998 led NBC's unprecedented $3.5 billion bid for every Summer and Winter Olympic Games from 2000 to 2008.[7] Several years later, NBC spent another $2.2 billion to secure the rights to broadcast the 2010 Winter Games and 2012 Summer Games.[8] To put the numbers in perspective, NBC was paying approximately twice as much for the U.S. rights as all European companies were paying combined.[9] NBC's commitment was such that General Electric, the network's parent company, accounted for more than 25 percent of all International Olympic Committee (IOC) revenues, a fact not likely lost on Comcast, which purchased a controlling interest in the network in late 2009.[10]

Although Ebersol remained bullish on the Olympics, from 2000 through 2006 TV ratings were inconsistent due to disadvantageous time zones and emerging technologies; this was perhaps best evidenced by the 2006 Winter Olympic Games in Turin. At that point, Internet usage was so widespread that the six-to-nine-hour time difference from Italy to the U.S. made it very easy for Americans to learn the results of important competitions prior to NBC airing them on a tape-delayed basis in primetime. Ratings were down 35 percent from 2002, and fell 25 percent from the 1998 Nagano Winter Games, which were the most recent Winter Games held outside the U.S.[11] Further compromising NBC was that several episodes of Fox's hit show *American Idol* beat Olympic coverage in head-to-head primetime ratings, and an episode of ABC's *Lost* also topped the Turin Games in ratings among young viewers.[12] In previous years, other networks seldom bothered to compete against Olympic coverage, but this time they were undaunted, given the television landscape in 2006.

As the 2008 Beijing Games approached, many wondered if the Olympics could regain their television luster.

Beijing 2008—The Olympic Games Make a Comeback

In 2001, the IOC awarded the 2008 Games to Beijing over more time-zone-friendly Toronto and Paris. China was an emerging nation on the international scene, both economically and in sports. After Mao Zedong and the Communist Party took control of the country following World War II, the nation had effectively closed its borders and shut itself off from the world. However, in the late 1970s, new leader Deng Xiaoping slowly opened the country's economy and started a national sports program. In 1984, China competed in the Olympic Games for the first time since 1948, and the country rapidly improved its athletic prowess to the point where many predicted it to win the medal count in 2008.

The 2008 Games were seen as an enormous opportunity for China to open its doors to the rest of the world. Economically, the country had already become a superpower, but the 2008 Games enabled China to demonstrate this progress to the world. This demonstration was on full display in the Opening Ceremony, as more than fifteen thousand performers took part in a spectacular show that cost more than $300 million to produce.[13]

"The Olympics are the ultimate unscripted drama, and the athletes and the setting are part of that drama," said David Neal, then executive vice president of NBC Olympics. "Beijing and China were a daily part of that story."[14]

Appreciating NBC's clout given its considerable rights fees, Ebersol persuaded the IOC to move the gymnastics and swimming competitions—two of the highest-rated Olympic sports—to the morning in Beijing so that they could be aired live and in primetime on the East Coast in the U.S., thereby mitigating the time-zone challenge brought about by the twelve-to-fifteen-hour time difference between China and the U.S. According to Neal, NBC began preparations for the broadcast more than five years in advance of the Games, and Neal himself made nearly twenty trips to Beijing in the years leading up to the Opening Ceremony in order to develop a working relationship with his Chinese counterparts and get a proper feel for the environment.

In addition, Ebersol and NBC embraced the Internet, using it to their advantage. While NBCOlympics.com always had comprehensive Olympic coverage, the site was elevated to a new level for the Beijing Games. Most Olympic sporting events were shown live on the website at no cost to the user, allowing NBC to announce it was broadcasting a record 3,600 hours of Olympic coverage (almost one-third of it online), up from 1,210 hours in Athens and 441 hours in Sydney. These Olympic webcasts, which featured the international feed but no broadcasters, provided an opportunity for fans of lesser-profile sports such as water polo, team handball, fencing, and modern pentathlon to catch all of the action live.

By 2008, NBC owned multiple cable stations and was able to broadcast numerous Olympic events on such subsidiaries as MSNBC, CNBC, USA, Oxygen, Universal HD, and Telemundo. In addition, NBC launched high-definition channels dedicated to basketball and soccer that could be seen on DIRECTV and elsewhere.

"More is better," Neal said. "The appetite on the part of the consumer is limitless. The fact that we offered so much was a huge benefit. There wasn't a sport that you couldn't find being broadcast somewhere. The more we could offer, the better."[15]

NBC used 106 broadcasters to cover the Beijing Games and employed nearly three thousand people to help with its coverage, many of whom were working out of temporary offices on the set of *Saturday Night Live* at 30 Rockefeller Center.[16] Because of its coverage of the Olympics for the past twenty years, NBC had gained considerable experience, and it showed in the excellent production quality. There were numerous technologies that NBC introduced or honed in its coverage, such as allowing viewers to more easily identify swimmers. The network also had used a familiar team of broadcasters, including Hicks for swimming, Al Trautwig for gymnastics, Tom Hammond for track and field, Mike Breen for basketball, and Costas in the studio. NBC's impressive work was rewarded with six Sports Emmys for its Olympic coverage alone, including Costas winning for best studio host.

The results of NBC's efforts proved phenomenal. The network, which had paid an estimated $893 million for the rights to the Beijing Games, sold more than $1 billion in advertising.[17] After initial ratings surpassed expectations, NBC sold its extra ad inventory, generating another $25 million in sales in the twelve days following the Opening Ceremony.[18] General Electric further benefited from the Games, as it is estimated that the Olympics may have helped the corporation generate $700 million in new infrastructure orders in China.[19]

In large part, the ratings for the primetime coverage proved to be high due to the mystique of holding an Olympic Games in China. But also, by airing the swimming and gymnastics events live, NBC allowed Americans to enjoy and celebrate in the shared experience that is often fundamental in any sports broadcast, as evidenced by the atmosphere at The Gin Mill the night Phelps broke the record. It certainly helped NBC that Americans competed extremely well in many events, winning the overall medal count in the process.

Through the first week of coverage, NBC captured an average of more than 30 million viewers a night. That average dipped to 27.7 million by the second week, but it was still a significant increase over Athens. The average Nielsen rating for the entire seventeen-day Olympic Games was 16.2 with a 28 share, and NBC estimated that 214 million people watched at least some of the Games, making it the most watched television event in U.S. history. That figure represented a 2.4 percent increase over the 1996 Atlanta Games and a 5.4 percent increase from the 2004 Athens Games. NBC dominated the competition during the Games—in the first week of coverage alone, the network had more viewers than the next closest twelve networks combined, marking the largest margin of victory for any network during any primetime week in Nielsen history.[20] NBC also showed its greatest gains in viewership among young males, a demographic that many thought was unlikely to grow for Olympic audiences.

The ratings increase trickled over to NBC's other programming as well. NBC's *Nightly News*, which was broadcast live from Beijing on many nights, saw its biggest lead over ABC and CBS evening news broadcasts since 2004.[21] Ratings for *The Today Show* also spiked. Cable ratings were similarly strong, as MSNBC's late-afternoon Olympic program saw an increase of 252 percent on one night, and CNBC nearly quadrupled its normal ratings.[22]

"There are only a handful of big events left on TV, but 'Event TV' still works in terms of aggregating a large and diverse audience," Neal says. "They enhance the brand identity of NBC in building a mass audience. 215 million American viewers watched some portion of our coverage from Beijing, which validates and speaks to the identity of NBC as a place to watch a truly big event."[23]

Sponsors were also quite pleased with their decision to advertise with NBC Olympics. A Nielsen IAG study found that advertising during the Olympic Games produced a better brand recall (+14 percent), message recall (+20 percent), and likeability (+33 percent) than advertisements during normal primetime hours. In addition, advertisements that carried Olympic themes enjoyed even better brand recall (+29 percent), message recall (+40 percent), and likeability (+33 percent).[24]

The Internet strategy also paid dividends for NBCOlympics.com, as ComScore data showed the site had 6.7 million unique visitors from August 4th through the 10th, 14.2 million from August 11th through the 17th, and 12.2 million from August 18th through the 24th. Nielsen, which uses a different metric to measure Internet traffic, reported that NBC attracted 4.27 million unique visitors from August 8th through the 18th, and reported a higher daily average than competitors such as ESPN.com and Beijing2008.cn.[25]

Still, it was interesting to note that both ComScore and Nielsen indicated that Yahoo! Sports' Olympic section garnered more unique visitors than NBCOlympics.com, despite the absence of live Olympic video streams. The disparity was much greater with ComScore than with Nielsen, and it could partially be attributed to Yahoo!'s status as a portal. However, it could also be a testament to Yahoo!'s own high-quality Olympic coverage. Regardless, NBC earned impressive engagement figures online, with Nielsen estimating that the average NBCOlympics.com user spent nearly sixteen minutes on its site, compared to less than seven minutes on Yahoo! Sports' Olympic section. NBCOlympics.com also delivered nearly seventy-five million video streams.[26]

An e-marketer study found that NBC actually under-monetized its web assets. The study estimated that NBCOlympics.com generated $5.75 million in video-ad revenue from the Games, compared to the $23 million in ad revenue from CBS's coverage of March Madness.[27] Some analysts indicated NBC could have earned more in revenue had it showed live video for the highest-profile Olympic events, or if it had agreed to distribute some video on other sites.

There was also a chorus of critics on the West Coast, where none of the prime-time broadcasts were aired live. The West Coast tape delays, and the tape delays of other sporting events, prompted John Skipper, executive vice president of content for ESPN, to say that if ABC and ESPN aired the Olympic Games, then much more of their coverage would be live. NBC has indicated that they continue to plan to air events on tape delay. "Loudly and clearly people say that they want to watch the events at the times that are most convenient to them," Neal says. "The numbers bear that out. It's a challenge, but also an opportunity."[28]

In the grand scheme of things, given its size and scope, NBC did a remarkable job covering the Games, and it had the ratings to prove it. The network remained optimistic about the strong ratings continuing for the 2010 Vancouver Winter Games, in large measure because of its North American location. In fact, the Vancouver Games proved to be the second-highest-rated Winter Olympics ever, bolstered by the compelling men's gold medal hockey game between the United States and Canada.[29] NBC will look to continue to innovate and offer strong broadcasts for the 2012 Olympic Games in London. The success of NBC's coverage for the 2008 Beijing Games led to indications from ABC and ESPN that they would bid to host the 2014 Sochi Winter Games and the 2016 Rio de Janeiro Summer Games. It remains to be seen how Olympic coverage will continue to evolve but one thing is certain: NBC will remain an opinion leader in this regard.

The 2008 Olympics represented a high-water mark in terms of readily available event-based television content. Even as televised sports continues to grow as a profitable entertainment medium, it is helpful to review the humble beginnings of televised sports as entertainment.

TV CONTENT: AN OVERVIEW

As previously mentioned, the first televised sporting event was a modest one, with approximately four hundred television sets picking up the feed from the 1939 baseball game between Columbia and Princeton universities. Despite the use of a single camera, the allure of sports on television would not be lost on those hoping to profit from it.

Five years later, the first sports broadcast on network TV took place with NBC's broadcast of the featherweight championship bout between Willie Pep and Chalky White. This boxing match aired on the corporate-sponsored *Gillette Cavalcade of Sports*, a variety show that remained a staple of sports television for twenty years.

Less than a decade later, in 1953, the Harlem Globetrotters appeared on *The Ed Sullivan Show*, which was viewed by an estimated 77 percent of U.S. households.[30] The Globetrotters, along with their undermanned competitor, the Washington Generals, would come to personify the early convergence of sports and entertainment on television.

Eventually, "made for television" shows emerged that routinely blended entertainment quality with athletic competition. ABC's *Superstars*, which began in 1973, showcased top athletes from different sports, such as pole vaulter Bob Seagren, soccer player Kyle Rote Jr., and football player O. J. Simpson, competing against each other in various athletic events.

Furthermore, while not initially positioned as a "made for television" event, the Super Bowl has certainly become just that, delicately balancing sports and entertainment, including the advertising spots shown during commercial breaks. First played in 1967, the Super Bowl has become a day-long event that captivates viewing audiences. From the hours of pre-game analysis to the half-time spectacle featuring A-list entertainers, the broadcast has successfully blended sports with entertainment, so much so that the Super Bowl is routinely the highest-rated program on television from year to year.

It is important to note that the early success of sports on television was not limited to broadcast networks. Cable channels such as WGN (1948) and TBS (1972) helped popularize the Chicago Cubs and Atlanta Braves, respectively, to national audiences in the years following their launches. In time, individual sports teams recognized an opportunity to increase revenue by controlling their broadcast distribution rights through the creation of regional sports networks; the New York Yankees' launch of the Yankee Entertainment and Sports Network in 2002 is the most prominent among such networks. Still, other teams have found it cost-prohibitive to be in the broadcast entertainment network business and have had great difficulty securing sufficient carriage. Such was the case with the 2005 failure of Carolinas Sports Entertainment Television (C-SET), a cable network owned jointly by the NBA's Charlotte Bobcats and Time Warner Cable.

Other cable networks also sought to take advantage of sports fans' insatiable appetite for televised sports, as evidenced by the historic roles of HBO's *World Championship Boxing* (1973) and Showtime's *Championship Boxing* (1986), which have been vitally important not only to the sport of boxing but also to the development and refinement of sporting events on pay-per-view.

As discussed earlier, sports on cable television changed dramatically with the launch of ESPN in 1979. In addition to televising games, the network became known for its unique and compelling packaging of sports and entertainment content and epitomized the convergence of sports and entertainment.

However, such packaging can prove difficult to craft. Unabashedly positioned to combine sports and entertainment, NBC and World Wrestling Entertainment jointly launched the XFL, a football league, in 2001. Although initial interest in the league was strong, interest rapidly declined because the XFL failed to deliver a highly entertaining brand of football to viewers while simultaneously underachieving as an entertainment vehicle.

Despite such high-profile failures, as the popularity of sports on TV grew, so too did rights fees charged to air the programming. In 1970, networks would pay $50 million to broadcast the NFL, and by 1985 the going rate was $450 million. Leagues such as the NFL were fully aware of their increasing ability to deliver young male audiences to advertisers—and were charging accordingly. Today, the NFL averages approximately $4 billion per year in broadcast rights fees; an amount over and above the revenue it generates from NFL broadcasts on the league's own network, which began in 2003.

As all sports and entertainment mediums continue to assess how best to deliver TV content, one thing is certain: doing so today requires an increasing reliance not just on technology but on technology that makes sports fans feel as though they are an integral part of the event.

NBC, through its packaging and distribution of the Beijing Olympics; ESPN, given its success with *College GameDay*; and the Ultimate Fighting Championship understand this as well as anyone in the television business.

ESPN'S *COLLEGE GAMEDAY*

Premiering in 1987, ESPN's *College GameDay* has been a Saturday morning mainstay since it left the ESPN studios in 1993 to broadcast live from Notre Dame Stadium prior to the matchup between top-ranked Florida State and second-ranked Notre Dame. The decision to begin broadcasting live and on location from the most compelling college football matchups or storylines in the country each week added a new dimension to the sports-viewing experience. The current *GameDay* team consists of host Chris Fowler and analysts Lee Corso, Kirk Herbstreit, and Desmond Howard, as well as feature reporter Erin Andrews. The first three have been together since 1996, with Howard and Andrews joining the team in 2005 and 2010, respectively. These five have not only shared their insight on the importance of the game at hand but, due to their very presence at the venue, continue to legitimize its significance.

GameDay has gained such popularity that thousands of fans routinely show up for the 9:00 A.M. EST start of the three-hour program—in large measure to show the rest of the nation watching on TV what the game-day and tailgate atmosphere is like at the host school. The University of Nebraska, for instance, continuously draws large crowds and had an impressive 15,800 fans on hand for the show prior to the game against Notre Dame on September 8, 2001.[31] *College GameDay* brings an enormous national spotlight to the host city and university, and therefore the host cities and schools work together to ensure a compelling execution. According to ESPN's executive vice president of content, John Skipper, ESPN has yet to have a host college turn *College GameDay* away. In fact, many schools have lobbied for *College GameDay* to broadcast from their campus because of the significant attention it brings to the university.[32]

Passionate fans stationed in the background of the *GameDay* set wear the home team's colors, wave team-spirited flags, and bring homemade signs intended to taunt the visiting team and needle the hosts—all while orchestrated cheers are being led by the host school's "spirit" team and mascot. The "Spirit Meter" segment encourages crowd noise and estimates the decibel level being generated behind the *GameDay* set. Spectators watching on TV are encouraged to go online to ESPN's *College GameDay* website and vote for their favorite sign in the background, further enhancing the interaction among the fan, the TV viewer, and the televised content. *GameDay* has gained such a cult-like following that Washington State University has created a network of fans across the nation that waves the university's flag in the background of the *GameDay* set. These fans have done so at every *GameDay* broadcast since 2003, underscoring the program's strong appeal.[33] This atmosphere surrounding *GameDay* has contributed to the show's averaging in excess of one million viewers per week for more than a decade.[34]

In addition to being curious about other universities' game-day experiences, viewers tune in to hear opinion and analyses, and it is this combination of broadcast elements that has enabled *GameDay* to average a 1.6 Nielsen rating over the past several years.[35] Skipper notes that the probability of success is strong given "the spontaneity and energy of the crowd, the drama of whatever's happening in college football and on the campus, and the level of preparation these guys [Fowler, Corso, Herbstreit, and Howard] have."[36]

GameDay differentiates itself from traditional pregame broadcasts with its interactive and boisterous nature. It begins with country music duo Big & Rich's hit song "Comin' to Your City," with revised lyrics mentioning several of the top college football programs in the country. Elements of the show that have evolved over time include segments such as "Speed Drills," in which Fowler asks Corso and Herbstreit a handful of questions they are required to answer in about a minute. Corso or Herbstreit are also asked to predict the biggest upset of the day in a segment titled "Upset Alerts," designed to generate excitement and dialogue throughout the day. Each of these elements contributes to *GameDay*'s ability to reach its core audience of active, college-educated, or soon to be college-educated consumers, between the ages of eighteen and thirty-four.

Celebrity guests such as retired college basketball coach Bobby Knight and NBA basketball legend Charles Barkley have been invited on-set. These guests are encouraged to participate in the banter between Corso and Herbstreit, as well as give their prediction on the winning team. Since 2005, current host and former Heisman Trophy winner Howard has led a live interactive segment on a small artificial field, where he describes the teams' top plays and how to stop them. This portion of the program deviates from traditional studio broadcasts and engages the audience in an interactive learning and entertainment experience.

GameDay's appeal has not been lost on sponsors who seek to reach the very demographic the show consistently delivers. In 2003, The Home Depot became the presenting sponsor of what has since been dubbed *College GameDay Built by The Home Depot*. When The Home Depot extended its sponsorship for three additional years in 2006, Roger Adams, SVP of marketing for The Home Depot, stated, "Consumers often decide on Saturday mornings exactly what home improvement project they plan to tackle for the weekend, so having a prominent presence on *College GameDay* provides us with a national platform to connect with our customers and offers The Home Depot brand a unique point of differentiation."[37] The Home Depot designed the current set for *GameDay*, which includes The Home Depot's logo in a prominent position on-set. The sponsorship includes commercial spots and The Home Depot–sponsored features during programming.[38] According to Front Row Marketing Services, The Home Depot, in a single airing of *GameDay*, has received up to fifteen minutes of broadcast exposure, worth over $1.1 million.[39] Furthermore, The Home Depot's sponsorship and promotional campaigns have allowed *College GameDay* to create and develop the personalities of the show's hosts through quirky commercial campaigns. Skipper views such campaigns and the character-building advertisements as critical to the ratings and personality of the show.[40]

In addition, Chick-fil-A sponsors the segment leading into "Mascot Movers," the preamble to the climactic moment of *GameDay* when Corso dons the mascot head of the university he is predicting will win that day's on-site game.

The success of *GameDay* has spawned two ESPN spinoffs: in 2000, a radio broadcast called *ESPN Radio College GameDay* and in 2005 a NCAA Basketball version, also called *College GameDay*. ESPN's *College GameDay* has garnered multiple Sports Emmy nominations over the years, including a 2008 win for "best weekly studio show." Not surprisingly, Skipper says "the sustainability of *College GameDay* is not something on the top of my worry list."[41] There is no doubt that *GameDay*'s nearly twenty-five-year contribution to the convergence of sports and entertainment via on-location broadcasting will have a long-lasting impact and will continue to be revered as a model for success.

While *College GameDay* has shown how the presence of a pre-game show can personify the foundation of sports and entertainment integration, burgeoning sports have utilized the entirety of this convergence to become more relevant to the sports-viewing public. The Ultimate Fighting Championship (UFC) is one of the most notable examples of this trend.

ULTIMATE FIGHTING CHAMPIONSHIP

Largely unknown a decade ago, UFC has emerged as one of the fastest-growing sports organizations due to its ability to successfully navigate the television landscape. Utilizing a unique mix of pay-per-view (PPV) broadcasts, reality TV, and DVDs, the mixed-martial-arts (MMA) organization has developed a dedicated and profitable fan base.

UFC was founded in 1993 by advertising executive Art Davie and Rorion Gracie, a master in Brazilian Jiu-Jitsu. They initially partnered with Semaphore Entertainment Group (SEG), a pioneer in PPV events, and, over time, UFC garnered a small but loyal following for its PPV events and was eventually purchased by SEG. The sport, which consists of participants practicing numerous martial arts crafts and takes place in a trademarked eight-sided ring known as "the Octagon," was promoted to viewers as "no-holds barred fighting." However, the violence of the sport was too much for some to handle, and in 1996 it so horrified Arizona Senator John McCain that he likened it to "human cockfighting." McCain sent letters to all fifty U.S. governors asking them to ban UFC events, and thirty-six of them obliged; UFC subsequently lost much of its revenue-producing capabilities. Despite UFC's concerted efforts to improve fighter safety by instituting new rules, it struggled to gain exposure, let alone acceptance.

As SEG neared bankruptcy in 2001, Las Vegas–based Station Casinos executives and brothers Frank and Lorenzo Fertitta established Zuffa, LLC. They then purchased UFC for $2 million and named boxing trainer and manager Dana White president. Zuffa continued to refine UFC's rules to ensure fighter safety—so much so, in fact, that a 2006 Johns Hopkins study found that MMA competitors were at no greater risk for serious injury than boxers.[42] The refining of the rules, along with Lorenzo Fertitta's industry relationships, helped UFC attain regulated status in most states which, in turn, fueled exposure, fan interest, and media coverage.

Despite this progress, Zuffa lost $34 million by the end of 2004. Knowing that they had to expose the UFC brand and its exceptional athletes to as many people as possible, the Fertitta brothers and White began pitching an idea for a UFC-based reality show called *The Ultimate Fighter*. The reality show would serve as a "Trojan horse" to put UFC on free cable television in millions of U.S. households. The show's concept was to feature a group of young MMA fighters living and training together, as well as competing against each other for the chance to win a six-figure contract from UFC. Although the television series was pitched to virtually every television company, not a single one would pay for it. Zuffa therefore decided to pay over $10 million to produce the series, and it was only under those circumstances that the Viacom-owned cable channel Spike TV agreed to broadcast it.[43]

"We thought it was a bad thing when we had to fund the show ourselves," Frank Fertitta recalled. "At the end of the day though, it worked out to be a huge benefit for us because we owned all the rights."[44]

The Ultimate Fighter first aired in January 2005 and quickly became a huge hit for Spike TV, particularly among the eighteen- to thirty-four-year-old male demographic. Viewers were engaged by the compelling personal stories of the fighters and were impressed by their athleticism and extraordinarily difficult training regimen. For many viewers, the show offered an introduction to MMA and UFC, and many of the top UFC competitors would make regular appearances. Furthermore, the term *UFC* had begun to seep into the vernacular as the word people used when discussing the MMA genre in general. The show continued to thrive during its tenth season, culminating in a season finale that averaged 3.7 million viewers with a peak of 5.2 million viewers during the three-hour telecast.[45] Highlighting the continued success of the franchise, the show averaged a series record 3.4 million viewers an episode, higher than many regular season games in mainstream college and pro sports on cable networks.[46]

Several competitors on *The Ultimate Fighter* have enjoyed successful MMA careers, so the show has afforded UFC a unique platform to build its future stars' brands. For UFC, *The Ultimate Fighter* has effectively become what college sports has been for the NFL or NBA, namely a training ground for athletes to polish their skills and develop marketable personalities.

"*American Idol* is the closest to what we are," Lorenzo Fertitta said. "On most reality shows, people don't care about the person after the show ends. People who come on our show have a career that you can continue to follow. Many of them have become stars in our sport."[47]

Spike TV quickly increased its UFC-related programming in 2005, airing *UFC Unleashed*, which featured complete fights from UFC's vast library. Later that year the network added *UFC Fight Night* and began broadcasting a series of live UFC fights throughout the year. Spike TV continued to see an impressive following among the male eighteen- to thirty-four-year-old demographic. The sport's bouts were real, unlike in professional wrestling, and offered more action than boxing. While boxing struggled to organize high-quality fights due to the large number of disjointed governing bodies, UFC had control over its competitors and was able to arrange attractive—and lucrative—match-ups. UFC and Spike furthered their relationship in March of 2010 when they announced that they were providing fans online access to episodes and fights from all ten seasons of *The Ultimate Fighter*.[48]

In turn, the cumulative effect of Spike TV's UFC programming had an impact on UFC's PPV events. In April 2005, *UFC 52* earned 280,000 PPV buys for an event featuring Chuck Liddell and Randy Couture, more than double the previous high.[49] By 2006, UFC events were generating more than 500,000 PPV buyers per event. *UFC 66* featuring Liddell and Tito Ortiz earned more than $42 million in PPV buys alone.[50] The company generated over $220 million in gross revenue through PPV buys in 2006, surpassing World Wrestling Entertainment's $200 million and the $177 million generated from boxing on HBO.[51] This success provided UFC an opportunity to further expand its business by later offering its fights at movie theaters throughout the United States, which started with UFC 111 in March 2010.[52]

UFC entered into negotiations with HBO about having the premium cable channel purchase the right to air UFC matches and related programming. According to the Fertittas, Zuffa decided against securing a deal. While they indicated the money involved was acceptable, they could not agree with HBO on issues about control over production of the broadcasts. "No one ever helped us along the way, so we had to become a producer and develop that core competency. That has been a big advantage for us," Lorenzo Fertitta says. "We were able to create an overall sensory experience that was completely different from boxing. So we didn't want to just hand off our brand to HBO. We weren't comfortable with letting them produce our product."[53]

To tactically expand its reach, UFC purchased World Extreme Cagefighting (WEC) in 2006 and has used the league for lighter-weight classes and to help develop fighters. WEC matches are aired on cable network Versus. In 2007,

UFC acquired Japan-based competitor PRIDE Fighting Championships and absorbed many of its top fighters, solidifying its grasp on the sport's talent. It is estimated that UFC generates as much as 90 percent of all revenue in the MMA industry.[54]

UFC's success with its PPV events has resulted in other business opportunities for Zuffa. The company sells DVDs of all its title fights, which regularly rank among the top-selling sports DVDs. UFC's video game *Undisputed*, which was published by THQ in 2009, was immediately successful, selling more than three million units its first year on the market.[55]

UFC has entered into several merchandising deals with its top fighters, for everything from clothing lines to action figures. UFC also negotiated deals with established sponsors such as Anheuser-Busch and Harley-Davidson, further securing UFC's position as a sports business leader. In 2007, *UFC 75* drew 4.7 million viewers on Spike TV, the highest-rated broadcast in the history of the network, contributing to UFC's ascension as a sports property worthy of advertising dollars.[56]

According to Lorenzo Fertitta, "UFC has spawned a certain type of lifestyle. There's a distinctive sense of community that's around UFC, which is a bit like surf, skate, or snow."[57]

Reinforcing its emergence as a lifestyle brand, UFC and the founder of 24 Hour Fitness, Mark Mastrov, announced the launch of UFC Gyms in 2009, the first major brand extension of UFC. The opening of the gyms was followed later in the year by the creation of *UFC Magazine*, which is published six times a year.

UFC has also seen impressive international growth, quickly finding popularity in France and Germany. By 2009, it had successfully extended its presence in Brazil and the Philippines through content and product licensing. While some sports, such as American football or baseball, are difficult for many non-Americans to learn at an older age, MMA is relatively intuitive and easy to understand. The Fertittas say that they are pursuing a strategy of having major networks in individual countries purchase programming, rather than making deals with larger pan-regional cable networks. These major networks are more popular within each individual country, although it does take longer to negotiate a larger number of deals. By decade's end, UFC was broadcast in 130 countries and territories, reaching over 450 million homes, and aired in nearly twenty different languages.[58]

UFC generated more than $260 million in gross PPV revenue in 2008, exceeding WWE's record for the greatest PPV revenue generated in a single year.[59] Boasting seven of the top-ten PPV events in 2008, UFC achieved more than six million PPV buys that year, firmly establishing Zuffa as an annual profit-generating business.[60]

Today it is estimated that UFC is worth over $1 billion, providing the Fertittas a handsome return on their $2 million investment.[61] Without question, their strategic use of television has been central to unlocking the sport's fan base and the revenue it is capable of generating.

TV CONTENT: THE BOTTOM LINE

The Beijing Olympics, *College GameDay*, and the Ultimate Fighting Championship all demonstrate the power of televised sports to build and extend brands, as well as deliver value to strategic partners, especially advertisers and sponsors. As similar properties look to the future of TV as a monetizable medium, they will have to remain keenly aware that the number of hours people spend watching TV continues to climb despite a plethora of other forms of entertainment. All the while, content remains king, as evidenced by sports leagues and related entities' desire to maintain control of their media rights. In addition, the recognition—indeed the embracing—of the fact that TV's evolution brings with it unique challenges and opportunities must be considered.

Watchful Eyes

Every year in the U.S. since 2004 TV viewing per household has surpassed an average of eight hours per day. In defiance of other forms of media and entertainment challenging TV's supremacy, the number of hours has actually steadily increased over this period.[62]

Despite the apparently rapid adoption of entertainment platforms intended to compete with—if not replace—TV, it will remain the dominant source for sports and entertainment viewing. This seemingly insatiable appetite for programming also yields opportunities for commoditized sports, such as Major League Baseball (MLB), whose regular season is the longest in sports. Leagues such as these, in which viewers may clamor for shoulder programming as much as they do to watch regular season games, have the opportunity to parlay this interest into complementary year-round programming.[63] This is seemingly best exemplified by MLB's launch of its MLB Network. Regardless of whether they are special events or regular season games, live broadcasts have the ability to drive viewership to the shoulder programming and vice versa, further cementing the relationship between fans and the sports they follow.

This continued competitive advantage will influence how media and cable companies conduct business, have an impact on advertisers and other media marketing organizations, and allow (emerging) sports leagues and teams to better connect with sports fans. At the same time, it will continue to create challenges for other forms of media distribution and live sports and entertainment.

NBC's coverage of the Beijing Olympics reinforced the power of TV as the ultimate form of media distribution. The Opening Ceremony was watched by more than one billion people worldwide, making it the most watched live event of all time.[64] Particularly impressive about this is that it occurred at the height of media fragmentation, highlighting the extraordinary power of appointment television. It also demonstrated that multiplatform coverage will not necessarily cannibalize the core broadcast.

Despite TV's ongoing cable-ization, and the ever-growing number of other traditional and new media outlets, major sporting events remain consistently DVR-resistant and aggregate engaged audiences, demonstrating global reach and staying power in the process. It is this reach and power that will continue to permit rights holders to generate billions of dollars from the licensing of their broadcast rights.

The prevailing strength of televised sports has bolstered those that make high-definition (HD) TVs and other peripherals—and vice versa. Households that watch sports have acquired HD sets at an accelerated rate compared with non-sports-viewing homes.[65] Moreover, sports fans in homes with HD sets and HD reception watch well in excess of an hour more of TV each day than the average person.[66] The symbiotic relationship among those that license sports broadcasting rights, those who manufacture televisions, and those who enjoy the programming from the comfort of their own living rooms has extended TV's life cycle and enabled industry participants to profit from it.

As consumer demand for televised sports remains strong, this allows satellite and cable TV providers to charge more for sports channels and related tiers, often to the consternation of fans and under the watchful eye of Congress. This has a rippling effect as sports leagues and teams, as well as advertising agencies and corporate marketers, pounce on opportunities to reach their target markets with greater precision. New or emerging sports leagues or properties will continue to realize the need to be on TV—not just to establish their credibility and to build their brands, but also to generate revenue. By entering into strategic partnerships in which the sports league or property and the broadcast company share the economic risk and returns, the parties have a vested interest in each other's success.

TV's continued strength, both in terms of hours watched and cumulative audience attracted, forces new forms of media to plan accordingly, as their impact on sports, while dramatic, will take longer than initially thought. Also affected by TV's entrenched position are live sporting events. The gap between the traditional game-day experience and the home-viewing experience has narrowed dramatically. The cost associated with attending live sporting events, when compared to the convenience of watching an event from one's family room, forces sports marketers to devise campaigns that persuade fans to part with their precious time and disposable income to attend in person.

Content Remains King

Controlling their own content enables sports entities to have near complete control over how their brands are positioned, extended, and reinforced. The ability to deliver consistent messaging to numerous constituencies affords them the opportunity to bypass traditional media distribution channels or otherwise use existing ones to drive viewership to their content-controlled programming. When doing so, sports properties such as UFC generate additional revenue streams while simultaneously diversifying the sports entity's business and reducing opportunities for piracy or other illegal uses of its content. Although a measure of objectivity is certainly lost, the upside associated with using any and all content to establish and grow viewer and fan interest outweighs it.

The decision by many governing bodies, sports leagues, conferences, and franchises to maintain ownership and control of their content has substantial ramifications for broadcast and cable TV networks and providers, advertisers and sponsors, athletes, viewers and fans, and even the federal government.

The proliferation of governing-body-, league-, or conference-owned networks such as the NFL and NHL Networks, NBA TV, and the Big Ten Network, as well as franchise-controlled networks such as the YES (Yankee Entertainment Sports) Network and NESN (New England Sports Network), not only permits these leagues and franchises to deliver programming targeting their most loyal fans, but also enables advertisers and sponsors an additional medium through which they can reach the demographic they seek. As these networks extend their offerings to include shoulder programming consisting of reality shows and other promotion-oriented programs that cover news and present analysis, the opportunity exists to reach a tighter, albeit smaller, audience. Versus, for example, which televises the NHL, attracts a very committed fan base, one that has demonstrated its interest in the sport and related programming by subscribing to the cable network. Advertisers, recognizing this strong viewer base constituting a loyal demographic, are able to craft marketing messages to this targeted consumer segment.

Among the considerations when doing so is the persistent need to establish strong working relationships and strategic alliances with cable TV companies, as they remain the primary distributor for such content. This will continue to grow in importance as the league-owned networks begin broadcasting more of their games on their own networks, fundamentally reshaping televised sports in the process.

College athletics and niche cable channels, and those that advertise and sponsor them, have an emerging opportunity when the content is controlled. Conferences such as the Big 10, and cable networks such as ESPNU, have the ability to increase the exposure of lower-revenue sports such as baseball, softball, lacrosse, volleyball, and golf, among others. Raising the visibility of these sports serves another critical function: it assists in establishing or building interest in them. Conferences and networks provide (prospective) advertisers and sponsors an attractive way to activate against these historically lower-profile sports—and do so while reaching a very coveted and brand-loyal audience in the process. The projected lucrative nature of these conference networks will continue to have a profound affect on college athletics, resulting in conference realignment. As the sheer number of options grows for advertisers and sponsors, league-owned and conference-owned networks, as well as those featuring new or emerging sports leagues, must remain vigilant to ensure that their marketing partners are receiving adequate value for their investment.

Athletes that might not have otherwise garnered much media attention continue to benefit as the league or conference in which they play increasingly controls and disseminates its own content. More extensive or deeper coverage of certain sports, for example, those featured in the Olympics—especially track and field and figure skating—enables athletes in those sports to build and solidify their personal brands in advance of the Olympics. This added, up-front exposure accelerates their ability to extend their brands during the Games, and to monetize them following the Games.

While fans welcome this added sports coverage, and may even be willing to pay a premium to watch it, the Federal Communications Commission and the NCAA, among others, will maintain a watchful eye on how sports organizations and their cable partners distribute sought-after content. This is because issues ranging from antitrust violations to the exploitation of athletes may arise under these conditions.

The End of "TV" As We Know It

In much the same way the traditional cell phone has morphed into a multi-dimensional, multiservice piece of mobile hardware, utilizing rapidly advancing technology in the process, so too has the TV. One example of this is the push toward televising sports in 3D, an opportunity ESPN plans to capitalize on with eighty-five live sporting events during the first year of the ESPN3D network.[67] Highlighting this push, the ESPN3D channel began televising the 2010 World Cup in June 2010. Generations removed from rabbit ears and the need to manually change channels, the TV remains the indispensable piece of in-home hardware levered as a medium to deliver the latest in technology to consumers, especially sports fans.

Beyond delivering increased clarity and quality of broadcasts, particularly for major sporting events, TVs are increasingly connecting to personal computers and other devices that facilitate the pulling and streaming of content. This in turn creates opportunities for greater consumer engagement as the ability to participate in social networking or simply keep current with one's favorite micro-blogger increases. As this transformation occurs, business opportunities are presenting themselves throughout the sports industry, for TV networks and new media powerhouses, as well as sports leagues, teams, and athletes. The advertisers and sponsors attached to these media and sports entities also stand to benefit as the offerings made available to consumers and fans continue to become more compelling. With the increased access to consumers comes the requirement that advertisers and sponsors refine their marketing messages, in terms of both style and substance.

This linking between TV and PC extends the consumer and fan experience, as traditional and new media companies foster working relationships that increase the quantity and quality of sports programming. For example, Hulu, the joint online venture among News Corp., Comcast/NBC Universal, and the Walt Disney Co., reshaped how TV programming is accessed. Over time, partnerships such as these that cater to consumer demand will be in the position to extract meaningful advertising and subscription fees linked to sports programming.

When consumer traffic is driven to and from traditional and new media platforms, as successfully accomplished by ESPN's *GameDay*, for example, myriad opportunities arise; opportunities that allow media conglomerates to direct, if not redirect, consumers to market-related programming. As fans continue to adapt to and embrace cross-platform initiatives, new media providers, realizing their ability to generate revenue from these activities, will begin to acquire sports broadcast rights, historically secured by traditional broadcast networks. New media conglomerates will be willing to pay more for a league or team's media rights, given their enhanced ability to monetize such rights across many platforms, including those associated with social media.

As this happens, sports leagues, teams, and even individual athletes will benefit as their increased, tactical reach will allow them to establish stronger connections with consumers and fans, both domestically and abroad—and do so more easily and far more cost effectively. In doing so, these sports leagues and related properties have the opportunity to establish and extend their brands in new markets. They also will be favorably positioned to generate additional (online) advertising and sponsorship revenue, an increase sure to be welcomed by athletes who, in many leagues, receive a defined percentage of such income.

TV CONTENT AND CONVERGENCE: FINAL THOUGHTS FROM FOX SPORTS'S DAVID HILL[68]

David Hill is the chairman of Fox Sports. Fox Sports maintains an ongoing leadership position in televising the National Football League and Major League Baseball. Hill shared his perspective on convergence and TV content with the SBI.

SBI: What are your thoughts on the convergence of sports, entertainment, and TV content?

HILL: For me, convergence has always existed. I have never been able to understand why people separate sport and entertainment—sport to me is the greatest form of entertainment there is. I came to sport very late after beginning my career as a television journalist. I had no desire to work in sports but I did enjoy playing them. I never watched sports because the thought of paying to watch sports was always alien to me and my family. Therefore, I was never much of a spectator and sport was never that important in my life. Sporting events were something that occasionally happened in my life, yet when an opportunity arose for me take a job as a sports producer, I thoroughly enjoyed it because to me it *was* entertainment.

SBI: How did your perception of televised sports change once you began working in the industry?

HILL: What was interesting for me was the difference between sports, politics, and economics. With politics and economics, you can promise everything and yet never have to deliver. With sports, there is a crucible of honesty and righteousness that forces people in the industry to actually deliver on their promises. The people that have made their lives out of sports are aware of this finality. It's not like an economist or politician that is never held to rights; you either win or lose in sports. You can't make excuses, you either failed or succeeded.

SBI: What differentiates Fox Sports from its competitors?

HILL: I don't really worry about our competitors or the tradition of sports. I didn't fall in love with sports; I fell in love with television. In order for television to stay current, it has to fit its consumers. As life changes and consumers change, television has to change as well to maintain validity. While at Fox I have done my best to not only stay current, but to also try to stay ahead of consumer change, making sure our sports product delivers and captivates audiences.

SBI: Where have you seen changes in the televised sports industry during your career?

HILL: Of all the things I've done in television, my most notable accomplishment was putting the score and time in a box in the corner of the screen. I received death threats about that, and television executives told me that they would never use it. My thought process was that when you sit in a stadium, you can see the clock and the score so why can't you do that at home? I have also changed broadcasts in many other ways. It has always been because I view televised sports as entertainment. What I've been doing the last few years at Fox Sports is remove things from the game such as full-framed graphics so that we get the viewer back to the action quickly—all of which is an attempt to make our coverage as minimalistic as possible. The ultimate goal is transparency for the fans. I believe this is what this generation wants. With its access to the Internet, there are no inner sanctums anymore. The consumer has the right to be everywhere and be in everything through total access. Not only do they have the right, they demand it.

SBI: How is technology changing your game-day presentation?

HILL: We are now broadcasting to a better informed audience than at any time in the history of television. Therefore, we have to be quicker, better, faster, and smarter. There has been a major change with the NFL pre-game show because we now work with more information and last-minute updates coming in from games. Because we are in competition with every website and every blogger, we also have to be more accurate. My background, where I started out as a copy boy at newspapers, taught me that you never publish anything until it is triangulated. That means that any alleged information you have only becomes a fact if you are able to check it with three separate sources. It's really the basic principles of journalism. In order to maintain our accuracy, we practice old-fashioned journalism in the modern age. I don't care if we're not the fastest but I do care that we are the most accurate. I expect Fox Sports to be the most trustworthy source for news.

SBI: How do you approach the formulation of new ideas for broadcast elements?

HILL: First and foremost, television has to be for the audience. I don't act on my ideas until I think about them for awhile and consider the ramifications. I've been very fortunate. For the last thirty years, I've worked for two remarkable media moguls: Kerry Francis Bullmore Packer in Australia and Rupert Murdoch with Fox. I've worked closely with them over the years, and as a result I've learned many lessons from both of them. One such lesson is that when you get an idea, keep it to yourself and don't let self-doubt keep you from doing it. Your first idea is always your best idea. You have to protect it and carry it out. When it comes to formulating new ideas I trust my instincts.

SBI: How much of a role do sponsors play in shaping your programming?

HILL: The great thing about television is that you are never in doubt about what the public thinks. You never have to worry because you get feedback a week later. If you make a change, you know a week later whether the audience liked it or not by whether they decided to watch again. We know that if we don't put out an attractive, intellectually stimulating, informative, and accurate package, they are not going to watch. In terms of sponsors allowing us to push the envelope, if our changes don't work we just won't have sponsors. When you work in the media, you don't have tenure. If you don't deliver you can be fired the following week. So, sponsors play a key role as they are able to voice their opinion with their checkbooks.

SBI: What is your process for making bidding decisions on television broadcast rights?

HILL: I've run sports divisions since 1977 in three different countries. What I do is set policy and make bets on decisions going forward. It's all about huge bets in terms of using your knowledge to choose the direction you think will be most successful. There are certain fundamentals that you look at, but eventually you have to commit one way or the other.

SBI: Where are the biggest challenges in terms of staying connected with fans?

HILL: There is no challenge at all because it is what we are paid to do. If you can hear, see, and respond to the fan, that is all that is needed to stay connected. Listen to your customer, anticipate their wants and needs, and be ready to deliver—if you do that, the challenges will be minimal if they exist at all.

2 VIDEO GAMING

THE WII

It's a Saturday night in Sherman Oaks, California, and twenty-six-year-old Devin Curry is hosting some friends at his apartment. Some are playing poker; others are just talking, enjoying a beer or a glass of wine. A room full of onlookers quickly turn their attention to the Nintendo Wii as Curry picks up his "Wiimote" control and begins bowling on his big-screen TV. "Oh man! Turkey!" he shouts, signifying that he has just bowled his third strike in a row.

Soon most people are staring at the screen. Diana, a college student visiting from Chile, is playing tennis against a newfound friend and, despite the fact that she has rarely played any form of video game, is holding her own in the match and having a great time in the process. Later in the evening, a group of guys will play a baseball game, using some of Devin's avatars, or "Miis," and a "Mii" named "Ice Cube" hits a home run off of "Phil Jackson."

The hugely popular Wii does not have spectacular graphics. Unlike many of its competitors, it's intuitive and has only a small handful of buttons on its controller. The Wii's signature advantage is that it allows real actions to have a virtual impact on its games, and it has created an activity that is the hit of this party, and many others like it around the world.

In 2008, Nintendo was sitting atop the video game industry thanks to its innovative Wii. This placement would have been unfathomable just a few years earlier. But how Nintendo achieved its lofty position, and where that success has led, has redefined the video game industry.

History of Nintendo

Nintendo was founded in 1889 in Kyoto, Japan, by Fusajiro Yamauchi as a small company that made Hanafuda playing cards. It enjoyed modest success throughout its early years until, in 1959, Nintendo partnered with Disney to produce and distribute playing cards featuring Disney characters. In large part due to the success of this Disney-inspired product line, the company went public on the Japanese stock exchanges in 1962.

As the company grew, it looked to create new business and experimented with a taxi company, a "love hotel" chain, a TV network, and a food company that made instant rice—all of which failed. In 1966, Nintendo began making toys and created the popular Ultra Hand, the Love Tester, and the Kousenjuu series of light gun games.

By 1975, it had entered the video game industry, securing the rights to distribute the Magnavox Odyssey home video game system in Japan. It then worked with Mitsubishi on developing a video game system, and released several arcade games in the late 1970s and early 1980s, none more popular than the 1981 release of *Donkey Kong*. The game created new licensing opportunities for Nintendo, and it earned the company nearly $300 million in its first two years.[1]

Two years later, Nintendo released the Family Computer, the "Famicom," in Japan, and it was an instant success, selling 15.2 million consoles and 183 million cartridge games.[2] The U.S. version, known as the Nintendo Entertainment System (NES), was released in 1986. Nintendo learned from the demise of Atari and other video game consoles during the video game crash of 1983 and 1984, when the market was flooded with low-quality games that had compatibility difficulties with various systems. Nintendo improved the quality of games available on its console by establishing strict licensing agreements with software developers. Every game had to be approved by Nintendo, blank cartridges were to be purchased through Nintendo, and the developed game was exclusive to Nintendo, with royalties going to the developer.

The NES was a rousing success, and it led Nintendo to expand its video game business to include the handheld Game Boy. Nintendo subsequently improved on its console system by creating the Super Nintendo, Nintendo 64, and Nintendo GameCube over the next two decades. Super Nintendo was the leading game console in the mid-1990s, outselling the Sega Genesis twenty million units to thirteen million units in the U.S., but Nintendo gradually lost competitive ground into the mid-2000s as its products lagged in graphics, features, and game play.[3]

The State of the Modern Video Game Industry—Pre Wii

By the mid-2000s, the video game console industry consisted of three major manufacturers: Nintendo, Sony, and Microsoft. Sony was the clear leader in the space, having launched the successful PlayStation in 1995 and the PlayStation 2 (PS2) in 2000, which, in 2005, became the fastest game console to sell over a hundred million units worldwide.[4] While the cost of the PS2 exceeded $300, it was very successful, in part because it doubled as a DVD player.

Microsoft struggled somewhat with the release of its Xbox in 2001. It found the creation of a new console division to be costly, and it initially was unable to differentiate itself substantially from the competition. Although it sold twenty-four million units worldwide, the Xbox division of Microsoft lost over $4 billion in its first four years.[5] In 2002, Microsoft enjoyed some success with Xbox Live, which allowed gamers to play against opponents online, and it forced Nintendo and Sony to follow suit.

Also in 2001, Nintendo released the GameCube, which sold twenty-one million units worldwide.[6] While Nintendo still had a loyal brand following, it had lagged behind both Sony and Microsoft in graphic capabilities, and several top game publishers did not even bother making games for Nintendo's console. It was also slow in developing online capabilities. Despite its third-place standing, the GameCube was profitable.

By the mid-2000s, all three console makers were pondering which direction to take their companies. Sony and Microsoft decided to offer significant improvements to their existing product, while Nintendo chose to offer a dramatically different type of product.

Sony elected to appeal to its core customers in creating the PlayStation 3 (PS3), which was designed to be the most technologically advanced game system ever created. Similar to the PS2, Sony wanted the PS3 to serve as a more complete home entertainment system, so it included the first Blu-ray 2.0 player and improved online play. However, the PS3 was so advanced that its release was delayed by over a year, and it was not released until late 2006. Production costs were also extremely high, as Sony paid $805 to produce a 20 GB unit and $840 to produce a 60 GB unit.[7] The PS3 retailed at $499 and $599, respectively for the two models, meaning that Sony lost an estimated $250 for every unit sold. In the first six months of production, Sony lost nearly $2 billion on the PS3.[8]

Adding to Sony's woes was Microsoft's Xbox 360, which also had excellent graphics and online play, but was released a year prior to the PS3. The Xbox was also more affordable, initially costing $299 and $399 for the premium edition. Still, the PS3 hasn't been a complete loss for Sony, as it helped the company's Blu-ray surpass Toshiba's HD DVD and become the industry standard. In addition, Sony has been able to reduce manufacturing costs and cut the retail price as it streamlines the production process.

The Nintendo Wii—A Blue Ocean Strategy

The term *blue ocean* was introduced in October 2004 in the *Harvard Business Review* by professors W. Chan Kim and Renee Mauborgne of INSEAD, but they had been writing about the concept since 1997. The blue ocean philosophy suggests that there are red and blue oceans in business. Red oceans are industries that exist today. They are crowded marketplaces that see intense, cutthroat competition that can become bloody; hence the term *red ocean*.

Conversely, blue oceans represent an untapped and unknown marketplace, which is untainted by competition. It is ripe for opportunity, and growth in these blue oceans can become rapid. Competition is irrelevant in blue oceans because the rules of the game have not yet been established. This strategy is not without risks, as it can be very difficult for companies to find blue oceans. A company may believe it has uncovered a new market, only to find the ocean to be more of a pond. Undertaking a blue ocean strategy forces a company to ask new questions about its target market and take a more holistic view of the industry.

Nintendo president Satoru Iwata was an early believer in the blue ocean approach and decided to apply it to the video game industry. Iwata was convinced that the casual—rather than devoted—gamer constituted the blue ocean within the video game industry. Echoing this sentiment was Nintendo of America president Reggie Fils-Aime, who believed the competition was focusing too much on satisfying the hardcore gamer at the expense of developing a new customer base, one including women, the elderly, and kids, all of whom might enjoy video games but who were simply overwhelmed by the latest and greatest advanced gaming systems.[9]

"Intellectually, yes, this sounds obvious," said Iwata in 2007. "But within Nintendo, among the shareholders, everywhere, there was resistance. When I first raised the idea, in 2003, nobody believed it was possible to broaden the games market."[10]

"The industry had found itself at a point where sales were leveling off," says Perrin Kaplan, former Nintendo of America vice president of marketing and corporate affairs. "If the video game industry had continued on its path, then it would not have been seen as innovative and robust. The industry really needed to shake itself up."[11]

Nintendo launched its new console in 2006 and selected the name "Wii" because it sounds like "we," meaning it's for everyone. It was spelled with two lower-case "i"s to symbolize two gamers playing side by side.

The Wii initially focused on sports games. Users gripped a "Wiimote control," swung it, and watched their actions mimicked in the video game world. The Wii retailed for $249.99 and included the Wii Sports package, which featured tennis, golf, bowling, baseball, and boxing games. It was also compatible with many popular sports games, such as EA SPORTS's Madden NFL, in which gamers could literally throw as if they were Indianapolis Colts quarterback Peyton Manning or stiff-arm an opponent as Adrian Peterson does as running back for the Minnesota Vikings. In addition, Wii users could download old Nintendo games, which added a nice touch of nostalgia for older generations and lapsed gamers.

Nintendo realized that it needed to market the Wii differently from its other gaming consoles. As a result, the marketing and communications group took a risk and began a grassroots viral marketing campaign. Nintendo asked nonplayers—including parents—to serve as ambassadors for the Wii, some of whom doubled as parental bloggers. Parents were impressed with the product because it offered a far more active game-playing experience for their children than the typical couch-sitting game console.

The Wii also appealed to senior game players who had difficulty exercising. The Wii made its way through retirement homes as a low-resistance but high-excitement workout.[12] In fact, several years later, the Wii earned the American Heart Association's seal of approval as its healthy check logo began appearing on the video game system packaging.[13] As previously stated, the Wii wound up being a hit at parties and was purchased by many people for social purposes—it even started popping up at office parties. The Wii's graphics were not quite as advanced as those of the Xbox 360 or PS3, but its target market of casual gamers did not demand that they be so, and it also allowed Nintendo to keep prices down.

"A lot of people don't have time to invest in multilevel, multichapter games,"

Kaplan says. "Some people have a video game skill from when they were young, or others don't have the skill yet, but in this stressful world, taking time out of a busy day for a little slice of joy is a great gift. They can all be told that they can give the Wii a try, and it's really intuitive and far easier—and way more fun—than they would have thought. It's also a way to spend time with your families."[14]

While Nintendo was having success with non-traditional gamers, the Wii also found its way into the home of many hardcore gamers who saw the system as substantially different from the Xbox and PlayStation consoles they had been using for years. These gamers would wind up owning more than one game console.

"One of the challenges is keeping the core gamer really happy," Kaplan says. "We said to them 'it may look simple to you, but you need to try it, because it's different from how you're used to playing.' So they tried it, and a couple of them who thought of themselves as skilled gamers were surprised that they weren't good right away and liked that challenge. But they also want a richer and deeper experience from games too—a variety, so Nintendo is paying a lot of attention to them to keep them engaged."[15]

The Wii was such an enormous success worldwide that Nintendo was having difficulty producing enough supply to meet demand. It was not unusual in 2007 to see those wishing to purchase a Wii form long lines outside retailers in the hope of securing a console to call their own. By the end of 2009, the Wii had sold more than fifty million units worldwide, a total sure to grow dramatically as new global markets are accessed.[16]

In the first six months of sales, the Wii was outselling its top two competitors six to one. In the first year after its release, the Wii helped Nintendo increase its profits by 500 percent and double its stock price, making it the second-most valuable Japanese company after Toyota.[17]

What's Next?

Looking into the future, Nintendo has continued to expand the Wii's sports offerings. In May 2008, Nintendo released *Wii Fit*, a game that features a balance board and allows users to engage in a wide variety of exercises from yoga to push-ups. The board keeps track of a player's weight and body mass index in an effort to keep the user healthy and in shape, as well as motivated. Several fitness centers began to offer classes featuring the Wii, further extending its application well beyond the core gamer. *Wii Fit* was the third-best-selling game of 2008 in the U.S., selling over 4.5 million units, despite launching midway through the year.[18]

To keep the Wii fresh and ahead of its competitors, Nintendo released the Wii Vitality Sensor in 2010.[19] The device, which clips to players' index fingers, takes into account the emotional state of those playing. According to Nintendo president Satoru Iwata, "With the sensor, we can tell whether you are breathing in or out. We can tell how nervous you are."[20]

Despite its success, Nintendo recognizes that it won't have the blue ocean to itself for long, as the competitive landscape in the video gaming industry has proven to be a dynamic one whereby success is measured in large part by one's next console offering, not its last—and Nintendo, Sony, and Microsoft know this better than anyone.

"An important part of success is for companies to create products that consumers do not realize they need," Kaplan says. "People used to be intimidated by gaming. They thought it was fun, but it was too complex, so they just thought they weren't gamers. It was a perception we knew they had, but we didn't articulate it that way. The Wii was something that they could do easily and have fun with."[21]

VIDEO GAMING: AN OVERVIEW

While the Wii has ushered in a new way for consumers to interact with their favorite games, the history of video games dates back more than fifty years. Considering the rapid evolution of this medium, it was unlikely that William Higginbotham, who created *Table Tennis for Two* to showcase a new analog computer during an open house at the Brookhaven National Laboratory, was aware of what would follow.

Unlike *Table Tennis for Two*, whose primary use was to showcase emerging technology, many acknowledge *Baseball* in 1971 as the original sports video game because it was created for the specific purpose of video gaming.

One year later Atari released the coin-operated arcade game *Pong*, the electronic table tennis game, which served to launch the video game industry as we know it today. Arcades for video games also became popular, as scores of young people flocked to them in the 1970s and 1980s to play.

As successful as arcade games eventually became, it was the development of the video game console that further popularized video games by bringing them into the home. The Atari 2600, often referred to as "The Godfather of Modern Video Game Systems," was introduced in October of 1977 and sold over thirty million consoles; it included an installed base that led to the sale of hundreds of millions of video games.[22]

However, in the early to mid-1980s the video game industry suffered because the market was saturated with low-quality games and consoles. The Atari 2600 had become outdated, and a compelling next-generation console had not yet been manufactured. Simultaneously, as their cost dropped, personal computers emerged as adequate substitutes for many consoles.

That would change in 1985 when Nintendo released its NES console system and, by 1987, the video game market had recovered, with U.S. sales reaching approximately $825 million.[23]

The NES was revolutionary for its time, offering high-quality games such as *Super Mario Brothers* and *The Legend of Zelda*. It also provided the most superior graphics of any gaming system to date while remaining quite user friendly. By 1989, the home video game market had reached $3.5 billion in sales in the United States.[24]

In the late 1980s, the landscape for sports video games began to change. In 1988, Electronic Arts (EA) released *Jordan vs. Bird* for the NES, which was the sequel to the 1983 computer game *One on One: Dr. J vs. Larry Bird*. Notably, these games were the first to allow users to actually play as if they were professional athletes. Five years later, Tengen released *R.B.I. Baseball* for the NES, which was the first game for home consoles in the U.S. that enabled gamers to play as if they were controlling a real professional team.

However, Tengen was unable to secure a license from Major League Baseball, which limited the game's authenticity. In fact, Tengen was not alone, as many publishers faced similar challenges that compromised the marketability of the games. Obtaining the proper licenses for sports video games has proven to be crucial in achieving success, as can be seen with THQ's WWE franchise, as well as EA SPORTS's *Madden Football*, which today has exclusivity relating to NFL team licenses.

Over the past twenty-five years, and due in large part to technological advancements and new industry entrants such as Sony and Microsoft, video game consoles have continued to evolve and attract players of all ages, who are now able to play in real time against gamers located anywhere in the world.

As video games grew in popularity, so too did sports-specific games. Publishers such as EA SPORTS, 989 Studios, Midway Games, THQ, 2K Sports, Activision|Blizzard, and many others have built impressive track records as industry stalwarts. Their games' strengths, much like those associated with the Nintendo Wii, are predicated on allowing players to become immersed in the action and controlling nearly every aspect of the game.

EA SPORTS has exploited its league licenses and has used enhanced game play as an important product attribute, so much so that its *FIFA* soccer game has sold a total of 65 million copies over fifteen years worldwide, generating revenue in excess of $2 billion.[25] THQ's *WWE Smackdown* franchise has achieved tremendous success as well, having shipped approximately forty-seven million units worldwide since 1999.[26] Similarly, Tony Hawk—profiled in Chapter 3—has established an extraordinary track record based on the video games carrying his name and likeness. "Tony Hawk" branded video games sold approximately thirty million units over a ten-year period, and have consistently ranked in the top ten in U.S. sales in the years they were released.[27]

With the emergence of new sports and new distribution platforms and channels, the video game industry continues to thrive and does so on a global basis, as evidenced by the success of THQ's WWE titles and the launch of Major League Gaming.

THQ'S WWE FRANCHISE

Founded in 1989 as an interactive toy and video game publisher, THQ (Toy Headquarters) develops and publishes content for a variety of video gaming platforms, including the Nintendo Wii, Sony PS3, Microsoft Xbox 360, and the Sony PlayStation Portable (PSP), as well as such portable devices as the Nintendo DS.

In 1995, Brian Farrell became president and CEO and changed the company's focus from that of a toy company that included the publishing of video games to a company *solely* focused on video games. The shift in focus enabled THQ to dramatically increase revenue in the years that followed, and made it one of the most profitable publishers in the video game industry.

Throughout this period, THQ secured long-term licensing agreements with numerous "content creators," including World Wrestling Entertainment (WWE) in 1998. The THQ-WWE licensing agreement consists of up-front commitments and guarantees, along with royalties paid on the basis of sales volume. The relationship between THQ and WWE has been extraordinarily successful for both companies, while simultaneously underscoring the convergence of sports, entertainment, and technology.

WWE, the branded leader in professional wrestling, bills itself as "an integrated media and entertainment company; one that has been the recognized leader in sports entertainment for more than 25 years."[28] Unlike the wrestling matches one might watch during the Olympics or at a collegiate match, WWE's events are positioned as entertainment, with its wrestler-characters competing against each other in matches that have predetermined outcomes. In essence, the WWE, under the leadership of Vince McMahon, has combined sport with theater to create a highly engaging form of entertainment.

This is best exemplified by the historically and consistently popular pay-per-view events WWE produces, particularly WrestleMania. For example, the twenty-fifth anniversary of WrestleMania, held in 2009, became the company's highest-grossing live event, with $7.4 million in ticket sales and $1.5 million in merchandise sales. Equally impressive, the event also garnered a record-breaking 105 million page views at the WWE website.[29] WWE's distinct ability to identify the value of convergence has resulted in annual company revenue surpassing $500 million by decade's end.[30]

Recognizing one another's strengths and ability to reach highly coveted audiences, THQ and WWE teamed in 1998 to create *Smackdown!* for the Sony PlayStation, the first in a series of games that would later become one of the most popular video game franchises ever.

"It all starts with WWE Creative and Vince McMahon. They've created a huge fan base with over-the-top and fun stuff," Farrell says. "At THQ we understand what needs to get built and we have a partner in Yuke's Co. [video game developer in Osaka, Japan] that knows how to build it. We try to make a highly entertaining game."[31]

This billion dollar video game franchise has achieved tremendous success over the years, having shipped approximately forty million units worldwide since 1999, cementing THQ's reputation as the top publisher for fighting games in the process.[32]

"We do iterate on the game like *Madden* iterates football or *NBA Live* [renamed *NBA Elite* in 2010] iterates basketball," Farrell says. "But we have to innovate each year and deliver something new. We're asking our consumers to part with a fair amount of money. You have to give them a compelling reason to do that or they won't. This is a sophisticated consumer. A lot of people in our industry underestimate the consumer, but they know the games well."[33]

Smackdown is now available on a variety of gaming platforms including the Sony PS3, Microsoft Xbox 360, and the Nintendo Wii, along with a number of mobile devices including Apple's iPhone, and remains an industry leader when it comes to game play. The video game franchise is based on what one might see in the ring at a WWE event, and allows gamers to play as their favorite wrestler-character with one important caveat: unlike in the WWE events, the video game outcomes of matches are not predetermined.

THQ has successfully recreated every aspect of what has made the WWE popular for decades, from wrestler entrances into the ring and the authenticity of the "wrestling moves" to the post-match celebrations. This reality reached new heights when the game was made available for the PS3 and Xbox 360. Given the advanced processing power and graphics of these consoles, gamers are able to immerse themselves in the total WWE experience.

"The video game experience is an extension on someone's passion and affinity for wrestling," Farrell says. "But our goal is to make the WWE accessible to everyone, even those who don't go through the turnstile or watch every week."[34]

THQ has created an online competition for the game as well, which includes online rankings in which gamers are ranked against each other—a feature reminiscent of the "top scores" screens that people have grown accustomed to in old arcade games. This feature enhances the competitive nature of the game and allows players to feel like they are a part of more serious gaming leagues, such as the emerging professional video gaming leagues.

While the core demographic for the game is males aged eighteen to thirty-four, THQ has attempted to expand the demographic for this franchise with marketing efforts that one might expect to see for big-budget movies.[35] For instance, approximately 75 to 80 percent of advertising for this franchise occurs on TV, and online advertising outweighs print ads by approximately two to one. Although the franchise is still advertised to its core gamers via avenues such as IGN, GameSpot, and WWE programming, efforts are increasingly targeting casual gamers, as evidenced by advertising during various college football bowl games and in *Maxim* magazine.

When companies such as THQ carefully blend sports, entertainment, and technology they are poised to succeed; when companies do so while also incorporating successful licensing strategies, they position themselves to dominate a portion—if not all—of an industry.

MAJOR LEAGUE GAMING

As seen with THQ's success with its online component of the WWE franchise, online gaming has become its own example of the convergence among sports, entertainment, and technology, improving the video gaming experience in the process.

New media entrepreneurs Michael Sepso and Sundance DiGiovanni capitalized on this new era of online gaming by taking the format associated with traditional sports leagues and combining it with video games to create Major League Gaming (MLG), which was founded in 2002. The two later continued the league's growth by raising $35 million from private-equity investors in two rounds of funding in 2006.[36]

The largest organized league and international sanctioning body for professional video gaming, MLG primarily operates through live competitions and its online website, www.mlgpro.com; it has also had distribution deals with the USA Network, G4 Network, and ESPN. When discussing the vision for MLG, Sepso stressed the importance of "building and balancing the company's business model around the authenticity and cultural norms of the competitive, multiplayer video gaming world in order to connect with its players."[37] This vision continues to be embraced by the investment community, as evidenced by Oak Investment Partners contributing an additional $7.5 million in venture capital in 2009.[38]

The MLG Pro Circuit provides teams of gamers the ability to compete while playing a preselected set of team-based games, such as *Gears of War, Modern Warfare,* or one of the games in the *Halo* series, during regular season events throughout North America. Players can also participate in Pro Circuit ladder tournaments that help them earn Pro Circuit Rank Points, which are used for seeding the larger regular season events and gaining reserved passes for upcoming Pro Circuit Events.

MLG's 2006 acquisition of Gamebattles.com helped extend the MLG brand by offering online tournament options that initially yielded over 460,000 users and 700,000 teams playing tournaments across forty game titles on multiple gaming platforms.[39] Further extending its brand presence, MLG aired shows about the league on the G4 and USA networks. The USA show, *MLG Pro Circuit*, aired on Sunday mornings and featured a behind-the-scenes look at the personal lives of a group of gaming professionals in addition to in-game competition that followed the seven-city season. Gamers who played the same games at home were now able to showcase their ability in a competitive setting which, in turn, was broadcast for other players to enjoy. While the two seasons of the seven-part weekly series brought additional publicity to the league, the Internet was ultimately deemed the best medium to market the league and its players. In addition, MLG management believed sponsors were more willing to buy online ads than television ads when hoping to reach their eighteen- to thirty-year-old male demographic. Demonstrating their belief that the Internet provided greater fan access, MLG pulled the shows off the air and redeployed their television producer to handle Internet programming.[40] This move proved successful, as the first Pro Circuit event for 2008 drew 12,000 people onsite and 750,000 video streams via mlgpro.com.[41] When reflecting on the television experience, Sepso spoke of turning a "non-linear story into a linear one" in order to fit it into a thirty-minute television show.[42]

Using the mlgpro.com website to broadcast tournaments and run the league, MLG quickly saw the number of unique monthly users grow dramatically from twenty-five thousand in 2006 to five million users in early 2008.[43] The site hosts over 700,000 online matches a month and registers, on average, five thousand new online tournament players each day.[44] Given the online growth, MLG has been able to attract an increasing number of sponsors, including Dr Pepper, Old Spice, Stride, Ballpark, Bic, Castrol, Tinactin, Hewlett-Packard, Hot Pockets, and GameStop.[45] Although there have been a number of competing leagues over the years, these sponsorships, coupled with MLG's methodical approach to growth and exclusive contracts with the top pro gamers in North America, have created a stable company that has survived where others have failed. The viral development of MLG as a sports league has contributed to much of MLG's success. When discussing why MLG has succeeded while others failed, Sepso underscored the need "to develop a business model that fits the needs of the participants rather than fitting the participants into a contrived model."[46] A key concept of MLG's development was treating it as sports league and maintaining a direct relationship with its sponsors. In addition, MLG has made it a point to own all its media production and distribution, which contributes to the strength of its sponsor relationships.[47]

In addition to sponsors, MLG has been able to align itself with media and development partners. In conjunction with ESPN, MLG has produced top-ten highlight videos of "in-game" plays that fans can see on the video game section of its website and at MLG's websites. ESPN3, the broadband network for live sports programming, is also being utilized to stream tournaments and live coverage of some events.[48]

The accessibility to MLG and the possible fame its players can receive is undoubtedly another draw for the league. Any person with the appropriate skill and access to the Internet can be the league's next big star. Highlighting the fame the league and its players had achieved, MLG entered into a special promotion in 2009 with soft drink maker Dr Pepper, which featured the league's number one team, Str8 Rippin, on approximately 175 million of its twenty-ounce bottles.[49] Gamer Tom "TSquared" Taylor, a member of the Str8 Rippin team and one of the league's biggest stars, was featured on the label along with MLG's own branding. This sponsorship and promotion signified the validity of the league, as it was the first time Dr Pepper had placed any of its sports league partners or sponsored professional stars on its label for national distribution.[50] Not only did the promotion feature gamers, it also provided fans prizes, access to the Gamebattles.com website, and exclusive content surrounding the Str8 Rippin team and the 2008 MLG season. As mentioned by Sepso, these major sponsorships allow MLG to reach levels of marketing through co-marketing that they otherwise would not be able to obtain with their budget.[51] Further reinforcing Sepso's comment, in late 2009 MLG entered into partnerships with EA, whereby MLG operated numerous competitions involving EA's popular sports titles, and headwear retailer LIDS, which offered an exclusive MLG fashion line.[52]

In 2010, MLG continued its innovative approach to sponsorship and video gaming by announcing the Doritos Pro-Gaming combine with the goal of finding new video gaming talent through online and at-site competitions.[53] Through each step of its development, MLG has succeeded by providing video game players at home the aspiration to become stars at one of their tournaments. From the at-home playing of their sponsors' games to the appearances at retail stores where the games are sold to the onsite tournaments that are streamed live online, MLG has provided a league that solidifies the link between gaming, entertainment, competition, and business.

VIDEO GAMING: THE BOTTOM LINE

The Nintendo Wii, THQ's WWE videogame franchise, and Major League Gaming all represent not only where video gaming has been but also where it is headed as an industry. Video gaming, which includes the sale of consoles, games, online downloads, and peripherals, is expected to grow to $68 billion in revenues by 2012.[54] As video gaming continues to evolve and reach new market segments, industry stakeholders must consider the extent to which their businesses will be affected by such issues as video gaming becoming more of a social and physical activity, resulting in more users per console. They must also closely scrutinize increases in mobile gaming, particularly gaming that utilizes phones and other personal mobile devices. Finally, stakeholders must pay keen attention to the increase in downloading video game game updates, extended versions, and other content, including virtual goods.

Leaving the Couch Behind

Due in large part to the continued success of Nintendo's Wii, video gaming has transformed itself from a being a relatively stationary activity with a contained number of players to an all-encompassing social and sporting activity, enjoyed by groups as well as individuals. Often referred to as gesture-based video gaming, this genre of gaming has caught the attention of many industry stalwarts who have seen the potential in non-sedentary gaming. Social video gaming, historically associated with the Wii, is a fun, cost-effective form of home-based entertainment. Exercise and performance-related gaming, such as Electronic Arts's *EA SPORTS Active* and Nintendo's *Wii Fit* and *Wii Motion Plus*, have taken this genre to a new level. Together, these gesture-based games have created opportunities for many in the sports business. Console manufacturers, game developers and publishers, sports organizations, advertisers and sponsors, athletes, and consumers and fans all feel the effects.

Console manufacturers, along with those responsible for creating and distributing these games, have already responded to consumer demand for increased interactivity. However, they will have to be even more proactive in their efforts since they seek to further broaden the consumer base of casual gamers. When doing so they are required to enhance game features that attract casual gamers while not disenfranchising hardcore players, a challenge that, properly executed, will increase the overall size of the market, which in turn will help offset increased development costs. It is important that they also strive to create games that cater specifically to each target market.

Console manufacturers and game developers will be supported in their efforts by advertisers and sponsors who seek to reach the extended (casual) gamer base. For example, as video game publishers deliver customized work-outs, supply real-time feedback, and provide downloadable content to those relying on a game for their workout routine, the attractiveness of (in-game) advertising, sponsorship, and cross-promotion will significantly increase.

Licensed image and content providers, especially sports leagues, teams, and athletes, become more important as consumers desire a strong connection to the product, whether it be linked to a physical workout or social activity. For instance, those playing *Guitar Hero* want to strum actual songs by their favorite artists, while sports fans may want to play as John McEnroe in *Grand Slam Tennis* for the Wii. As this trend continues, the size and scope of social gaming competitions—and even gaming leagues structured around such content—will increase.

Overall, consumers that may not have considered themselves gamers are now responsible for much of the industry's growth and future success. Ultimately, this results in the further mainstreaming of the video game industry and creates the opportunity for incremental revenue generation for all industry participants.

Pay and Play As You Go

Mobile gaming, which has been heavily promoted and encouraged by Apple's iPhone, Google's Android, and the Blackberry family of smartphones, continues to grow rapidly. Revenue is projected to more than double between 2008 and 2012, with estimates suggesting total revenue of $13.5 billion by 2012.[55]

The flexibility and scalability that come with portability, even if the quality of game play is compromised due to less robust user interfaces, extends the gaming market for both hardcore and casual gamers. The rapidity of techno-logical advances, when coupled with the revenue upside associated with mobile gaming, will have a material effect on the sports business industry.

Console manufacturers, game developers, and publishers, along with phone manufacturers and telecom providers, will vacillate between being partners and competitors. Sports leagues and governing bodies responsible for licensing and the oversight of intellectual property, in this case personal digital rights, will also have a vested interest, as will the athletes themselves as they and their rep-resentatives recognize an opportunity to monetize their personal brands. Consumers and fans, especially those that continue to "pull" this content toward them given their interest in video gaming, stand to materially shape the future of this part of the industry, a future certain to include improved quality of mobile sports video games dictated by consumer wants and needs.

Console manufacturers risk losing meaningful market share as their traditional consumer base spends more time and resources on mobile gaming. As time and attention are siphoned away from console-based video games, these manufacturers will be forced to more actively engage developers and publishers in an effort to maintain their clout. This is particularly important given that game developers and publishers will be allocating incremental resources to reaching mobile gamers. Developers will be required to work with phone manufacturers to ensure proper technology integration, as well as simultaneously adapt their own game production to the mobile game user who seeks shorter games with less developed storylines. If both strategies are successfully implemented, these developers have the opportunity to extend their brands as the market segment continues to grow.

By creating deeper and more integrated strategic alliances with telecom companies that offer exclusive games or content, brands have cross-promoted one another and helped grow the market segment together. As "apps stores" continue to gain prominence, carrier exclusivity will evolve and the telecoms will be forced to address developers' ability to design for an entire platform rather than single (or multiple) carriers. Regardless, incremental value will be gained by phone companies as revenue increases with games downloaded onto their phones. Consumers may be more likely to stay with a cell phone company because of desired mobile gaming availability, while the telecom providers are poised to offer customizable data packages and service plans that optimize revenue generation.

Mobile gaming now presents sports leagues and their athletes with unique and targeted opportunities to reach their core fan bases while also establishing a bond with casual fans that enjoy mobile gaming. Given that so many sports leagues have entrenched sponsorship deals with telecom providers and routinely license their rights to those manufacturing and distributing video games, the possibility of forging deeper and more integrated business partnerships exists. Properly constructed, these alliances will facilitate new entrants into sport sponsorship given the brand affinities of the demographics their combined reach delivers, namely brand-loyal consumers who consider themselves sports fans.

Downloading the Future

Online video games are forecasted to generate $12 billion in 2011, a four-fold increase since 2005.[56] In the U.S. alone, the number of online gamers is projected to grow to more than 180 million in 2012, an increase of more than 17 percent from 2009.[57] Not surprisingly, the sports business industry is paying close attention to the impact this growth will continue to have, particularly as it relates to emerging revenue streams. This growth, fueled in large part by convenience, cost, and ease of play, is now being complemented by attendant increases in revenue brought about through such developments as the increase in micro-transactions, including the purchase of virtual goods, and the emergence of professional video gaming leagues.

The transition to online gaming and related business activities will continue to materially influence console manufacturers and game developers, as well as retailers reliant on traditional unit sales, (sports) brands hoping to resonate with consumers online and, of course, gamers.

The ongoing migration to online gaming, while not spelling doom for traditional console games, continues to force console manufacturers and their developers to adapt to the shifting paradigm. Hardware and software companies must create new avenues for consumption and align with other brands in an effort to remain top of mind as the industry becomes more fragmented. Retailers, chiefly those specializing in video games, are as vulnerable as the "mom and pop" bookstores were when Amazon and other online outlets began to dominate the retail book industry.

Working with their strategic partners, video game franchises, including THQ's WWE and UFC franchises, must be nimble enough to deliver compelling games through this medium (as well as the mobile medium) without harming the core brand. Mitigating this challenge is the opportunity for the console manufacturers and developers to work with brands to ensure authenticity that leads to additional revenue generation. As mentioned earlier, micro-transactions represent but one increasingly monetizable market segment. The ability to purchase virtual goods ranging from in-game element upgrades, such as deeper levels of penetration and improved weaponry, to avatars wearing officially licensed sports merchandise has created a burgeoning market, one anticipated being in excess of $3 billion by 2012.[58]

Popular (lifestyle) brands and licensors, including sports leagues, franchises, and athletes, have the ability to help extend this market because many consumers have a strong affinity for their brands. For instance, a New York Yankees fan may be willing to pay a nominal fee to have his avatar outfitted with a Yankees cap. This type of purchase not only further personalizes the online experience for the consumer, it also authenticates it while simultaneously deepening the connection between the brand and the consumer. It also provides incremental licensing revenue. Sponsors and advertisers will dedicate more resources to this evolving form of marketing over time and will rely on it to amplify the core brand through enhanced cross-promotions. For example, that same consumer who purchased the virtual Yankees cap can be provided a discount on the "real thing" upon his next visit to the stadium or local sporting goods store.

Compelling and increasingly sophisticated online gaming experiences will continue to foster higher-end, organized participation, well beyond that of casual gamers. While MLG is certainly the most established league organized to date, others catering to additional market segments will emerge. As they do, all involved—including regulatory agencies and consumer advocacy groups—will have to work to ensure the integrity of the activities, particularly given ongoing issues of fraud and piracy.

Ultimately, the marketing and business development opportunities associated with online gaming will increase revenue for savvy brand marketers, whether they are console manufacturers or sports leagues, while at the same time delivering a more personalized, customized gaming experience for consumers.

VIDEO GAMING AND CONVERGENCE: FINAL THOUGHTS FROM EA SPORTS'S PETER MOORE[59]

Peter Moore is the president of EA SPORTS, a label of Electronic Arts, Inc. (EA). EA SPORTS is the world's largest sports video game publisher, with hit video game franchises such as Madden NFL Football, Tiger Woods PGA Tour Golf, FIFA Soccer, *and* NBA Elite. *Moore shared his perspective on convergence and the video game industry with the SBI.*

SBI: How has EA SPORTS approached the convergence of sports and entertainment in the video game industry?

MOORE: We have built our mission around personal access to the emotion of sports. We create a virtual simulation of the entire game itself and bring it to life in your living room. We utilize the power of the hardware to have cinematography levels that allow us to bring sports to life in an entertaining, immersive, and broadcast-style manner. Online has also provided us the ability to bring disparate people together through the networks that exist with the PS3 and Xbox 360 systems. This has enabled us to connect people in the millions in ways that weren't previously possible.

SBI: How have you seen video games affect convergence, and vice versa, on a broader scale beyond consoles?

MOORE: The roles have started to reverse as video game manufacturers have been able to develop and provide technology back to the broadcast people. *Virtual Playbook for Madden NFL* on the ESPN network utilizes the 3D *Madden* engine to push broadcast analysis past the telestrator. Coaches and players have grown up learning the game of football through video games like *Madden*. There's now a tipping point where fans get their knowledge of the game from video games. In fact, polling has shown that *Madden* video gamers have a greater knowledge about football and its strategies, history, and structure than people that play the game in real life. We are now a mainstream staple in the way people consume sports.

SBI: From an industry evolution perspective, what has been the most significant development over the past few years?

MOORE: There's been an evolution from playing by yourself to playing with a friend that comes over to your house to the current generation of network gaming. Online services such as Xbox Live provide no boundaries in providing personal access to the emotional aspects of sports via your console. EA SPORTS is more of a sports entertainment brand than a video game brand. The democratization and globalization of sports can now be furthered by the technology that is brought together through online video game play. Games are now seen as a dynamic service that reflects the day-to-day reenactments of what is happening in that particular sport.

SBI: What are some specific areas where EA SPORTS has taken advantage of convergence and differentiated itself from not just the video game marketplace, but other forms of entertainment?

MOORE: We bring people together interactively. We compare ourselves to brands such as Nike, adidas, ESPN, Fox, and Sky Sports because we are a sports entertainment brand that conducts its core business in video games yet has a broader influence on the world of sports. For instance, we offer digital trading cards for our *FIFA Ultimate Team* feature that you can download and buy. This generated tens of millions of dollars for us in the six months following the game's release. Another example is our *NCAA Basketball* franchise, which allowed players to download and play the NCAA tournament with the sixty-four teams that were selected on that day before the tournament even started. Nobody gets you inside the game and provides passion and emotion with the game experience like EA SPORTS. Nobody contacts millions of people in a truly interactive manner like we do by firing up your system, putting a game in the tray, and putting on your head set.

SBI: What are some EA SPORTS initiatives that the consumer should be excited about?

MOORE: Our Dynamic DNA system with our *NBA Live* franchise [known now as *NBA Elite*] was used by some teams to track the daily tendencies of players before they played their game that night. Player performance is adjusted according to the player's play in real time and is reflected daily in our video games. We have an upcoming experiment with our golf franchise. *Tiger Online* is a web browser game based on subscriptions and micro transactions such as new golf courses and digital versions of new golf clubs. This takes away the need for consoles, eliminates price as a barrier to entry, and provides convenience, as people can pick it up and play at a moment's notice on the Internet.

SBI: How do you bring lapsed gamers back into the fold when many games and controllers have become so complex over the past ten years?

MOORE: Approachability is important and, as a result, we are trying to make games more accessible with training modes through our *Madden* game where you can learn how to throw, run, and tackle. The Wii allows us to utilize a different experience that makes it easier for lapsed gamers to get involved. The Wii has allowed us to break down those barriers. The *Tiger Online* game addresses this as well with a simple "click and swing" system which anyone that has used a mouse can do. Our approach is, "If you can do email, you can play *Tiger.*"

SBI: How is the video game industry's revenue model changing, and how must EA SPORTS respond to this new paradigm?

MOORE: Much like the music industry's challenges, we are facing direct consumer digital downloads. We need to evolve as a publisher. We are aware that five-to-ten years from now consumers may not be driving to the store to pick up discs. We are evolving to a direct-to-consumer digital delivery where

maybe it's not $60 a year for *Madden*, but instead $30 to update to new stadiums, uniforms, and other updates game players find of value. Consumers
will be able to download directly at the precise moment everything is launched
online without leaving their home. This may be many years in the future, but as
we are seeing with other forms of digital media, convenience, speed, and flexibility are now paramount in the consumer's mind.

**SBI: What role do you believe the console manufacturers will play going
forward?**

MOORE: There will still be some form of hardware that is needed to facilitate a game experience. The consoles interpret the user's actions and put them
on the screen. Gesture control, which Microsoft and Sony have undertaken,
may be sufficient to change the game experiences enough that the controller
becomes your body and you don't have to push buttons. Hybrid games may be
the future with controllers and body motions being reflected on the screen.

**SBI: Can you describe how EA SPORTS balances marketing campaigns
and branding initiatives?**

MOORE: Within the last year we have undertaken more of a brand campaign than a franchise campaign—one that emphasized game situations more
than the games themselves. These ads celebrated what sports video gaming is
all about by championing the undertaking of playing sports games, and what
gamers love and cherish about the emotional access we provide to sports via
our titles.

**SBI: What challenges and/or vulnerabilities does the video game industry
face in the years to come?**

MOORE: Although video gaming is a form of entertainment, and many
believe entertainment to be somewhat recession-proof, we now know our
industry is susceptible during economic downturns. Gamers have become
more selective, and fewer games are selling more units. The big games are going
to get bigger, and the smaller games will become less important, with retailers
possibly not even stocking those games. The brand campaigns emphasize the
joy of gaming and the joy of "the win," as everyone enjoys winning, especially
when it comes to video games.

**SBI: As someone at the forefront of their industry and the technology
surrounding it, what advice can you give the sports business community at
large?**

MOORE: The key is to provide personal access to the emotion of sports. I'm from Liverpool and I live and die with my team. No other medium has this type of passion, emotion, and is part of the deep core of who we are. You need to leverage everything from a business perspective, but without destroying the passion and emotion that we all love about sports.

ATHLETE BRANDING

DAVID BECKHAM

On the afternoon of July 21, 2007, the center of the sports world was the Home Depot Center in Carson, California. Executives from Anschutz Entertainment Group (AEG), the owner of Major League Soccer's (MLS's) Los Angeles Galaxy, paced around their suite in anticipation.

Their view showed a sold-out stadium, one bustling with twenty-seven thousand fans, including numerous celebrities such as Eva Longoria, Katie Holmes, and California Governor Arnold Schwarzenegger, who entered the stadium via red carpet, reminiscent of a Hollywood movie premier. On the field a slew of ESPN television cameras prepared to broadcast what would turn out to be the highest-rated MLS game in the history of the network—despite it being an exhibition match between the Galaxy and perennial English Premier League power Chelsea.[1] All of this because David Beckham represented the future for an eleven-year old sports league that desperately wanted to elevate its stature. Months earlier, the British soccer sensation had agreed to a monumental five-year contract with the Galaxy, which could pay him up to $250 million, including endorsements.

For weeks, ESPN had run advertisements comparing Beckham's arrival in the U.S. to that of the Beatles coming to America. Understandably, most of those in attendance didn't just come to watch a soccer game; rather, they were in attendance to be part of a spectacle, an event that was as much about entertainment as it was about soccer. They were there to get a glimpse of Beckham, the global brand who was sitting on the bench with a badly sprained ankle.

Despite the injury, Beckham had to play—there was simply too much riding on his premier to have it any other way. Much to the delight of all those associated with soccer in the U.S., he took the field in the seventy-eighth minute and played for the balance of the Galaxy's 1-0 loss.

"Start of Something Big" read the *Los Angeles Times* headline the next day, with the sub-head announcing, "Beckham makes a brief appearance, but his influence is clear to his teammates and his opponents, who predict big things for him."[2] *Times* columnist Bill Plaschke, who just days earlier had declared himself "Bored by Beckham," changed his outlook in a piece headlined "Beckham's Magic Shows."

MLS had transformed itself in a matter of twelve minutes. But was it enough to elevate the sport's status in the United States on a permanent basis? Was David Beckham's brand strong enough and portable enough to make soccer a major sport in this country?

Soccer in the United States

While soccer is the most popular sport in the world, it has always been well below football, basketball, baseball, and numerous other sports in the U.S. in terms of commercial appeal.

The North American Soccer League (NASL) was founded in 1968, and it existed in relative obscurity until, in 1975, the New York Cosmos signed the legendary Pelé. Pelé's arrival was soon followed by several international stars that included Italy's Giorgio Chinaglia and Franz Beckenbauer of Germany; these arrivals spiked interest in the Cosmos and curiosity about the budding league.

Other NASL teams quickly attempted to replicate the success of the Cosmos by signing foreign stars—many of whom were well past their prime—to large contracts. The league also expanded to twenty-four teams, as it tried to spread the game nationally. Yet the NASL clearly was not ready for such rapid growth. Soccer had not quite taken hold in many markets around the U.S., and there simply was not an in-depth knowledge of the game or a large enough fan base. The NASL was not able to generate the revenue quickly enough to support rising player salaries, and there weren't enough markets interested in the sport to support the league's rapid expansion. The NASL folded in 1984, and professional soccer would not return to the U.S. for another twelve years.

During the 1980s, America witnessed impressive growth throughout the youth soccer sector. Suburban parents were enrolling their children in American Youth Sports Organization (AYSO) and other youth leagues across the nation. Soccer was relatively inexpensive to play, it was safe, and it helped children stay fit. By the early 1990s, soccer had become the top organized participatory sport in the U.S. for children of both genders.[3]

Hoping to spread the game further, the international soccer association FIFA awarded the U.S. the right to host the 1994 World Cup, and it proved to be a huge success. Americans jumped at the opportunity to see the best soccer players in the world, and the country's large football stadiums helped make it the most attended World Cup ever.

With the success of the World Cup, U.S. organizers promised they would start a professional soccer league and, in 1996, the ten-team MLS was launched. Unlike the NASL, MLS would seek to grow at a slower and more manageable pace. The league utilized a single-entity ownership structure that ensured cost certainty because owners invested in the league and served as franchise operators, not owners. It employed a strict salary cap, and, with the goal of developing American soccer players, it limited the number of foreigners. Also, unlike the NASL, MLS had several owners who had experience in the sports industry with other organizations, such as Philip Anschutz, Robert Kraft, and Lamar Hunt.

MLS initially incurred financial ups and downs, but stabilized once more teams began building soccer-specific stadiums. Attendance in the league grew from 13,700 a game to 15,100 in 2006. AEG, whose founder Philip Anschutz fervently believed in the sport's promise in the U.S., was heavily involved in the development of MLS, at one point running half the league's teams. AEG subsequently would build stadiums for these franchises and then sell the teams to local investors or operators, with the exception of the Galaxy, which it kept.

Despite MLS's newfound stability, there remained a sense that it still required a shot in the arm in order to stand out in a cluttered sports marketplace. AEG and MLS, having learned from the NASL's demise, and recognizing the trends in U.S. soccer, believed Beckham would be just what the sport needed to take it to the next level.

David Beckham—Building a Brand

David Beckham has established and extended his world-class brand through his success on the field and his high-profile pursuits off it.

Regarded for his gritty team play and bending free kicks, he has proven to be one of the top players in the world. Simultaneously, the name Beckham has become synonymous with celebrity off the soccer pitch. His marriage to already-famous Spice Girl Victoria Adams contributed to his carefully honed and crafted celebrity image, creating fame matched by few in the entertainment world. While extremely popular in his home country of Great Britain, he also has considerable crossover appeal worldwide. He has used this appeal to serve as an ambassador for the brands he endorses, as well as for the game of soccer.

Born to working-class parents in London, Beckham signed with Manchester United at age seventeen and went on to become one of the best players in the world. During his time with Manchester United, he earned a reputation as a winner, guiding his team to six Premier League titles in an eight-year period and winning the 1999 Champions League title. In 1999 and 2001, Beckham was the runner-up for FIFA Player of the Year.

On-field performance alone does not explain why Beckham is such a revered icon in the sports world, as there have been numerous superstars whose talent has matched or exceeded Beckham's over time. What differentiates Beckham is that he has carefully branded himself as the ultimate celebrity athlete, living a high-class life of glamor and extravagance. In 1999, following his marriage to Adams, the couple was quickly dubbed "Posh and Becks." The duo routinely appeared in tabloids and, in fact, often fueled this interest themselves, as evidenced by such events as their $1 million wedding, complete with golden thrones for the bride and groom.[4] Over time, their lavish London home was dubbed "Beckingham Palace."

Beckham quickly extended his emerging celebrity by surrounding himself with global entertainment icons. Singer Elton John and actress Elizabeth Hurley became godparents to Beckham's children, while he simultaneously developed close and public friendships with other celebrities, including Tom Cruise and Katie Holmes. Beckham continued to draw attention to himself by changing his hairstyle regularly, from long hair to a Mohawk to entirely shaving his head. He posed shirtless in several magazines and branded his own cologne.

He secured endorsement deals for several "hip" products, including Police sunglasses. He also was signed by adidas for his soccer playing skills, as well as by Gillette, to hone his new masculine image. By the mid-2000s Beckham's major sponsorship deals were paying between £2 million and £3 million annually, and the *Times of London* estimated that he made over £20 million a year in endorsements alone prior to signing with the Galaxy.[5] Beckham's life was so glamorous and so seemingly perfect that he was called the quintessential "metrosexual" by the man who invented the term.[6] Even Beckham admitted that he didn't mind being an icon for both straight and gay men.[7]

"In this day and age in sports and entertainment, there's so much going on that it's hard to rise above the noise," former AEG Sports president Shawn Hunter says. "[Beckham] has a brand that can stay relevant. He's relevant across cultures and in a wide variety of media."[8]

At the same time, Beckham began feuding with Manchester United and its famous coach, Sir Alex Ferguson, who believed Beckham's celebrity had become a distraction. Beckham spent months in long, drawn-out contract negotiations with Manchester United for his "image rights" and, by 2003, the team had decided to sell his contract to the Spanish soccer team, Real Madrid, for $50 million. There, Beckham earned $37 million for his image rights alone, and in his first six months in Madrid, the club sold more than one million jerseys. Real Madrid sold $600 million worth of shirts and other soccer merchandise during Beckham's tenure with the team, increasing merchandising profits by 137 percent, this despite not winning a La Liga title until Beckham's final season with the club.[9]

Real Madrid realized enormous financial success with Beckham because his brand had transcended the British borders and had attained global appeal. Beckham was wildly popular in Asia, particularly in Japan, where he became an attraction during the 2002 World Cup. He was so beloved that his Mohican haircut became one of the most popular styles in the nation—for women. Beckham became the face of Vodafone's mobile phone, the J-phone, and he sold chocolates for a Japanese company that created a three-meter high chocolate statue of him.[10] Beckham's fame grew such that Motorola made him a "global ambassador."

The film *Bend It Like Beckham*, about an Indian girl playing soccer in England—in which Beckham didn't even appear—was a worldwide hit in 2002–03. It also furthered the image that Beckham was a man who wanted to spread the goodwill of the game worldwide to those of both genders and all walks of life. He partnered with AEG in 2005 to build the David Beckham Academies in Los Angeles, Brazil, and England for youth soccer players.

Beckham has succeeded in branding himself by both maintaining a high level of play on the field and successfully blending off-the-field self-promotion with the assistance of complicit paparazzi. Beckham has been very consistent in how he has refined and extended his brand. While he epitomizes the modern-day sports celebrity in terms of visibility, he has largely avoided the pitfalls of celebrity by maintaining a humble and down-to-earth working-class attitude. He has always valued and supported his family in public, and this has given Beckham a sense of authenticity that is often missing from today's athletes.

"He's very smart. It amazed us how humble he was," Hunter says. "His brand really evolved through his success on the field and then his alignment with global brands."[11]

Beckham has also been bold with his brand, always attempting to take his celebrity status in new directions or to new heights. Both on and off the field, Beckham represents an ideal vision for much of the viewing public, making him the ideal fit for a growing league in need of a difference maker.

Bringing Beckham to Los Angeles

Even before Beckham signed with the Galaxy, he was the most recognizable soccer player in the U.S. A poll conducted by the marketing talent agency Davie Brown Entertainment showed that 51 percent of Americans knew who Beckham was, whereas Landon Donovan, arguably the best American soccer player in the world and a Galaxy teammate of Beckham's, was known only by 9 percent of those polled.[12]

AEG had already witnessed success with the Galaxy before the 2007 season. The team was averaging in excess of twenty thousand fans per game, the highest in the MLS. Throughout MLS the belief existed that the timing was optimal for the league to make the transition from secondary status to that of a premier U.S. sports league. In an effort to accomplish this, MLS changed its rules and enabled each team to exceed the salary cap in order to sign a foreign star; ideally international players that could help boost attendance, increase television ratings, and assist in growing the league's roster of sponsors.

By 2006, at a time when Beckham's on-field prowess had begun to fade in the eyes of many Europeans, he was intrigued by the opportunity to expand his brand into the lucrative U.S. market, especially in Southern California, where his iconic status far outflanked his ability as a soccer player. Hollywood's proximity offered Beckham a new distribution channel for his celebrity lifestyle, and it afforded him new endorsement possibilities and even an option to expand his career into the motion picture industry.

So while Beckham was still playing for Real Madrid, he signed with the Galaxy to begin playing in the middle of the 2007 season. The five-year deal was laced with sponsorship and endorsement opportunities. Beckham would receive $5.5 million annually from the Galaxy. He would also receive approximately 50 percent of all jersey sales and share a portion of revenues generated by the Home Depot Center. In total, he could earn up to $250 million over the course of five years.

The massive deal included arrangements with sponsors such as Pepsi and Gillette to help promote his presence in the U.S. while seamlessly pitching myriad products. The opportunity also provided numerous benefits for Victoria Beckham, not the least of which was a Spice Girls Reunion Tour that was organized by AEG; conveniently, AEG also hosted many of the concerts at their facilities. The deal also included a clause that would allow Beckham to own an MLS team at the end of his playing career.

"People didn't realize it was a thirty-month process to bring Beckham here," Hunter says. "[AEG president and CEO] Tim Leiweke deserves a lot of credit for this. He had the vision and was able to get the stakeholders to buy in."[13]

Deal Analysis

The outcome of Beckham's move to America proved to be decidedly mixed. An ambitious appearance schedule, one designed to drive value not only to his brand but to all those that had invested in him, was compromised due to the nagging ankle injury. After he played in just a handful of games due to persistent injuries, the Galaxy announced on August 31, 2007, that he would likely miss the remainder of the season.

Because MLS had back-loaded the Galaxy's schedule with road games designed to showcase Beckham around the country, sold-out crowds nationwide were left to watch a struggling Galaxy team play without the icon that so many fans had paid to—and expected to—see.

Still, in that first year, MLS and the Galaxy reaped substantial rewards due to the Beckham signing. Games in which Beckham was scheduled to play drew 75 percent more fans than the average MLS game. After Beckham arrived, league attendance grew 49 percent, while overall MLS jersey sales increased by 780 percent; the Galaxy alone sold 600,000 Beckham jerseys during his time in Los Angeles. MLS Internet traffic was also up 80 percent in 2007, as fans from all over the world wanted to follow brand Beckham.[14] The Galaxy saw a 16.5 percent increase in attendance in Beckham's first year with the team, and were able to plan a lucrative preseason Asian tour. The club generated $13.3 million in new revenue three months before Beckham even arrived, including a five-year $20 million jersey sponsorship deal with Herbalife, which fit in perfectly with Beckham's own brand.[15]

"Herbalife was the easiest deal," Hunter says. "Other prospects were not sure they'd come. They needed to see [Beckham] on the field first. Herbalife helped push the other deals through."[16]

However, Beckham's star began to fade in the U.S. Due to injuries, he was unable to control his brand for the first time in his career. Off the field, the buzz surrounding his arrival quickly died down. On the field, however, the Galaxy did see an attendance bump with Beckham in uniform in 2008 (up 7 percent from 2007 and 25 percent from 2006)—averaging nearly a sellout a game—and the Galaxy's road attendance was nearly ten thousand fans a game higher than that of any other MLS team.[17] But beyond Beckham, interest in MLS remained relatively level. Games in which Beckham played drew 23.2 percent higher ratings than games he missed.[18] After the 2008 season, ESPN cancelled its weekly MLS broadcast and moved MLS games to ESPN2. Also in 2008, the MLS Cup final between New York and Columbus earned the lowest rating in the league's championship history on ABC, which moved future MLS Cup broadcasts to ESPN. While Beckham's presence helped the league when he was on the field, he failed to boost the appeal of MLS when he was not playing. A microcosm of the league's reliance on Beckham and its ongoing struggle to gain a foothold with the public, the 2009 MLS Cup final, featuring Beckham's Galaxy against Real Salt Lake, drew a .7 rating; an increase of 17 percent from the prior year's Beckham-less final.[19] However, Beckham's appearance was not enough to prevent the final from drawing the second-lowest rating ever for the MLS Cup, a fact somewhat mitigated by 2009 being the first year the final was shown on cable network ESPN instead of ABC.[20]

In parts of three seasons with the Galaxy, Beckham played for four different coaches, including a brief stint under his recommended coach Ruud Gullit. Beckham seemed unhappy with the quality of MLS play, there was reported infighting within the organization, and Beckham became uncharacteristically distant from the media. He also apparently longed for the European game, and missed numerous Galaxy games to play for England in international matches.

Following the 2008 season, the Galaxy loaned Beckham to Italian club AC Milan at his request. The move was reportedly made so that Beckham could keep up his fitness level, but Beckham played well for the Italian team and soon thereafter requested a permanent transfer. The Galaxy were not willing to relinquish their prize investment easily; however, they were hamstrung because Beckham had an out clause that activated after the third year of his contract. Following extensive negotiations, the Galaxy ultimately agreed to let Beckham finish out the entire 2009 season with AC Milan and rejoin the Galaxy in July of that year. Milan reportedly paid the Galaxy $6 million to keep him for a few more months, while Beckham contributed an estimated $3 million on his own to help compensate AEG for the fallout from sponsors.[21] Meanwhile, the Galaxy reduced all 2009 ticket prices by an average of 10 percent.

The controversy surrounding Beckham's time with the Galaxy did not diminish his worldwide appeal. Shortly after the deal with Milan, Beckham appeared in a major advertising campaign for Motorola. He was also selected to be a spokesman for England's bid for the 2018 World Cup. At the same time, Beckham had not completely soured on MLS, as he not only agreed to return to the Galaxy for another half season in 2010 (despite having the ability to opt out after the 2009 season), but also stated his intent to exercise a clause in his contract allowing him to purchase an MLS franchise at the end of his playing career.[22] While Beckham's playing career may have reached a crossroads after he tore his Achilles tendon in 2010, an injury that precluded him from playing for England in that year's World Cup, he remained an integral and high-profile part of England's World Cup presence.

Part cautionary tale and part personal branding success story, David Beckham highlights the issues athletes are presented with once they attempt to extend their brand beyond their exploits on the playing field. With this in mind, it is helpful to explore the attributes that contribute to building a personal brand, as well as to examine those who have successfully maximized their branding opportunity.

ATHLETE BRANDING: AN OVERVIEW

Simply stated, a brand is a collection of perceptions in the mind of the consumer.[23] Brands are largely intangible and are established and built over time by communicating and reinforcing core attributes and characteristics. A personal brand is composed of people's perceptions about a particular individual and is what differentiates us from one another. It is the sum total of an individual's personality and takes into account reputation and character.

Like other prominent brands, successful athlete brands are established through the combination of a unique and recognizable set of qualities that serve to create value and differentiate the brand. Properly developed, positioned, and cultivated, an athlete's personal brand can transcend the worlds of sports and entertainment, ultimately providing lucrative opportunities for not only the athlete but the organizations he or she represents.

Throughout history athletes have leveraged these qualities, including charisma, authenticity, believability, and the ability to convey marketing messages, to enhance their own brands while simultaneously adding value to those brands with which they are affiliated.

Some of the earliest examples of athlete branding in the twentieth century can be linked to the growth and popularity of the Olympic Games. As the Games grew, so too did opportunities for certain athletes who possessed a balance of athletic achievement and notoriety. Johnny Weissmuller, winner of five Olympic gold medals in swimming in the 1924 and 1928 Games, leveraged his fame to become a Hollywood movie star. He parlayed his athletic prowess by landing the famous role of Tarzan in *Tarzan the Ape Man*, which, in 1932, not only became one of MGM's most successful movies ever, but also spawned a series of highly profitable sequels. Weissmuller bridged the gap between sports and entertainment, developing an indelible "brand" around the famous Tarzan scream, which was eventually granted registration by the U.S. Patent and Trademark Office.

Years later, Edson Arantes do Nascimento, aka "Pelé," dominated the sports landscape on his way to becoming the world's greatest soccer player. He led Brazil to three World Cup titles, in 1958, 1962, and 1970, and was so respected and revered that some have even credited him with stopping a war as, in 1967, both sides in Nigeria's Civil War agreed to a forty-eight-hour ceasefire so that Pelé could play an exhibition match in Lagos, the nation's capitol.

Statesman Henry Kissinger went so far as to suggest that Pelé had made the transition from superstar to mythic figure—and Kissinger would know, since he helped broker a deal to bring Pelé to the New York Cosmos of the NASL in 1975 in an effort to build interest in soccer throughout the United States.[24]

Pelé's tremendous on-field success has afforded him opportunities at success off it. He has endorsed such products as MasterCard, Pepsi-Cola, and Brazil's state-controlled oil company, Petrobas. At the age of seventy his personal branding opportunities remain compelling, as in late 2009, Pelé launched his own cleat and apparel manufacturing company, Pelé Sports AG.[25] While Pelé ·has succeeded in some ventures, his failure with others highlights the tenuous nature of success off the field. Attempting to further craft his personal brand, Pelé is represented by William Morris Endeavor, IMG, and Prime Licensing, each of which believes it can parlay his life story and athletic prowess into substantial revenue.

Transcendent personal brands of the era were not limited to team sports heroes. Robert Craig "Evel" Knievel achieved great success as a motorcycle daredevil in the late 1960s and throughout the 1970s. Knievel attempted numerous dangerous jumps, and though he didn't always succeed, he built a worldwide following that admired his bravery, showmanship, and humble small-town roots. His death-defying stunts were among the highest-rated programs on ABC's *Wide World of Sports*, which enabled him to monetize his brand in conjunction with everything from movies and TV specials to music, toys, and collectibles. According to toy industry executives, Knievel helped save the industry in the 1970s, as the Evel Knievel Stunt Cycle, among other Knievel toys and collectibles, generated more than $300 million in sales during the 1970s and early 1980's.[26]

As evidenced by the personal brands highlighted here, the opportunity exists for a small number of optimally positioned athletes to stand out from their peers and, in the process, assist their business partners in building brand recognition and generating revenue. Two athletes who have distinguished themselves in this regard over the past several years are action sports legend Tony Hawk and NBA All-Star Yao Ming.

TONY HAWK

Tony Hawk is among a small handful of athletes whose personal brand has achieved iconic status. The development of Hawk's personal brand has occurred symbiotically with the emergence of skateboarding, as well as with the growth of action sports overall. As the top brand in this rapidly growing sports category, Hawk helped create the market for action sports, while simultaneously extending his own brand in the process.

Three pillars underscore Hawk's broad brand appeal. First, he personifies "cool." His skateboarding performances are dazzling and have inspired millions to not only watch but also take up his sport and consume his branded products. A pioneer, Hawk has been a trendsetter, crafting the style that defines modern skateboarding—a style and resulting brand that resonates particularly well with young people. The second pillar of Hawk's brand is his accessibility. It's not just that Hawk makes himself available to fans but also the great lengths he goes to in order to make skateboarding accessible to young people and to offer opportunities for them to experience his sport in a variety of ways. The final pillar of Hawk's exceptional personal brand is his clean-cut image. He is one of the few athlete brands that can be authentic to young people while at the same time garnering parents' admiration, because he represents values that parents embrace, namely hard work, humility, and respect.

Hawk was a phenom from a very young age and, by the time he reached sixteen, was widely regarded as the best skateboarder in the world. While he no doubt was extremely athletic, it was his fearlessness in attempting death-defying stunts, such as being the first skateboarder to ever complete a "900" (two-and-a-half rotations) in competition, that memorialized his "coolness." However, Hawk's dazzling performances tell only part of the story as to why young people routinely rank him as their favorite athlete. By its nature, skateboarding is a counterculture sport, and Hawk has understood this positioning well. He has successfully enabled corporate America to market him to the masses without compromising his core fan base.

In addition to mainstream corporate endorsements, including those with Campbell's Soup, AT&T, and Heinz, and instead of aligning with traditional sportswear and sports equipment companies such as Nike or adidas, Hawk has developed his own brands. Today, many skateboarders ride a Tony Hawk–branded Birdhouse skateboard or wear styles from Hawk Clothing, which was acquired by Quiksilver in 2000. Consequently, he has been the trendsetter in the skateboarding market, helping establish and build the market while at the same time leveraging this growth and his personal brand to monetize the opportunity.

"One major characteristic of [Hawk] is his authenticity," said Will Kassoy, then senior vice president of Activision|Blizzard, the publisher for Tony Hawk's video games. "Especially today with the Internet, you can't spin something some way. People know if something is lacking pretty quickly. He brings his authenticity to every product that he endorses, and it's quality. He manages his brand in an equity-appreciating way."[27]

However, when Hawk first began skateboarding, and it became apparent that he would excel at it, a market for him to generate revenue from his emerging personal brand did not exist. So his father, Frank, founded the National Skateboarding Association, the world's first professional league. Despite this, in the early 1990s skateboarding's popularity floundered and Tony Hawk nearly abandoned the sport. Fortunately for Hawk, ESPN created the X Games in 1995, which provided him the ideal platform to showcase his talents. This exposure was vital to developing Hawk's brand, as millions of Americans and, shortly thereafter, worldwide audiences were awestruck by his unequaled skills.

For nearly two decades Hawk has tirelessly worked to promote his sport and ensure that it and he remain highly relevant. In an effort to solidify his brand and the sport, he founded the Boom Boom HuckJam Tour, an action sports event that visits over twenty cities. The events are set to live music and regularly sell out, generating upward of $20 million annually in ticket revenue, sponsorships, and merchandise. The Tour is intended to share the excitement of action sports with potential fans who would not otherwise have the opportunity to see action sports in person. Hawk makes sure to sign as many autographs as possible, making a personal connection with each fan whenever he can. To complete the personal branding connection, some Tour events are held at Six Flags locations, a few of which have leveraged the popularity of the Tour by building Tony Hawk–branded roller coasters. These rides have allowed parkgoers to experience the thrill associated with being a world-class skateboarder while doing so in a low-risk environment, albeit one that literally reinforces the Hawk brand at every turn.

Hawk has also successfully extended his brand through his production company, 900 Films, which has produced the best selling instructional sports video ever, as well as established more than four hundred skate parks in low-income areas through the Tony Hawk Foundation.

"He's been a huge evangelist for the sport of skateboarding," Kassoy says. "He's been willing to do things that may not have been as financially lucrative for him if he thinks it can popularize the sport further."[28]

But perhaps none of Hawk's brand-building ventures have been more successful than his video game series, *Tony Hawk's Pro Skater*, which has generated sales in excess of $1.1 billion.[29] In terms of sports video games, only John Madden's NFL game has been more successful. Hawk actively collaborated with Activision|Blizzard on the game's development—to ensure it was relevant and representative of his perspective on the sport. According to Activision|Blizzard, more than 75 percent of the game's players don't own a skateboard, enabling *Pro Skater* to further develop the sport into the mainstream of society, making Tony Hawk a household name—even to those that only know his pixilated likeness. In recent years, Activision|Blizzard has retooled the Hawk series to offer some new looks, and has released several new Hawk games, such as *Tony Hawk's Underground*, *Tony Hawk's Proving Ground*, and *Tony Hawk: Ride*, the latter of which features a skateboard-shaped controller.

Kassoy believes that Hawk's "authenticity, his credibility with his fans, is highly predicated on the attention he puts into the products he makes. He turns down more licenses than he associates with. He's very selective. He wants to make sure that the projects he works on are brand accretive. This is contrary to the approach of many other athletes where they simply license their name onto a product without making sure it's authentic and quality, thus ensuring a recipe for failure."[30]

Finally, Hawk's brand is one of the few that not only resonates with kids but also appeals to parents. "Parents are thrilled to look at this guy not tattooed up head to toe, a guy who wears a helmet when he skates. That's the one they want their kid to think is cool," says Pat Hawk, Tony's sister and COO of Tony Hawk, Inc.[31] Hawk has stayed out of trouble and exudes a certain humility and graciousness, regardless of time or location. He seemingly has no ego, and appears driven only by his passion for skateboarding. That passion is impressive to parents, as is Hawk's work ethic, both of which contributed to his becoming the superstar he is today.

Hawk's signature brand traits are not universal to successful athlete brands. As is the case with Yao Ming, other personal branding pillars can be bundled to build a profitable athlete brand.

YAO MING

Yao Ming's personal brand is so compelling that it spans multiple continents. As the first premier Chinese basketball player to reach the NBA, Yao has the hopes and dreams of a nation invested in his success. He also represents an opportunity for the NBA to further expand its brand into a burgeoning Chinese market, as well as throughout the rest of Asia.

Significantly, Yao's branding success has not only been linked to his basketball skills. Standing seven foot, five inches, Yao is one of the tallest players in NBA history, yet his good nature and warm smile contribute to an image of a gentle giant that appeals to advertisers and fans alike.

Yao is the child of two Chinese basketball stars—Fang Fengdi and Yao Zhiyuan—and he was identified at a very young age as a potential basketball star himself. By the age of thirteen, and already six foot, seven inches tall, Yao trained rigorously at the Shanghai Sports Technology Institute and, by the time he was twenty-one, he had led the Shanghai Sharks to the team's first Chinese league basketball title in over fifty years. Seven years later he purchased the financially struggling franchise in an effort to restore its standing.

Emerging brands, including personal brands, are marked by their distinctly recognizable qualities and high perceived potential value which, if properly nurtured, can result in the brand becoming an important part of business—and culture.

In Yao's case, his physical stature and athletic prowess were just the differentiators the Chinese government was looking for; attributes they felt compelled to leverage. So much so that, as one Chinese media source suggested, "Yao Ming is a business card for China."[32]

Following his performance with the Sharks, Chinese officials allowed Yao to enter the 2002 NBA draft, provided he turned over half of all his future earnings to Chinese government agencies.[33] Although Yao was the first overall selection in the draft, Nike had expressed interest in him years earlier, and believed that his well-developed personal brand in Asia could help the company extend its brand both domestically and abroad. Accordingly, Nike signed Yao to a four-year endorsement contract in 1999. At the conclusion of the contract, and hoping to parlay Yao's personal brand status, Reebok lured him away from Nike in 2003 and signed him to a ten-year deal estimated to be worth $7 to $10 million annually.[34]

Reebok was among the companies hoping to take advantage of Yao's global notoriety during the 2008 Summer Olympics in Beijing by creating a special shoe for him featuring traditional Chinese dragons, as well as the customary Chinese colors of white, gold, and red.

This familiarity in China provided a great opportunity for Western companies looking to expand market share in China, and vice versa for Chinese companies looking to grow in the United States. Coca-Cola launched an international campaign in 2008 featuring both Yao Ming and fellow NBA superstar LeBron James. Such a campaign was rare for the company since it seldom uses athletes in international campaigns because so few are relevant on a global scale.

Yao's personal brand has been recognized by *Forbes* magazine, which has consistently ranked him among China's wealthiest and most influential celebrities.[35] According to NBA deputy commissioner Adam Silver, "Yao has an amazing wit. He's very smart. His English is very good. He has a terrific sense of humor, and is very engaging. Yao is also multifaceted in terms of his knowledge of politics, other sports, art, and fashion. He's well read, and I think that's one of the things that makes him particularly appealing to marketing partners. He's charismatic. There's no question he's a fantastic ambassador for the NBA."[36]

The Founder Group, one of the official corporate partners of the Rockets, is a Chinese IT conglomerate. It sought to parlay its relationship with the Rockets and, by extension, Yao, to help build brand awareness and increase business in the United States while simultaneously reinforcing its brand to the massive global audiences routinely tuning in to watch the Rockets.

The NBA similarly recognized Yao's value as a catalyst for further growth in Asia and around the world. In 2008, the NBA formed NBA China, a new entity that would conduct all of the league's businesses in Greater China and help grow the game of basketball. Yao's success in the NBA—both on and off the court—provided a Chinese face on the sport's biggest stage and led to increased interest in NBA basketball among Chinese fans. With the creation of NBA China, the league has enhanced its direct connection to the country, leading to opportunities to grow the league's business, as well as positively influence more young Chinese basketball players hoping to develop into premier professional athletes. "China has very sophisticated basketball fans, and there is a long history of basketball being played in China," Silver says, noting that the popularity of more successful NBA stars such as Kobe Bryant and LeBron James dwarfs that of Yao's in China. "We market the game of basketball in China, and we market the NBA. The Chinese fans love NBA-quality basketball and the style and presentation of the game. Yao is certainly an important component of that. It was a long time coming, but there's no question that Yao was a shot in the arm for that."[37]

Yao's appeal as a "gentle giant" has also made him popular with advertisers. Off the court, he displays humility despite his size, which fans find welcoming. He even continued to live with his parents well into his NBA career, and that helped give him the image of a good-hearted family man. On the court, Yao is known for his strong fundamentals, and he has always been lauded by coaches for his desire to improve. In short, his nature and overall "story" have helped him build an attractive brand for sponsors.

"What's surprised me most about Yao is how sensitive he is as a person, and the burden he carries about what he feels the expectations are from the Chinese people when he plays for the Houston Rockets and for China," Silver says. "You can see it in his face. He's been very reluctant to be put out in front of other players. He wants to be treated like every other player. Part of that is culture, in terms of China valuing the team over the individual. I think that's one of the reasons why basketball, as a team sport, does very well in China."[38]

Over the years, Yao has had a variety of endorsement deals, with companies including Visa, McDonald's, Apple Computer, Gatorade, and Chinese mobile phone company Unicom, and now earns approximately $25 million a year from endorsements.[39]

Yao has also parlayed his international fame and extraordinary personal brand to assist charitable organizations. He formed The Yao Ming Foundation, which initially was focused on rebuilding schools following the devastating 8.0 earthquake that struck China in 2008, then on supporting numerous youth programs in both China and the United States thereafter. Yao's philanthropy is not limited to his own foundation, as he also supports a number of others including the Chi Heng Foundation, the China Youth Development Foundation, Project Hope, and the Red Cross.

While Yao's on-the-court efforts were placed on hold due to a season-ending and career-threatening foot injury during the 2009 NBA playoffs, he has maintained his off-the-court efforts by rebuilding his former Shanghai Sharks team and expanding the game of basketball in China.

As such, Yao has been able to cultivate a strong international brand by building upon the uniqueness with which it was launched, developed, managed, and extended. Both he and his business partners, including the Chinese government, have been able to parlay his global success to benefit the growth of their own brands.

ATHLETE BRANDING: THE BOTTOM LINE

David Beckham, Tony Hawk, and Yao Ming have successfully developed and extended powerful and monetizable personal brands. Professional or amateur athletes that have and choose to project charisma and personality—and combine these attributes with athletic prowess—tend to be ahead of their colleagues when building their personal brands. The following guidelines highlight how athletes will continue to establish, build, and monetize their personal brands, while simultaneously appreciating myriad influences and stakeholders that have an impact on their ability to do so. Before looking at these, it is important to highlight the fact that not all athletes strive to become personal brands, preferring instead to remain out of the limelight.

Personal Brands Are Born

Opportunities to create and foster personal brands are presenting themselves at earlier and earlier ages for athletes and entertainers. Encouraged by parents, refined by coaches, and fueled by corporate interest, young athletes who demonstrate exceptional skills and charisma, or otherwise differentiate themselves from their peers, are favorably positioned to establish, publicize, and subsequently monetize their personal brands.

They are able to do so because those individuals marketing products and services realize that consumers are making purchase decisions and developing brand loyalty earlier in life. Marketers seek personal brands such as Tony Hawk that resonate with their target demographic, particularly relatively impressionable target audiences who may be determining initial product or service preferences. The stakeholders affected by this are numerous, ranging from the emerging personal brand's family and entourage to those marketing and managing amateur and professional athletics, as well as the media, corporate shareholders, and advocacy groups.

For every Tiger Woods that putts against Bob Hope on *The Mike Douglas Show* at the age of two, there are countless others who never have the opportunity to resonate with consumers so early—if at all. Certainly Woods is the exception, and clearly he was not appearing on the show for the express purpose of building his long-term personal brand. However, in today's sports marketing world, one all too often populated with overzealous "stage" parents, unscrupulous family advisers, marketing representatives, and overbearing coaches and personal trainers, athletes must treat the initial personal brand creation process carefully. Young athletes who are positioned for stardom at early ages may not fully realize the impact this may have on their ability to participate in sports—let alone succeed. Some invariably will risk their amateur status and potentially be forced to forego highly regulated, organized domestic athletics as they get older, whether this is at the high school or collegiate level. Regardless of the level of participation, an inability to fully feature one's athletic prowess can undermine the ability to establish and extend a personal brand.

Special interest groups will gain traction as young athletes become marketable entities. Parental advocacy groups, labor lawyers, and even the civil rights movement may insert themselves in the process, potentially leading corporations inclined to sponsor young athletes to scramble for cover following shareholder concern. Pursued inappropriately or handled indelicately, the early positioning of personal brands will be compromised if overshadowed by those believing the young athletes are being exploited. Alternatively, stakeholders will always exist that advocate the early development and exposure of these personal brands. Regardless of one's position, the ability to brand build is compromised when mitigating factors such as these arise.

Personal brand building at such young ages also will have an impact on colleges and universities, requiring them to alter their recruiting strategies as younger stars capitalize on their abilities prior to entering college. While the athletes may benefit in some cases, especially when surrounded by a management team capable of executing comprehensive marketing and business development strategies in the era of new media, the overall "personality" of amateur athletics, including the NCAA, will be fundamentally altered.

Professional sports, provided they can navigate inevitable conflicts, may be among the largest benefactors. Although contracts increasingly will take individual player branding campaigns into consideration, professional sports leagues and teams indeed benefit from having athletes with established personal brands, particularly those that have already been favorably positioned for years prior to turning professional. This will help leagues and teams by leading to higher TV ratings, incremental turnstile-related income, and increased sponsorship. Along the way, concerns will be raised as leagues and teams more fully integrate sponsors with team activities. For instance, when sponsors' logos are included on team jerseys, conflicts surely will arise between athletes endorsing one brand and the team for which they play striking sponsorship deals with a competitor. Even so, the industry should be able to monetize this eventuality, provided athletes, their agents and unions, and the leagues can determine how best to share the revenue and do so without diluting any of the brands involved. Such developments will lead to changes in collective bargaining agreements and individual player contracts. If these developments are unsatisfactorily addressed, labor strife could emerge, leading to strikes and lockouts.

The Messenger and the Message Are Controlled

Prolific, well-defined (and defended) barriers between athletes and fans and customers have been removed. The ability to bypass traditional, entrenched media outlets such as the broadcast networks when it serves an athlete's purpose accelerates the personal branding process. This acceleration can result in the building of a compelling personal brand or assist in reinforcing the fact that an athlete is but a caricature of himself.

The ability of an athlete to craft a personal brand, concisely communicate the attributes of it, and parlay these achievements allows for the building of incremental value. This is especially the case when successful athlete brands transcend sports, as is the case with David Beckham and Yao Ming. Monetizing personal brands beyond simply the sports "space" broadens opportunities for, and extends the impact to, a wide range of stakeholders. Notable among these stakeholders are not only the brands the athlete is aligned with but also new means of media distribution and technology; emerging sports, leagues, and events; and, of course, consumers and fans.

In this message-direct world, athletes have the opportunity to communicate the depth and breadth of their interests, ranging from philanthropic associations to outside business interests and post-sports-career desires. While communicating a well-rounded personal brand no doubt pays dividends to the athlete's sport, whether it is team or individual, it also delivers tremendous value to the brands endorsed. The more believable and sought after the connection between the athlete and the consumer or fan—the tighter the perceived relationship—the better for the corporation, provided this connection does not appear manufactured or gratuitous.

Technological advances, especially "social media" that help consumers and fans feel closer to their favorite stars (to include living vicariously through them), continue to generate business opportunities for those that provide services to athlete brands. Given that barriers to entry will remain quite low, seasoned marketers and business professionals who demonstrate savvy in the areas of public relations, community relations, media relations, and crisis management will uncover opportunities to serve as spokespeople when these personal brands are taken directly to the consumer or fan—and done so on a global basis, instantaneously. However, just as these technological advances can help, the ever-increasing access to athletes and their personal lives has the potential to damage a brand as well. Should this occur, it will have far-reaching impacts on both the personal brand and the companies utilizing the brand.

On a relative basis, secondary and emerging sports leagues and special events such as lacrosse and women's soccer, as well as individual sports, may benefit from this direct-to-the–consumer-or-fan opportunity. Lacking the traditional media reach afforded the major sports leagues, this sports tier may be more agile and better able to take advantage of viral marketing linked to personal brands. Unencumbered with numerous, exclusive sponsorship and cross-promoting relationships, these sports properties have as an advantage the ability to more credibly harness emerging, viral marketing channels. This is not to say that they will surpass the marketing reach and muscle afforded the major leagues and global sporting events, merely that they may have a unique opportunity given their industry standing.

Endorsements Become Strategic Partnerships

Historically, endorsement deals between athletes and corporations have been largely transactional. That is, athletes have agreed to market or promote a particular product or service in exchange for a defined set of benefits, usually a quantifiable fee and the complimentary use of the company's goods or services. But because certain athlete brands are becoming increasingly valuable, and the entities they have traditionally endorsed have become noticeably more risk-averse, the relationship between them will continue to migrate and become more of a strategic partnership.

Such partnerships will more closely link longer-term pay, including equity, to an athlete's commitment to the brand, as well as to performance on the field and throughout the community. Startups and established companies alike will feel the impact of this migration from business transaction to marketing alliance, as will the athletes, their agents or business managers, and even amateur athletics and consumers and fans.

Upstart companies will be inclined to forge these partnerships, as they often need to break through market clutter—even if doing so costs them a percentage of their company or sales. Athletes, especially those that are willing to commit time and resources to a fledgling business, may find the upside greater than entering into traditional endorsement deals—especially now that such deals have become more difficult to secure. In addition to equity, athletes may gain voting rights and the ability to train or prepare for a meaningful career at the company upon retiring from competition, among other important business benefits.

Such a commitment places an even greater premium on the athlete's personal brand, as athletes not only become a more integral part of the company they represent but also have a more direct impact on the athlete's earnings ability, dependent on their behavior on the field and in the business community. In short, these strategic partnerships place an increased onus on personal brands, and more closely link risk and return to all parties involved.

Established companies that may not be able to offer endorsement packages that have a meaningful upside (such as equity participation) may struggle to attract compelling spokespeople. They will be forced to alter course, either by changing their compensation models or altering their approach to sports marketing by diversifying away from high-profile athlete-spokespeople.

The establishing of these strategic relationships will require agents and business managers to negotiate "mini-mergers," whereby contractual relationships between parties will carry with them added financial and marketing exposure. As these relationships take hold, amateur athletes considering whether to forego eligibility in exchange for entering into such partnerships will similarly need a wide range of guidance, placing an added emphasis on the acumen of their family and advisers.

Because these athletes will have incentive to closely monitor their personal brands, all those doing business with them will benefit, not the least of which will be the teams for which they play and the leagues they represent. Over time, consumers and fans will benefit from this as well, as their favorite athletes will be less likely to compromise their personal brands in ways that will lead to suspensions or otherwise bring disfavor to their team.

Corporations that successfully identify and then integrate compelling athlete brands into their marketing campaigns are poised to see increases in sales, enhanced shareholder value, or both. Compelling athlete brands that are able to actively engage consumers and fans, and do so while appreciating the nuances and developments just described, will continue to monetize their personal brands on a global scale.

ATHLETE BRANDING AND CONVERGENCE: FINAL THOUGHTS FROM IMG'S SANDY MONTAG[40]

Sandy Montag is a senior corporate vice president of IMG Sports and Entertainment and is managing director of its Clients Division. IMG is a premier sports, entertainment, and media company that represents top athletes and entertainers. Montag shared his perspective on convergence and athlete branding with the SBI.

SBI: How is IMG positioned to take advantage of sports marketing and the rapidly evolving area of athlete branding?

MONTAG: IMG is very well suited in terms of determining how our clients fit into the worlds of sports, entertainment, and business. From the day he launched the company, IMG founder Mark McCormack had an international vision for it. We were in countries before they were countries. We have always been stronger internationally than domestically. Today, we have seventy offices in thirty countries and twenty-six hundred employees. This scope has been the basis of what makes us successful and unique. I can call employees around the world to help out with various projects we have, and this is important because they may have a perspective I lack. This is a key advantage that speaks to the vision of Mark McCormack in the early 1960s. Our other key advantage is that we have divisions that enhance our clients' careers. IMG has been vertically integrated for years. Being involved in TV production and distribution, event management, and other areas of sports business enables us to more completely represent our clients and extend their personal brands.

SBI: As it relates to personal branding, how has the sports marketing landscape changed as sports has become more aligned with entertainment?

MONTAG: Throughout my twenty-five years at IMG the biggest change has been the proliferation of the platforms available to athletes and entertainers. In terms of content and entertainment platforms, money-making opportunities, and public relations and exposure platforms, there has been a great expansion. When I started in the mid-1980s it was the beginning of cable TV, while satellite radio and the Internet were nonexistent. Today's world provides a broad look that is almost overwhelming in terms of marketing opportunities available to athletes and entertainers. A primary example of this is John Madden. We signed a deal with Electronic Arts (EA) in the mid-1980s for a football computer game. At the time, EA was only able to make an eight-on-eight football game (as opposed to eleven-on-eleven) due to technological constraints. As a result, the first *Madden* football game did not come out until 1989 because John was unwilling to put his name on a game that was not authentic. The overall impact of this historic example highlights how the different platforms allow sports to become a more complete—and profitable—entertainment experience featuring well-known talent.

SBI: What athlete brand has IMG represented that has taken advantage of these multiple platforms?

MONTAG: Again, consider Madden. For his brand, we went into video games, entered into a deal with Verizon for cell phone applications, created a Sirius satellite radio show, and developed his own website—all in addition to supporting his broadcasting career. We also represent both Peyton and Eli Manning, who have been quite involved in mobile and web marketing initiatives as part of their overall endorsement responsibilities. We take individual clients and look at them beyond the scope of just putting them on television. We look at what other applications allow us to expand not only their brand, but also the brand they are representing.

SBI: What management challenges exist in this era of athlete marketing and branding?

MONTAG: I don't think the challenges are overwhelming, because you have to realize there are only so many athletes or entertainers that are brands. By brands I mean, names like Madden, Manning, or Timberlake, where you don't have to say the first name to know who they are. They transcend sports and entertainment and, as a result, you can negotiate licensing deals for them. On the other hand, you may have great athletes and entertainers that may be able to endorse products, but you cannot take them to the next level. You have to be realistic about who you represent and how they fit into the world. We're honest in terms of communicating this reality to our clients—we're not going to promise our clients that they will be a star with their own video game because there are only three people—Tiger Woods, John Madden, and Tony Hawk—that have their own game. Provided we remain honest and disciplined as the number of marketing platforms grows, the challenges will continue to be manageable.

SBI: Do you think athletes understand the dynamic nature of this marketing environment, one increasingly shaped by new media?

MONTAG: Athletes generally tend to have all the new gadgets so they are aware of what options are out there and just how accessible news, information, and entertainment have become. They don't need to be taught about these platforms as much as they have to be shown how to take these new media options and turn them into brand builders and money makers rather than allow these emerging platforms to harm their personal brands and, by extension, the companies they endorse.

SBI: How does IMG acquaint, or otherwise brief, its clients with potential endorsement opportunities?

MONTAG: We are hands on by taking them to meetings and maintaining a very interactive experience with them. Generally speaking, I don't believe in doing a deal just for money—it has to be the right fit for a client. For example, with Eli Manning, we had an opportunity to work with Verizon. Instead of just jumping at the chance, we took Eli out to Verizon headquarters and brainstormed with their creative content team to create an idea that made everyone comfortable. I believe getting clients involved and making them feel like they are part of the process is essential to maximizing your likelihood of success, both as it relates to the success of a marketing campaign and the establishing or extending of an athlete's brand.

SBI: What about the sponsoring company's perspective? Given the 24/7 news and entertainment cycle, how does IMG address their growing reticence about working with athletes?

MONTAG: In today's society with the Internet, your life can change in an instant. Companies are gun shy about using athletes and entertainers for endorsements because if they do something publicly that is unprofessional or embarrassing to that company, it can be a real detriment to all brands involved. Ten or twenty years ago before we had the Internet or cell phone cameras this wasn't as much of an issue. As I see it, this is one of the negatives of the new technology we have today. There is a lack of privacy where if an athlete or entertainer goes out to eat, there will be hundreds of pictures of them at that restaurant by the end of the evening. So if you're a corporation that is paying a lot of money to have an athlete represent your brand, you have to be careful. This is why I believe it is important for both the athlete and the company to get to know each other better through the process. This helps ensure that they both make an informed decision about working together. Even so, we are all aware that this process isn't perfect, but we do all that we can to mitigate any potential downside to both the athlete and the corporation.

SBI: On a macro level, how does IMG maintain its leadership position in terms of athlete management and branding?

MONTAG: In athlete management we focus on, and only work with, "A-level" clients. I believe that the number of brands that we represent and place in sports and entertainment will shrink over time because there are a limited number of global brands. The key for IMG is to identify where we are going to be next year or what is going to be hot in two years. We must remain creative in order to stay ahead of everyone else by thinking down the road, and doing so on a worldwide basis, instead of thinking about what happened yesterday here in the U.S. Fortunately, given IMG's structure and reach, we are poised to remain a global leader in athlete branding.

Part II

AWAY-FROM-HOME CONVERGENCE

Consuming sports while "away from home" is now at the core of convergence. Consumers demand that they be able to enjoy the benefits associated with this convergence, when and where they choose, as well as select the manner in which they choose to be affected by it. Increasingly, and much to the delight of sports fans, this convergence now prominently includes taking advantage of the integration of sports and entertainment while away from home.

"Away-from-home" convergence is defined as the consumer's ability to view, listen to, or participate in sports at his or her convenience while running errands, traveling for work or pleasure, at the office, and so on. Fan demand to consume sports while away from home has transformed the sports industry and created a new set of producers and stakeholders hoping to monetize this rapidly growing area of sports business. Cell phone manufacturers and telecom service providers, media programmers and distributors, fantasy sports providers, and others, including those that operate gambling properties and operations, are eager to reach those so interested in sports that they must have access to them around the clock.

These producers and stakeholders provide advertisers a compelling and targeted platform for marketing to a traditionally hard-to-reach consumer population. Monetizing the evolution of away-from-home convergence remains in its infancy in terms of the financial upside awaiting those that master these consumer touchpoints. To be sure, those that consistently deliver an enhanced fan experience will not only reshape the sports business industry but also profit handsomely in the process.

As described in Part I, radio provided Americans with the ability to listen to sports and entertainment from the comfort of their own living rooms. As important as the ability to listen at home to radio broadcasting was, it lacked in comparison—from the standpoint of convergence—to the Galvin Corporation's introduction of the first commercial car radio in 1930. With this single product extension, sports fans were able to listen to sports on the drive from work or during long car trips. This enabled them to follow legendary sports moments without being tethered to their living rooms.

Among the earliest and greatest moments to be heard while away from home was New York Giants broadcaster Russ Hodges' call of Bobby Thomson's game-winning home run in 1951. Those tuning into WMCA-AM radio shared in the excitement when the Giants beat the Brooklyn Dodgers as Hodges shouted, "THE GIANTS WIN THE PENNANT! THE GIANTS WIN THE PENNANT! THE GIANTS WIN THE PENNANT! THE GIANTS WIN THE PENNANT!" The Galvin Corporation may have initiated the era of away-from-home convergence with the car radio, but it was Hodges' famous description of the home run that made this form of entertainment real to those sports fans honking their car horns as a sign of support for their Giants.

The idea of consuming sports while on the go was not limited to the car radio. It also included other out-of-home experiences. For many, the convergence of sports and entertainment—and the ability to consume them while away from home—had close ties to motion pictures. Sports on the big screen has played an important role in the entertainment industry. Since the humble beginnings of the motion picture industry in the United States, numerous amateur and professional sports have been featured in the movies. For example, the early days included the first baseball short, Thomas Edison's *The Ball Game*, in 1898; this was followed seventeen years later by the first feature-length baseball film, *Right Off the Bat*.

In addition to these initial presentations, documentary-style news reels and films became popular, especially those describing major boxing matches of the era. A significant example of the blending of sports and entertainment in Hollywood was Abbott and Costello's legendary skit "Who's on First," which first appeared onscreen in the 1940 film *One Night in the Tropics*. Abbott and Costello provided sports fans with their first taste of sports entertainment that they literally could see without being present at the game itself. That same year, Ronald Reagan played the role of star Notre Dame football player George Gipp in *Knute Rockne: All American*. Shortly thereafter, in 1942, Gary Cooper starred as New York Yankees legend Lou Gehrig in *The Pride of the Yankees*.

Unlike today's entertainment environment, which allows for movies to be watched virtually any time and anywhere, watching sports-themed movies during the middle of the twentieth century was very much an "away-from-home" activity highlighted by the Saturday matinee and the always popular drive-in.

Since this period, and because the studios recognized the power of sports as entertainment, sports have maintained a strong presence on the screen and have been featured in myriad genres, particularly dramas and comedies. The decades that followed provided numerous examples, including *The Hustler* (1961), *Rocky* (1976), *Chariots of Fire* (1981), *Jerry Maguire* (1996), and *Talladega Nights: The Legend of Ricky Bobby* (2006).

Beyond radio and the movies, today's sports fans also have the ability to consume sports, including sports movies, on their cell phones and laptop computers. Mobile technology providers are quick to realize the growing demand for sports information while simultaneously appreciating the urgency of delivering news and information to fans. Other industry stakeholders, such as those in the gambling business, have welcomed this new platform and believe it is helping drive their businesses, both domestically and abroad.

As mobile technology features and applications improved to include the use of digital data, the ability to consume sports while away from home took a quantum leap forward and, in the process, forever changed how sports were consumed. Technological advances also provide the fastest and most compelling evolution of the formerly distinct sports and entertainment worlds. These advances simultaneously demonstrate and reinforce the merging of sports and entertainment.

Distributing sports content to fans' cell phones provides consumers with a level of convenience and immediacy formerly unavailable to mass audiences. Delivering content this way not only allows fans to be "in the know" but, perhaps more important, makes them feel as though they are "the first to know" about critical sports news and information. They feel empowered in the knowledge that they are immersed in the information flow, and delight in knowing—nearly in real time—when their favorite player has just been traded to their favorite team. For example, when future Hall of Fame pitcher Randy Johnson was traded from the Arizona Diamondbacks to the Yankees, a New York Yankees fan living in Phoenix, Arizona, didn't have to wait to surf the web or watch *SportsCenter* to find out. Regardless of how fans welcomed this breaking news, one thing was undeniable: the news of the trade found them—they did not have to search far and wide to learn about it.

Not surprisingly, and because the growth opportunities appear endless, stakeholders in away-from-home convergence have been, and will continue to be, quite diverse. Companies and organizations such as AT&T, Apple, MLB, Sony, Disney, EA, and Yahoo! may participate in different industries, but through away-from-home convergence they are now directly connected to one another. This form of convergence provides stakeholders with new market opportunities at a time when each seeks new and improved methods for reaching specified target markets.

The landscape of away-from-home convergence is marked not only by established and entrenched stakeholders, but by new entrants as well. Part II will examine how the traditional and non-traditional sports properties and leagues alike have utilized this merging of sports and entertainment to engage fans. Also analyzed in this section will be how the technology and service firms have enabled this convergence to take place, and are continuing to foster its growth. The strategies and tactics of new industry participants will be explored, as will be the impact convergence has on the consumer experience.

Finally, Part II will touch upon emerging modes of convergence that may have a measurable impact on our appreciation and understanding of it. Specific chapters will analyze the major stakeholders and examine how each hopes to continue to benefit from sports and entertainment becoming one.

Focusing on the Internet, Chapter 4 details how the online evolution has enhanced the fan experience. The Internet has forever changed sports marketing and content delivery, providing sports properties a compelling opportunity in the process. While Internet accessibility can be found in consumer's homes, its ubiquitous nature outside the home is what places it in the away-from-home category. Major League Baseball's (MLB's) own new media company, MLBAM, will be analyzed to explore how developing content pipelines to reach and engage fans can be profitable. In addition, websites that provide detailed news and information about athletes, such as Rivals.com, and sites dedicated to leveraging sports to build social networks, such as Citizen Sports Network, will be reviewed. Examples cited throughout this chapter are aided by key insights from industry executives Bob Bowman—CEO, MLBAM; Dave Morgan—then Executive Editor, Yahoo! Sports, now Executive Editor, Yahoo! North American Audience; Jeff Moorad—member of BOD, Citizens Sports Network; and George Bodenheimer—President, ESPN.

An in-depth look at how portable and mobile devices provide sports content will be discussed in Chapter 5. This chapter also considers different avenues through which mobile content can be consumed, and draws compelling examples from Verizon, EchoStar's Sling Media, and Nike+ to reinforce key points. Finally, this chapter will examine the competitive landscape and how this affects the future of convergence, as well as identify limitations and lessons learned throughout the evolution of mobile technology. As in the other chapters, the thoughts of noteworthy executives are featured, in this case from Terry Denson—VP, Content Strategy and Acquisition, Verizon; Blake Krikorian—founder, Sling Media; Michael Tchao—then GM, Nike+, now VP Product Marketing, Apple Inc.; and Larry Witherspoon—then CEO, Tickets.com.

The increasingly prevalent and important role played by gambling is the topic of Chapter 6. Historically, gambling and sports have had a dynamic, and oftentimes controversial, relationship with one other. Today, however, industry stakeholders are progressively uncovering and leveraging ways to work with and through traditional gambling channels to generate revenue. Leagues, such as the World Series of Poker; gambling-dedicated websites, including Betfair.com; and even cities, especially Las Vegas, are all utilizing sports-oriented gambling's enhanced role to drive their businesses. Contained in the discussion of gambling's impact on sports and entertainment will be insight from Jeffrey Pollack—former Commissioner, WSOP, now Executive Chairman, Professional Bull Riders, Inc.; David Yu—CEO, Betfair; Terry Jicinsky—SVP Marketing, LVCVA; and Frank Fahrenkopf, President and CEO, American Gaming Association.

4 THE INTERNET

MAJOR LEAGUE BASEBALL ADVANCED MEDIA

On the evening of September 19th, 2006, the Los Angeles Dodgers are play-ing the San Diego Padres at Dodger Stadium in a game that has important playoff implications. The Padres lead 9-5 in the bottom of the ninth inning and appear poised to take a 1.5 game lead over their division rivals in Major League Baseball's (MLB's) National League West.

Four hundred miles to the north in Berkeley, California, Dodger fans Tom and Eddie Berman are watching anxiously in Tom's apartment. The Dodgers' Jeff Kent steps to the plate and hits a home run. Then J. D. Drew homers. The Padres bring in future Hall of Fame pitcher Trevor Hoffman, who promptly gives up a home run to Russell Martin. Marlon Anderson follows with an amaz-ing fourth homer in a row, and the Dodgers have tied the game. The Padres score a run in the tenth inning, but Nomar Garciaparra hits a dramatic walk-off two-run home run for Los Angeles, and the Dodgers take over the division lead with an incredible 11-10 victory.

Tom and Eddie are screaming in the apartment, and their cheers are so loud that they receive multiple complaints from neighbors (presumably fans of the Dodgers' main rival, the San Francisco Giants). How are Tom and Eddie watch-ing this game in Berkeley? After all, the game is not broadcast on any local channel in Northern California, nor is it on ESPN, FOX, or any other station that airs baseball nationally. The Bermans do not have a satellite dish either. Instead, Tom has purchased a package on MLB.tv that allows him to watch every Dodger game directly from his computer. As a grad student at UC Berke-ley, he has taken advantage of features offered by MLBAM to demonstrate his passion for the Dodgers all season long. Hundreds of thousands of fans rooting for the other twenty-nine teams have followed suit as well.

The Beginning of MLBAM

Major League Baseball formally created MLBAM in January 2000. Previously, MLB teams had created their own websites and operated them independently from the league. The quality of those sites varied considerably, and that inconsistency made it difficult to cohesively promote the sport and the league as a whole. MLBAM centralized all teams' new media operations into one organization, as MLB believed that its teams could generate more revenue by combining their efforts.

At the urging of MLB commissioner Allan H. "Bud" Selig, all thirty teams were to own an equal share in the new venture. Each team had planned to invest $1 million annually for four years, for an estimated startup cost of $120 million, and each team would share equally in its revenue.[1] Initially, there was some skepticism about the venture, as it was starting on the heels of the "dot-com" bust, but baseball pressed forward. MLB continued with a structure that fundamentally positioned it for long-term success. MLB president Bob Dupuy played a key role during MLBAM's formation by persuading eight team owners to serve for free on MLBAM's board. Working together, this group was instrumental in fashioning a workable structure for what MLB believed to be a historic business opportunity.

"I thought then that in the history of this game, this would be as important a date as when Pete Rozelle got the NFL clubs to share revenue," Selig said in a 2007 *Newsweek* interview. "And nothing has changed my mind."[2]

It turned out that MLBAM needed only $75 million in investment prior to turning a profit, amounting to a cost of just $2.6 million per club—about the same expense as a backup infielder.[3] Each team has already been repaid, and the profits of MLBAM have been reinvested back into the company.

Nine months after founding MLBAM, Bob Bowman was recruited to be its CEO. Bowman brought an interesting set of credentials to the company. A graduate of Harvard College and the Wharton School of Business, Bowman became the state treasurer of Michigan at the age of twenty-seven. He later served as CFO of Sheraton Hotels and later still became president of ITT. In the late 1990s, he briefly led e-commerce site Cyberian Outpost. MLB executives believed that Bowman's diversity of experiences made him a great candidate to lead MLBAM through the ever-changing and difficult-to-understand Internet industry.[4]

At the same time Bowman was hired, MLB changed its league domain name from MajorLeagueBaseball.com to MLB.com. The latter URL had by coincidence been owned by Morgan, Lewis, and Bockius LLP, a Philadelphia-based law firm that has done work with MLB. But MLB recognized the value in using a shorter and easier-to-type domain, so it reached a deal with the law firm.

Bowman overhauled MLB.com in time for the 2001 season and, initially, the site was laced with errors in reporting results and player statistics. Bowman revamped the site again in time for the 2002 season, and from then on MLBAM flourished.

MLBAM Thrives

The backbone of MLBAM's success has been its ability to broadcast MLB games live on the Internet. With a small handful of exceptions, nearly every MLB game is now available on MLB.tv, a service that began in 2002. Over time, the quality of MLB.tv's live streams gradually improved to the point at which watching a game on a computer felt like a perfectly normal viewing experience to most users.

It is this feature that has separated MLB.com from the other league websites. While all league sites have offered a plethora of statistical information, updated rosters, schedules, and other useful facts, MLB was the first major professional sports league to allow its content to be aired live on the Internet. For the first time in 2008, the NFL experimented with streaming live video by showing *Sunday Night Football* on both NBCSports.com and NFL.com. Later, a deal with DIRECTV allowed for NFL games to be broadcast online through the satellite provider's web portals. NBA.com initially had highlights and other programming available on its website, but only later ventured into showing games live via NBA League Pass Broadband.

By 2008, MLB.tv boasted nearly a half-million subscribers, who paid between $80 and $110 a season.[5] A 2009 switch in media players from Microsoft Silverlight to Adobe Flash further improved the quality and reliability of the video streaming (also allowing for DVR-like functions), which likely contributed to MLBAM enjoying a considerable increase in subscribers; by 2011, at its current pace of growth, the site could have as many as one million subscribers. MLBAM has also expanded its video streaming capabilities to include Mosaic, a program that lets users watch up to six games at once. It should be noted that games on MLB.tv are not available to fans in local markets or any other area where a game is televised.

MLBAM has also succeeded because baseball is a sport that is uniquely suited to the Internet. There is a wealth of statistics in the sport, and these can be dissected every which way on MLB.com. Furthermore, it has the largest inventory of games, with each team playing 162 times during the regular season, and following the sport is a daily ritual for many fans. Aside from television, baseball fans can keep track of games through a game-tracker feature called "GameDay" if they do not wish to pay for or use video streaming, and still have a great sense of the action on the field. MLB.com currently averages over fifty million unique visitors a month, making it one of the most visited sports sites in the world.

"We are a destination site, pure and simple. We have an unswerving devotion to our fans and to our revenue model," Bowman says. "95 percent of our content is free, but 5 percent of it is paid. We try to create the best paid content for fans. Also, we are benefited because we have fifteen live games a night and forty-five hours of programming. We have more live programs in a week than a network. That creates advantages if you can scale."[6]

Bowman adds, however, "I don't think advertisers are a bottomless pit. So I don't think you can rely solely on advertisers paying you money just to be associated with your content for revenue."[7]

But games and stats alone do not tell the story of MLBAM's success. Bowman has aggressively pursued a wide range of business deals that have continued to grow the site. More than one-third of all MLB game tickets are purchased through MLBAM, nearly thirty million tickets a year.[8] Users can log on to their team's home site, check the view from a wide range of seat locations, and print their tickets from home.

In 2005, MLBAM purchased Tickets.com, which serves numerous MLB teams and also sells tickets for concerts and other sporting events. Recognizing the growth in the secondary ticket market, and realizing its stigma had effectively worn off, Bowman and MLBAM struck a deal with StubHub in 2007. Ticketholders now can sell their tickets to StubHub through a team's website, and StubHub can, in turn, resell a hard-to-obtain ticket. In the past, Bowman has called ticketing "the mother's milk" of MLBAM's revenue.[9] "The owners have embraced and accepted secondary ticketing," Bowman says. "It will lead to more and more knowledge about how tickets are priced."[10]

MLBAM is also in the retail business, selling more than $80 million a year in team merchandise.[11] In the twenty-four hours after the Boston Red Sox won the 2004 World Series, the team's first in eighty-six years, MLBAM sold more than $5 million in Red Sox paraphernalia.[12]

MLBAM does not limit itself to baseball though. For a time, the company held a stake in World Championship Sports Network (WCSN, now Universal Sports), which broadcast major events for many Olympic sports. It has also leveraged its capabilities to run the websites for Major League Soccer, Minor League Baseball, the Association of Volleyball Professionals (AVP), IceNetwork.com, TigerWoods.com, and the National Pro Fast Pitch League, with live streaming of all softball games. In addition, it has operated the websites for some local television stations, such as those for the New York Yankees–owned YES and the Mets-owned SNY. In the non-sports arena, MLBAM runs the websites for such musical acts as Bob Marley, Elton John, and Guns N' Roses. While some of the aforementioned sports leagues would eventually prefer to run their own websites, the core competencies that MLBAM has developed allows them to offer a more cost-effective short-term solution.

MLBAM has been very progressive about expanding into the mobile space. For a small fee, fans can receive regular updates on their team sent directly to their mobile phones. MLBAM content is programmed to be available for over 160 types of phone and has expanded to offer audio broadcasts of games through a deal with Sprint.[13] The for-pay *MLB At Bat* application has been particularly popular for Apple's iPhone and iPad, allowing fans to listen to the audio of any radio announcer for any game, along with a gametracker that shows precisely where each pitch was thrown and each ball hit. In 2009, using patented technology, MLBAM made live video streaming available for two games a day, only for out-of-market games.[14] Prior to the announcement about live streaming, *MLB At Bat* was already the number one selling application in the iPhone store, with 210,000 subscribers; the free *At Bat Lite* version served to extend this success.[15] By year's end, MLBAM had launched a 99 cent pay-per-game option for the iPhone that contributed to a broader consumption of the league's content.

MLBAM offers more than thirty different services, many of which are sponsored and provide MLBAM with additional revenue. Aside from the previously mentioned features, MLB.com offers fantasy baseball and a "Beat the Streak" game that gives $1 million to anyone who correctly guesses a different player that will get a hit for fifty-seven consecutive days—one longer than Joe DiMaggio's legendary record.

MLBAM employs journalists who cover each team, independent of the club. While the coverage is never excessively critical, the quality of reporting attracts more users. The site also features MLBlogs, which includes blogs written by players, team executives, and even celebrities. Today, MLB.com offers numerous shows on its site, and its content offerings have grown so large that the company needed to purchase a $500,000, thirty-eight-foot video production truck—a normal purchase for a television station, but a rarity for a website.[16] In 2009, MLB launched its own television network, which enhanced MLBAM's production capabilities and created some synergies between the two entities.

The company was approached by several investment banks in 2005 about undertaking an IPO that some analysts estimated could have been worth nearly $2.5 billion; by 2008, that estimate had risen to $5 billion.[17] MLBAM has declined to make the offering though, partially due to MLB's concerns about making its club finances public.

"The conclusion we reached was that it's better to be a better company than a good stock," Bowman says. "The cost of being public is too high. It's added disclosure and added liability. It adds a level of complexity that we probably don't need right now. There are only two reasons to go public: one is that you need capital, and we don't need a lot of that right now. Two is that you want to pay back the founders. Well, most owners are satisfied that they'll get their payday at some point."[18]

MLBAM Questions for the Future

MLBAM has faced challenges in recent years that have led some to question which avenues it may—or should—pursue in the future. In 2008, the U.S. Supreme Court ruled against MLBAM in a case involving licensing rights for player statistics in fantasy leagues. Previously, MLBAM had licensing deals with companies such as ESPN.com and Yahoo! Sports that paid between $2 and $2.5 million a year.[19] The combined amount of these deals totaled nearly $20 million.[20] MLB had paid the players' union $50 million over a five-year period to obtain those rights. The court judgment led ESPN to opt out of a $20-million-per-year deal with MLBAM in 2008 that, in addition to fantasy, also included various video rights.[21] However, ESPN wound up negotiating a new deal with MLBAM in 2008 for $210 million over seven years.[22] The agreement gave ESPN a wide variety of digital rights on ESPN.com, ESPN3, and ESPN Mobile. It also allowed ESPN to stream MLB games it broadcasts live on its own interactive platforms, such as Sunday Night Baseball and the annual Home Run Derby.

MLBAM has also been engaged in a dispute with SlingBox, which is discussed in greater detail later, regarding rights for Internet video content. In addition, some large-market teams are quietly making noise about wanting to capture local revenue on broadcasts through MLB.tv.[23] Several teams have grumbled about the lack of control they have over their own web sites.

"[MLBAM] really needs to help us with our local needs because every team knows its own market and they all differ," then Dodgers chief executive Jamie McCourt said at the 2009 IMG World Congress of Sport. "You can't have a cookie-cutter page. It really is a major opportunity to work together and evolve in a different way."[24]

MLBAM has said it would pursue a more focused strategy with regard to providing outside sports websites. It is also believed that WCSN was not profitable for MLBAM, whereas some of its other league initiatives have been.

"The simple fact is that unless you've got an unbelievably large audience, or an unbelievable commitment to a long-term view," Bowman says, "then it's hard for us to support a Cadillac sports site, which is what the fans want, while you're being paid Honda payments."[25]

Going forward, MLBAM's success will be dependent on its continued ability to adapt to changing technology and to innovate. Accordingly, MLBAM further embraced technology by launching MLB.tv for Sony's PS3 video gaming system for the 2010 season. PS3 owners subscribing to the for-pay service are able to watch games streamed through their system live in HD.[26] Historically, MLB had a reputation of being the sports league that was most resistant to change and slow to evolve. That reputation has largely changed due to the success of MLBAM and Bowman's groundbreaking work. MLBAM has found ways to generate revenue at a time when many are skeptical about the ability of new media companies to deliver a profit.

"Frankly, we'd like to have a twelve-month product," Bowman says of the challenges MLBAM faces. "The biggest issue we face right now is churn, after baseball season ends."[27]

MLBAM is one of a few Internet-based sites that continues to play a vital role in shaping how fans consume sports. Its ability to offer an increasing amount of access to consumers—regardless of their location—not only has provided teams and leagues with another touchpoint from which to market themselves, but has also extended the entertainment value of sports.

THE INTERNET: AN OVERVIEW

Access to and interactivity with sports news, information, and entertainment have substantially increased since the Internet's early days. Fans interested in checking scores, statistics, or highlights can now log on to the Internet via their nearest computer or PDA. This 24/7 access has transformed sports while simultaneously adding to their entertainment value.

This hasn't always been the case, as the Internet in its early days was fragmented and consisted largely of message boards and the listing of scores through online portals such as America Online, Compuserve, and Prodigy. This began to change in 1994 when ESPN and Prodigy partnered to form ESPNET. The new service initially provided fans text and pictures, and eventually led to audio and video clips, as well as the ability to exchange messages with prominent sports figures and ESPN commentators.[28] Following the Prodigy agreement, ESPN and the Internet media company Starwave broadened the reach to satisfy sports enthusiasts' demand by starting ESPNET.Sportszone.com in 1995; in 1998 it was renamed ESPN.com.

1995 also witnessed the launch of Sportsline USA. Dedicated to sports-related information and entertainment, Sportsline quickly became a rival to ESPNET.Sportszone.com. After CBS acquired a 22 percent stake in Sportsline in March 1997, the website officially changed its name to CBS Sportsline. It included real-time information on a wide range of sports-related content, from the major U.S. team sports to European Cup soccer and cricket. Sportsline also created and marketed official Internet fan clubs for more than a dozen of sports' biggest superstars, including Wayne Gretzky, Michael Jordan, Shaquille O'Neal, Cal Ripken Jr., and Tiger Woods.[29]

On the heels of Sportsline's launch, *Sports Illustrated* and Yahoo! Sports both entered the space, in 1996 and 1997, respectively. The well known magazine's Internet counterpart, later branded SI.com, brought much of the sports entertainment content available in its magazine to the Internet, including articles by renowned writers and behind-the-scenes pictorials of its famous swimsuit issues.

Yahoo! Sports began as a site that offered comprehensive information and coverage of sports leagues and sporting events worldwide while also providing sortable statistics intended for those playing fantasy sports. In addition, Yahoo! Sports provided original content from *The Sporting News* and from sports events; it also made scores and statistics from SportsTicker®, top stories of the day, and player profiles available to information-hungry fans. This initial focus on fantasy sports enabled Yahoo! Sports to surpass ESPN.com in 2008 as the top sports site in terms of unique site visitors.[30] Yahoo! further expanded its hold on sports with the acquisition of Rivals.com and Citizens Sports Network, both of which are discussed later in this chapter.

Realizing the opportunity to deliver content to fans, and to do so while closely managing their messaging, sports leagues developed their own web presence. Each league took its own approach to entering the realm of online content. Majorleaguebaseball.com and NBA.com launched in 1995, while the NFL entered into a partnership with ESPN Sportszone in 1996 for what was thought to be less than $1 million to produce the NFL.com website.[31] As a result of the Internet's growth, just two years later, after a prolonged bidding war between CBS Sportsline, Fox Sports, and ESPNET Sportszone, the NFL closed a deal to receive $10 million over a three-year period for the right to partner with the league.[32] Following the initial model of the other major sports leagues, the NFL allowed its individual team owners to operate their own team-affiliated websites, which were then hosted on NFL.com.[33] As concerns about Internet rights increased, the leagues began to take control of the team sites, which were all hosted and linked from the individual league domains.

The league involvement with the Internet provided unprecedented access for fans and thus enhanced the connection the consumers had with their favorite league or team. For example, the NBA provided fans audio and video clips of their favorite teams, as well as a link to ESPNET SportsZone to obtain live scores, stats, and news.[34] Eventually, fans were permitted to buy tickets and merchandise from these sites, further cementing their connection to their favorite sports, teams, and players.

The vast array of sports-related Internet options has enabled fans to fully immerse themselves in all aspects of the sporting experience. No longer relegated to merely "consuming" sports by watching games in person or on television, fans now participate in the dialogue and even produce their own content. With the advent of sports blogs, fans are an integral part of the sports entertainment experience—active participants in the process rather than just interested bystanders. Sites such as deadspin.com, kissingsuzycolber.com, and everydayshouldbesaturday.com highlight the way bloggers have successfully combined sports and entertainment online.

These fans-turned-content-producers have become a vital—and profit-able—part of the sports business landscape. With so many fans now consuming and producing content it is no surprise that sports-related news, information, and social networking applications have become wildly popular; nor is it surprising to learn that sponsors and advertisers are keenly interested in reaching these fans. As discussed in the following sections, Rivals.com and Citizen Sports Network are among those monetizing this consumption and production.

RIVALS.COM

An outpost for more than eleven million high school and college sports fans, Rivals.com has transformed the way amateur sports are covered.[35] Rivals was launched in May 2001 after CEO and president Shannon Terry led the effort to purchase and license the remaining assets of the Seattle-based Rivals Networks and subsequently rebrand it Rivals.com. The website is a compilation of over 160 sites that feature information on everything from Canadian high school athletes to University of Southern California football. Each major college athletic conference and its members' major sports programs are represented, as are "preps" sites delivering coverage of high school sports throughout North America. Because such comprehensive coverage had been missing from the marketplace, Rivals.com and its chief competitor, Scout.com, were rapidly embraced by information-seeking fans.

Fans visiting Rivals.com are divided into two groups: those that pay a monthly membership fee of $9.95 (or annual fee of $99.95) and those that merely frequent the "free" message boards.[36] These membership fees account for more than half of the company's revenue, with the balance generated from advertising and syndication fees.[37] In addition, according to then executive editor of Yahoo! Sports Dave Morgan, the local reach of the individual Rivals sites is attractive to advertisers and sponsors in terms of drawing from specific demographics in different parts of the country.[38] Paid registrants are allowed access to the premium articles and message boards on the "home" site where they subscribed, as well as being provided access to additional restricted areas throughout the Rivals network. Access for nonpaying fans is limited to the free articles and free message boards containing less detailed information. In addition to access to more comprehensive information and statistics, paid registrants also have access to a text message alert service that keeps them abreast of breaking news about their favorite school or recruit.

Many of the sites available through the Rivals.com network are independently hosted by web operators that have their own staff of reporters and writers charged with covering the site's respective teams and sports. These independent sites routinely feature news about who each school is recruiting and what is going on "behind the scenes" with the respective sports programs, including interviews and articles on the current sports season. While this is a significant draw for many fans, the community message boards are often what attract fans to the sites daily. The open discussion on these boards creates an online sports bar of sorts where fans meet to discuss and argue about various topics, while simultaneously gleaning information from so-called "insiders" that may or may not have connections to a sports program or specific recruit.

While the most popular affiliated sites have upward of 1,000 daily visitors, major events tend to demonstrate the vast number of fans that interact on these sites. National signing day, the first day high school seniors can sign letters of intent to attend the college of their choice, drives over 75 million page views and 1.5 million unique visitors to the Rivals network.[39] The demographic generating this massive amount of traffic has attracted sponsors such as Nike, which was a presenting sponsor for Rival.com's recruiting channel, and Verizon, which sponsored a March Madness countdown clock on the Rivals network.[40] Increased traffic is also witnessed at individual team sites when a high school player announces his intention to sign with a particular school on national signing day, or when a school's coach is about to be hired or fired. The latter brought 16,000 basketball fans to the Rivals University of Kentucky site on the day the school hired basketball coach, Billy Gillespie.[41]

In July of 2007, Rivals was acquired by Yahoo! for an estimated $100 million.[42] The Yahoo! acquisition was spurred by the company's need to reach the very desirable college sports fan demographic.[43] As Morgan stated, "The acquisition was important to Rivals because Yahoo! brought financial backing, a broader audience, and insights gained that Rivals otherwise could not have recreated."[44] This was particularly important given the fierce online competition from new media outlets seeking to build and maintain monetizable communities. Not only did the acquisition help attract advertisers, it also provided content creators with an incredible amount of user-created content through the message boards.[45] An additional development driving the acquisition was that other media outlets, such as ESPN, were starting their own recruiting coverage, while Fox Interactive Media was acquiring Scout.com. Rivals.com also provided Yahoo! a ready-made brand with an entire network of sites from which customers felt a sense of brand loyalty.[46] This built-in base guaranteed Yahoo! an increase in daily traffic, a key metric by which success is measured.

Rivals has continued to offer members services such as national player rankings, online video highlights, player cards, an online searchable player database, and official visit lists, and it produced video features on the top players in the country.[47] This vast amount of information at the disposal of millions of fans has helped increase anticipation leading up to national signing day. Daily updates on what the top players in the country are "thinking and doing" have created an intense following that serves as an offseason complement to the hugely popular college football and basketball seasons. Fans accustomed to waiting until the start of the next season for comprehensive news and analysis about their favorite sport are now fully engaged throughout the year as they follow—and participate in—the ebbs and flows associated with recruiting and coaching changes.

While the NCAA polices the universities in terms of how much contact they can have with high school student-athletes, the same cannot be said for those delivering content about amateur sports. The need for continuously updated recruiting information and analysis has occasionally placed Rivals reporters in a position in which they contact these coveted student-athletes as much as, if not more than, the college coaches recruiting them. This, along with allegations of some site reporters using their relationships with the athletes to steer recruits to certain schools, has increased the scrutiny given sites such as Rivals and Scout. Ultimately, these sites must balance their pursuits or run the risk of jeopardizing their core revenue sources, especially at a time when they seek to diversify and expand their presence offline. As Rivals has been brought under the Yahoo! sports umbrella, these issues have lessened as a result of the increased credibility that comes with being part of an overall media organization.[48]

For example, Rivals has been heavily involved with prep bowl games and scouting combines, which feature many of the top high school players in the country. Throughout the week of practice prior to the events, Rivals reporters and site representatives interview the athletes and observe practices that allow them to filter the information back to subscribing members as an added perk to their subscription. It is this added value that Rivals has labeled its "Ultimate Fan Experience" because it delivers fans exclusive access to expert content and information.[49]

This full-featured experience through vast multimedia exposure has helped extend the brand beyond its roots. Rivals has taken what was once a simple sports recruiting service and turned it into one that provides fans extensive sports entertainment options beyond those historically limited to in-season activities. As a result, the development of high school sports stars has become interconnected with the world of college sports and new media, enabling stakeholders to profit from this evolution.

CITIZENS SPORTS NETWORK

Utilizing many of the key factors surrounding Rivals's success, Citizen Sports Network (CSN) capitalizes on sports fans' innate desire for community through new means and new distribution channels. CSN has numerous products on social networking sites such as Facebook, MySpace, and hi5, for a total of over six hundred team applications for fans, fantasy sports sites, and high school sports social networking. However, CSN did not always focus on sports-oriented social networking.

In September 2005, Mike Kerns and Jeff Moorad co-founded ProTrade, the San Francisco–based company that would eventually become CSN. Kerns was the former chief of staff at Steinberg & Moorad Sports Management, a premier sports representation firm. He and Moorad were able to attract former Kleiner Perkins principal and San Jose Sharks co-owner Kevin Compton and former Moorad client and San Francisco 49er tight end Brent Jones as investors. Their first employee was Jeff Ma, a former member of the MIT blackjack team who served as the inspiration for the main character in the book *Bringing Down the House: The Inside Story of Six MIT Students Who Took Vegas for Millions* and the subsequent movie *21*. Later, Moorad became a general partner and the CEO of the Arizona Diamondbacks and is presently the vice chairman and CEO of the San Diego Padres; he remains a CSN board member.

Using Ma's math skills and Kerns's business acumen, the pair evolved Pro-Trade to be a new kind of fantasy sports site. Rather than offer typical fantasy games, ProTrade allowed users to buy and sell players or teams as if they were stocks. Like any stock, players and teams had "price to earnings" ratios, and users were challenged to create the most valuable portfolio in a wide variety of competitive games, played with friends and strangers alike. Much of the value of the players or teams was determined by algorithms developed by Ma, and ProTrade actually sold some of those algorithms to sites that had various fantasy games, including MLB.com and ESPN.com.[50]

Users did not spend actual money, as there are substantial hurdles involved with Internet gambling in the U.S., but they did pay anywhere from $5 to $50 to compete in various games with the opportunity to win prizes (some games were free of charge). ProTrade retained several high-profile pitchmen to help sell its product, including Phoenix Suns point guard Steve Nash and Dallas Cowboys Hall of Fame quarterback Troy Aikman. Ma also worked with well-respected executives to refine his algorithms, such as former Los Angeles Lakers and Memphis Grizzlies general manager Jerry West; Oakland A's general manager Billy Beane; and the late Bill Walsh, former San Francisco 49ers head coach and executive. In total, ProTrade raised $12 million in venture capital to finance the company.[51]

After nearly two-and-a-half years Kerns recognized that it was time to change the company's direction. While ProTrade was a well-organized site that offered unique games in a wide variety of sports, both domestically and abroad, senior management believed their user base had peaked at approximately 250,000. The process of buying and selling players like stocks may sound like fun, but it seemed too complex for some. Also, the inability to trade with real money may have hindered interest for some sports fans and gambling enthusiasts.

"ProTrade was—and still is—very important to us, but by itself simply doesn't have enough scale to really achieve the kind of ambitions we're after," said Kerns in April 2008. "We've kind of maxed it out."[52]

Accordingly, in April 2008, ProTrade was rebranded as CSN and sought to succeed as a premier sports entity in the social networking space. The opportunities in social networking were clear; after launching in 2004, Facebook had grown phenomenally to have over a hundred million users worldwide, and it had become a fixture in the lives of many college students and young adults. Its primary rival, MySpace, had roughly the same number of users, while hi5 had more than seventy million. In May 2007, Facebook began allowing outside software developers to design Facebook applications, and CSN joined in the fray.

"The idea of shifting the Pro Trade stock market concept to (Citizen Sports) seemed like a no-brainer, as we saw the explosion of social networking," Moorad says. "While ProTrade remains a brand of the company that we're very committed to, we were excited to play a more active role in the social networking space."[53]

Through a mere soft launch of team applications for fans of numerous sports worldwide, as well as several sports-related games on Facebook, CSN had attracted 1.5 million users that generated over $1 million in revenue by April 2008—more revenue than it generated in any prior calendar year.[54] Virtually all of the revenue came through advertising, as the applications offered advertisers more direct and unique ways to target specific demographics.

Emboldened by this early success, CSN set out to launch a high-quality fantasy football application on Facebook for the 2008 season. Like social networking, fantasy sports has also grown rapidly and had become mainstream by the mid-2000s. The timing to take advantage of the combination of social networking and fantasy sports seemed ideal, as Nielsen data indicated that in late 2007, nearly twelve million web users visited one or more fantasy football sites on a monthly basis, with the average user spending one hour and forty-five minutes at a league-hosted site.[55] Moreover, in 2008, the Fantasy Sports Trade Association reported that nearly thirty million people in the U.S. and Canada participated in a fantasy sports league, an increase of 54 percent from the previous year.[56] Sports fans simply love to act as real general managers, engage in transactions with their friends, and effectively gamble with others on their predictions for specific players' performance.

"Sports is a common denominator for many, regardless of social position or otherwise. It's a connector," Moorad says. "Specifically, football has shown itself to be a driver to that marketplace. Fantasy football is a way to track the pro game in a more in-depth way than a typical newspaper sports section. It's also a bonding tool. There are people who play in leagues for years and become fast friends."[57]

Facebook appeared to be a natural site to host a fantasy football game, largely because it already supported the interactions between groups of friends. To establish its game, CSN partnered with *Sports Illustrated* and its website, SI.com, in a revenue-sharing deal. For CSN, SI.com offered brand recognition and a sense of legitimacy about its fantasy game. SI.com also became the exclusive sales arm for CSN, and it offered expert opinions from many of its well-known writers. For SI.com, using CSN and its quickly developed expertise in

Facebook applications, as well as Ma's highly advanced algorithms, allowed it to gain ground in fantasy sports games, where it had fallen well behind industry leaders Yahoo! Sports and ESPN.com. For the 2009 NFL season CSN registered in excess of one million players for its fantasy game, twice the prior year's total.[58]

Continuing this momentum, CSN partnered with MLBAM in 2009, whereby MLBAM sold advertising within CSN's baseball-related Facebook applications. The two also partnered on other cross-marketing and promotional initiatives, leading CSN's Kerns to suggest, "There are similarities to this with our deal with *Sports Illustrated*, but here there's more of an element of our building our products in part with MLB.com technology, which we think is great, and is the kind of thing we want to do more of."[59]

CSN's rapid penetration in this area has not been limited to U.S.-based sports leagues; its Facebook fantasy game for the English Premier League (EPL), one of the world's most prominent sports leagues, experienced tremendous initial growth. Heading into the 2009 EPL season, CSN forecasted more than one million registrants for the game, which was sponsored by Pepsi Max and Ford.[60] In fact, by 2009, CSN had become the third largest fantasy sports provider, only trailing the aforementioned Yahoo! and ESPN.[61] This no doubt drew Yahoo!'s attention, as it reached a deal in March 2010 to acquire CSN, thus expanding Yahoo!'s scale and influence in the digital sports media industry.[62]

Such strategic partnerships yield clear opportunities. According to Moorad, "The power and allure of social media has become evident with our sponsors. The social networking space is huge. As advertisers continue to spend more money in the space, they can focus on not only the ability to reach consumers, but to reach them in a rifle-like manner. To reach a very defined demographic is becoming even more important to the advertising world. As marketers become savvier with their approach, I think that Citizen Sports is perfectly positioned to help them extend their brands."[63]

It remains to be seen how successful CSN will be with its fantasy products on social networking sites and through its iPhone application. However, given the high engagement figures on fantasy sites, which are very appealing to advertisers, and the increasingly wide-scale usage of social networking sites, it would appear that CSN, with Yahoo!'s influence, is poised to succeed given its first-mover advantage in social networking fantasy games.

THE INTERNET: THE BOTTOM LINE

The growth in both sports-related content on the Internet and the creativity associated with it has been dramatic given the enhanced interactive experiences provided by such companies as MLBAM, Rivals, and Citizen Sports Network. These organizations and other well-positioned and financed competitors will consistently be primed to adapt to emerging technologies. As they do so it will remain incumbent upon them to demonstrate to industry stakeholders that they are delivering quantifiable results, whether defined as brand-loyal subscribers, incremental revenue, or other distinguishable metric(s). In the process, online industry leaders will work diligently to ensure that profitable subscription models become reality. If this is to occur, much improved customization must be delivered to increasingly global audiences that utilize social media, and such customization must be done despite the fact that consumer wants and needs tend to outpace the industry's ability to easily and cost-effectively deliver technology.

Subscription Models Take Hold

Although slower to take hold than many industry stakeholders would have preferred, online entities have begun to monetize their assets through subscription-oriented content and programming. Exemplified by MLBAM and Rivals, when loyal customers are presented with content specifically tailored to their needs as consumers and fans, meaningful revenue can be generated. When consumers and fans are provided unfettered access on a global basis to their favorite sports content, including teams and athletes, numerous stakeholders stand to benefit, while others must alter their approach to generating revenue and building brand value. Internet businesses, sports leagues, governing bodies, franchises, and athletes are directly affected. So too are those that have historically funded sports, such as the television networks, sponsors, and advertisers.

As online media continues to evolve in the sports space, and does so tactically through delivering more complete and compelling sports content to desirable target audiences, it must consider two important challenges. It must anticipate ongoing backlash from consumers and fans who historically have accessed such content for free. The extent to which the backlash will be mitigated will certainly be a function of the quality and cost of the content delivered. Second, although piracy is somewhat less of a concern for live sporting events, the industry must guard against both it and archival content being commandeered without permission, payment, or both. As these obstacles are overcome, private equity and venture capital firms will continue to take notice, further accelerating growth opportunities and the potential for asset appreciation among myriad industry stakeholders.

Demand for services will grow as distributors of Internet content continue to improve their capabilities, ultimately permitting those in sports to deliver far more robust, branded, and live sports content to fans. Those that own and distribute online content, through the most important new distribution platform in sports, are well positioned to play a far greater role in the sports industry. This not only will include targeted cross-promotions to drive service adoption and extend subscription packages, but also will include more extensive sponsorship of leagues, events, and teams. Simultaneously, if the industry is capable of addressing piracy, which continues to threaten stakeholder interest, and delivers high levels of customer service, then it will be positioned to have a further impact on the sports business industry; an impact that may eventually include franchise ownership. This will not occur until or unless sports' media distribution paradigm, which is guided by revenue generation and affected by the public sector, changes.

However, sports leagues and governing bodies, particularly those with compelling content, committed fan bases, and access to capital, will be inclined to go it alone. For example, MLBAM historically has generated approximately half of its total revenue from fans that pay in excess of $100 per season to view live games over the Internet.[64] Established Internet properties that offer an intriguing additional platform for advertisers, sponsors, and of course the league's own franchises and players are ideally situated. Once league-owned and operated sites become cost effective and achieve critical mass, they will be able to use this presence when discussing future broadcast rights packages with television networks, highlighting the ability to stream their own games as leverage.

Emerging leagues or those that are less entrenched online can lever the Internet to build their brands, experimenting with new applications and services in the process. Regardless of the extent to which a league or team is an online powerhouse, they all have the opportunity to generate incremental revenue through ticket and merchandise sales, as well as the ability to monetize international markets over time. These opportunities are extremely important since revenue from online advertising at such sites may be slow to develop, given their smaller audiences.

Individual franchises also stand to benefit, especially in terms of global branding. The Chicago Cubs and Atlanta Braves built national followings given their early relationships with WGN and TBS, respectively. Internet-based content that strikes a chord with fans worldwide enables all sports franchises to build their brands on a global basis and then to monetize this enhanced value in much the same way as leagues.

Athletes, including amateur athletes, have the opportunity to accelerate their personal branding given the growth of their respective league's online presence. However, the extent to which athletes eventually derive a portion of overall Internet revenue secured by the leagues will become a major point of contention in future labor negotiations. Forecasting revenue emanating from online content could lead to labor strife as, historically, leagues and players' unions have had difficulty determining how best to share known revenue streams, let alone evolving ones like those associated with new media.

Technology Enables Customization

Rapidly advancing technology has dramatically improved the ability to customize content for consumers and fans. Customization, which brings fans closer to their favorite teams and players, simultaneously empowers sports marketers who can now reach a coveted demographic with great precision. By understanding the likes and dislikes of fans, as well as uncovering their consumption patterns and preferences, numerous industry stakeholders can develop and extend their brands while generating revenue in the process. These opportunities are not limited to Internet businesses, sports leagues, franchises, and advertisers. Opportunities are also created for those that aggregate and disseminate (marketing) data and information and support those investing in sports, particularly sponsors and the television industry. Through a better understanding about target markets, the return on investment associated with sports production and consumption will increase. This presupposes that consumers and fans continue to embrace such customization and do not feel as though their privacy is being jeopardized or that the customization is otherwise intrusive from a marketing perspective.

As technology evolves and consumers and fans are afforded a greater opportunity to access their favorite sports content whenever and wherever they choose, new media companies—here including "traditional" media companies such as television networks that are moving into the space—must work with sports leagues and teams to provide even more compelling access to live content. For instance, ESPN utilizes its ESPN3 Internet technology to give fans multiple camera angles from which to choose when watching certain sporting events. While it can be argued that such technology represents advancement in television programming, it is important to consider that the television industry is striving to mimic the real-time, interactive nature of online sports. This is similar to the way that televised sports have added broadcast elements that cater to the video game generation. Historically, video game makers strove to replicate the actual sports experience in order to be viewed as authentic; today, it is televised sports that continue to customize their broadcasts in order to deliver a compelling game presentation to a younger, more tech-savvy and demanding audience.

Moreover, traditional media companies are also hoping to take advantage on the local level, particularly as the newspaper industry undergoes unprecedented change resulting in consolidation or elimination of many daily papers. Television networks that take advantage of these changes in print journalism are favorably positioned to attract advertisers and sponsors. Rather than allow the migration from television to the Internet to have a negative impact on their overall approach to content distribution, television networks are continuing to protect and defend their territory, and do so not only online but increasingly on local levels. ESPN's launch of city-specific ESPN.com websites in major metropolitan cities is one example of a major broadcaster relying on the Internet to protect and extend its core television offerings. By delivering local content at a time when local newspapers are retrenching, ESPN has the opportunity to carve out local market share, but only if it delivers authentic and accurate local content, as discriminating fans will not embrace anything less.

Should media companies fail to credibly deliver compelling sports content, fans will look elsewhere for the sports news, information, and analyses they seek. Over time this will lead to consumers' willingness to pay (more) for the content they deem important or complement their demand for content by further embracing bloggers.

As sports, television, and the Internet continue to converge, these entities will benefit from striking comprehensive strategic alliances; they may also choose to merge. Because of their ability to customize content, online companies may eventually move into television. While the programming may not closely resemble television as it is known today, these companies may blend sought-after content delivery with the ability to reach an attractive demographic better than others. Eventually, Google, Yahoo! or other emerging new media giants may secure the "broadcast" rights to major sports leagues and events. Their ability to customize content and deliver targeted (global) audiences will allow them to monetize these rights beyond their acquisition costs by providing advertisers and sponsors an improved marketing platform. Conversely, leagues such as MLB have already responded, establishing a foothold in the new media space given the success of MLBAM, which looks and feels more like a television network every season. Other sports-oriented sites, such as Rivals, are able to similarly communicate the benefits of customized content to advertisers and sponsors seeking to reach brand-loyal consumers and fans.

In addition to customization enabling teams to increase engaged audiences on a global basis, it also serves as a catalyst for venue attendance and the spending surrounding it, such as that on concessions and merchandise.

Harnessing Social Media

The sports industry's ability to tap into fans' deep interest in, and commitment to, social networking sites remains fertile territory. With most sports-oriented websites containing at least a modicum of social networking, what was once a phenomenon is now becoming lucrative for those in sports business. Sites such as Rivals and CSN have combined sports content with personal interaction in ways that allow them to form deep bonds with their customers. As the ability to monetize social networking gains further traction, sports industry stakeholders will be among those that profit the most, as the attachment between fans and the sports teams and athletes they revere the most remains strong. The growth in these interactive, interpersonal experiences provides sports marketers and brands viral, cost-effective opportunities to reach targeted customers with accuracy and authenticity. Also afforded a compelling marketing platform are sports leagues, teams, and athletes who welcome the chance to personally connect with fans willing to spend time and money on sports-related content. At the forefront of this ability to connect with the fans are micro-blogging sites that allow fans to directly communicate with their favorite athlete. However, the impact on television and other forms of media is becoming significant.

Sports marketers' ability to immerse brands in social networking sites has created a level of marketing precision previously unavailable through other media platforms. At the very least, these brands have the ability to have their marketing messages tactically reinforced via social networking. As this continues, sites offering a deep and engaging experience with sports fans will attract incremental advertising and sponsorship, often at the expense of more traditional media outlets.

When these brands align with sports leagues and teams to communicate jointly to consumers and fans, the opportunity increases exponentially. As brand and sports marketers partner with these sites to optimize consumer and fan interaction and usage, all parties benefit from the economies of scale, resulting in increased shareholder and sports franchise values brought about by revenue increases over time. As previously indicated, athletes benefit from such developments in two ways. First, they are poised to build or extend their brands on a global basis, which aids their efforts in securing endorsement deals. Second, athletes, through the collective bargaining process, will eventually capture a significant portion of the revenue created by leagues given their relationships with social networking sites.

With athletes, coaches, and even team owners providing consumers and fans direct access to their thoughts and observations before, during, and after sporting events, the impact on traditional media is immediate and dramatic. Revenue opportunities, once confined to television, radio, and print, are shifting because social networking sites are better able to deliver tightly segmented markets. Certain forms of sports media, especially television, may not be harmed provided they allocate sufficient resources or otherwise form strategic alliances in the social networking space designed to promote interest in live programming. For athletes, these developments bring with them potential limitations. While there is no doubt that social media enables athletes to develop, refine, and extend their brands, the likelihood exists that many will be compromised by their high-profile indiscretions. Athletes seeking to be entertaining and relevant may ultimately harm their personal brands by violating league or team mandates, or simply by underappreciating the impact their comments may have on team members, sponsors, or, most important, the consumers who purchase their endorsed products and the fans who look forward to their next game.

THE INTERNET AND CONVERGENCE: FINAL
THOUGHTS FROM ESPN'S GEORGE BODENHEIMER[65]

George Bodenheimer is the president of ESPN. ESPN is the preeminent sports and entertainment company, with deep penetration into all facets of sports entertainment. Bodenheimer shared his perspective on convergence and the Internet with the SBI.

SBI: How has the Internet shaped ESPN's business the past couple of years, and how will it continue to do so?

BODENHEIMER: The Internet has provided us with tremendous opportunities since we launched ESPN.com over fourteen years ago. Since we primarily provide fans news and live games, the Internet helps us provide information fans want to know in real time. We can no longer wait for the six o'clock *SportsCenter* to provide fans updates. *SportsCenter* is live during the day now, and ESPN.com changes every couple of minutes depending on the news. We have to update all of our media in real time and make it easy for our fans to find—especially given their well-demonstrated appetite for new media. We also look at what we term "the best available screen." The customers we are serving are avid sports fans, and they look for the "best available screen" when they are ready to consume sports. If you are a fan and are away from home, you are going to use your computer or cell phone for information. We are trying to serve all of our fans on any and all of those screens in real time, all of the time—they won't settle for anything less.

SBI: How do you maximize these new technology platforms?

BODENHEIMER: Let's use college football as an example. Fans can have their mobile phone alert awaken them in the morning at the start of ESPN's College GameDay telecast. Then, between the website and ESPN's mobile and television broadcasts, there exists steady preview material until the day's games begin. At the same time, fans can log on to ESPN3.com to watch several other college football games simultaneously while chatting with other fans, and having the ESPN or ESPN2 game available on their HD set. Through the ESPN3.com site, fans can also receive information from the ESPN research and analysis group in real time. ESPN.com also offers fans the "Virtual Press Box," which is a moderated real-time feed that includes all of the ESPN analysts at the game; the analysts in Bristol, Connecticut; selected fan comments; updated stats; and poll questions presented to the fans on all the games currently taking place, as well as the upcoming evening games. Now fans have an incredibly immersive experience that begins Saturday morning and doesn't conclude until the last game that evening. Fans can continue following the events as well through ESPN mobile television. The product that is being produced from these football games is much more expansive than what was being produced a few years ago—when it was primarily just the game. Now, there are many products that are extracted from one football game, and we are able to use the Internet as a hub for much of it.

SBI: What have been the most prominent technological advancements?

BODENHEIMER: The quality of the video online and through mobile phones has greatly increased through the years. Audio is also very important for the fan. Podcasting has become a significant business for us in terms of audience and advertising. We also have an ESPN Radio application for the iPhone that allows fans to open the application and listen to personalities like Tony Kornheiser no matter where they are. These advancements help us deliver the highest-quality fan experience, and we believe the rapidly improving video and audio capabilities encourage our fans to spend more time with our online offerings.

SBI: What do you believe will be the most compelling advancement in the years to come? Maybe one that the industry is still refining?

BODENHEIMER: For us the answer to that question is 3D. We began by producing the 2009 USC-Ohio State football game, X Games, and golf in 3D. However, there are plenty of questions regarding business models, exact technologies, and how it gets into the home. Ultimately, it will be a superior upgrade in viewing experience, especially for sports—but we have to be very careful not to compromise the ESPN brand when taking advantage of it. What I mean by this is that we must make sure that the quality of the 3D experience is consistent with what fans expect from ESPN, whether this is on their TV or laptop.

SBI: What are the biggest hurdles facing 3D?

BODENHEIMER: Getting into the home is our first job. Next, we do not have a complete feel for the cost that we will incur to produce high-quality sports product in 3D. Interestingly, there won't be a problem with display devices because those will be on the market very quickly and the cost should not be excessive. The issue will be making it work as a business. When we look back at ESPN HD launching in 2003, there was no business model. We were uncertain of which format to choose, however we decided on what was best for our fans. We are viewing 3D in the same way in terms of producing and distributing 3D product at high levels of quality for the fans. On a macro level, we appreciate that they will be utilizing 3D on a variety of platforms.

SBI: Where has ESPN been able to monetize its new media services?

BODENHEIMER: We always seek value for the content that we produce. We have a dual revenue stream model in television. For ESPN.com, we are looking at multiple revenue streams consisting of premium content—our ESPN Insider service—on the Internet, supported by advertising revenue as well. We know the content we produce is highly valued by our distributors and our fans. We are also pursuing other models such as ESPN3.com, where we license a broadband network to Internet service providers and they deliver it to their customers. Nobody has that model, yet we know that it is a proper model in terms of building a sustainable service that has quality content on it. Quality content costs money, and sports in particular has unique costs, and thus we are very focused on building businesses that go beyond the advertising model. However, we have to be careful not to compromise the fan experience in the process.

SBI: What advice would you give others in the new media business?

BODENHEIMER: If you have products and services that serve fans, that really take into account what they want, you will make it work and be able to monetize it. You have to talk to your fans and customers all the time. We receive consumer feedback in real time in many ways, including electronically and via customer calls and fan feedback centers and now through Twitter. That allows us to monitor how our fans feel about our products and what they want from us to improve their experience. For example, with college football, we monitor Twitter to find out what fan responses are to ESPN3.com or whether there are any technical problems or issues. As a company we also organized our ad sales around a single multimedia sale. This prompted us in the content group to approach our product in the same way. We have been able to renew the college *GameDay* franchise around The Home Depot and utilize the *Virtual Press Box* in conjunction with Microsoft. Understanding the value of these products for advertisers is also part of our plan. It boils down to making sure our fans have the best possible experience and then it is up to us to make sure our business partners can connect with them in compelling ways.

SBI: How does ESPN maintain its leadership position?

BODENHEIMER: As I suggested, we never lose sight of the fan. We also keep a very keen eye on our business partners, including our distributors and advertising partners. We even established and operate a media lab in Austin, Texas. This lab allows us to demonstrate to advertisers the kinds of products and advertising vehicles we have at our disposal. For instance, we use biometrics that study people's eye movements and perspiration levels as they interact with media. This kind of research adds value for our advertising customers by reinforcing to them just how closely we know what our fans are thinking and wanting. In short, we use real research to demonstrate the value of advertising across our various platforms.

SBI: What are ESPN's biggest challenges going forward?

BODENHEIMER: There are few barriers to entry for those hoping to enter some of our businesses, especially online. Also, our business partners are oftentimes our competitors, including leagues, cable distributors, and phone companies. Competition and choice are therefore among the biggest challenges. As a result, a strong brand is going to matter even more. We have a great position with sports fans where they gravitate to ESPN on a daily basis. If we keep our brand strong by zealously improving products, developing new products, being first to market, and remaining focused on our fans, we can continue to be successful and overcome these challenges.

MOBILE TECHNOLOGY

VERIZON V CAST

They were commercials that seemed to appear on TV during every sporting event in 2007. In one, a sports reporter interviews a tuxedoed Mike Joiner, who is identified as the "MVP of today's Baxter-Donahue wedding." Joiner rattles off sports clichés about it being a "team effort," and a replay of him at the altar as best man is shown while he watches a gamecast of the "Chicago-St. Louis" game on his cell phone.

In another, a woman identified as Sarah Fiske is interviewed in front of a house after being named "MVP of the Anderson baby shower." The reporter asks, "What was the toughest part for you, Sarah?" She responds, "You know, like I said, pretending that I actually wanted to be here. But I was able to stay focused and watch highlights from a bunch of college hoops games." A replay is shown of Sarah at a hopelessly boring ladies event while she's watching highlights of college basketball on her Verizon V CAST mobile device complete with ESPN MVP. Then, in a moment of hilarity, her angry sister Nancy tries to drive away without giving Sarah a ride home.

Other Verizon V CAST commercials that would appear throughout the year featured a man on his honeymoon, colleagues at an excruciating work-related conference, and even a man with two paramedics in an ambulance. The point of these ads is fairly clear: they demonstrate that, thanks to sports-related content, even the least-desirable situations can be ameliorated. All preconceived notions of time and place are thrown out the window, as one can be close to sports virtually anywhere and anytime. Fans everywhere are now capable of watching gamecasts, updating their fantasy sports team roster, or viewing highlights courtesy of emerging mobile technology.

For ESPN, the new service provided a dramatic change in strategy after some early forays into mobile technology went awry. For Verizon, a partnership with

ESPN Mobile offered a quality sports brand to complement its breakthrough V CAST technology and service offering that had already been making waves. The partnership seemed to be a perfect match, but as mobile technology continues to evolve, the value of such alliances remains fluid.

Verizon and V CAST

Verizon was formed in 2000 after Bell Atlantic acquired GTE for $52 billion. The merged companies were renamed Verizon as a combination of the words *veritas* and *horizon*. Verizon grew steadily throughout the 2000s, especially after its 2005 acquisition of MCI. By the time Verizon acquired Alltel in 2009, it had moved ahead of AT&T and Sprint Nextel to become the number one wireless provider in the U.S., with nearly eighty-five million subscribers.[1] It had also been shown in numerous surveys to have the strongest brand loyalty among consumers when compared to other wireless providers, largely due to its wide-reaching network.

In the early 2000s, Verizon was one of the most aggressive wireless companies in investing in video technology on mobile devices, technology that was already proving to be popular in Korea and Japan. Verizon began by spending billions on building a 3rd Generation Evolution Data Optimized (3G EV-DO) wireless network that initially was in a few select markets and eventually rolled out nationally to most major markets. This BroadbandAccess network was separate from its normal mobile phone network because its purpose was to allow high-quality video content to play on Verizon mobile devices.

In September 2004, Verizon launched V CAST, which could support this video content. Playing at an impressive fifteen to seventeen frames per second, the service could work only on V CAST-enabled phones. At first, the service was available in only 14 markets, and within the first year it worked on fewer than two million of Verizon's then fifty million subscriber phones.[2] By 2007 those numbers had increased to more than one-third of Verizon phones being V CAST-compatible in over 170 metropolitan markets.[3] Today, more than half of all Verizon phones are V CAST-enabled, and few new phones are sold without the technology.

V CAST allowed users to watch clips and, in some cases, full episodes of their favorite television programs on their cellular phones. These included programs on major broadcast networks and cable stations such as NBC, ABC, Fox, CNN, Comedy Central, and others. In addition, Verizon aggressively pursued rights in the sports sector. Although Sprint signed a $600 million agreement with the NFL for wireless video content in 2005, Verizon actively pursued individual team rights and secured a majority of National Football League teams.[4] At roughly double the cost of a normal sponsorship deal, Verizon became a sponsor of a team and was able to show a variety of content through the V CAST network, including coaches' shows and press conferences.[5]

Other early Verizon deals included one with perennial NBA all-star Shaquille O'Neal to air a special show about his life, a *Sports Illustrated* show offering special commentary from former magazine columnist Rick Reilly, and one with NBC to deliver content from the NHL and Triple Crown horse races. V CAST also offered the most advanced video game play of any mobile device, and Verizon introduced subscription pay games, including a deal with Electronic Arts to offer *Madden NFL 06*. The cost was $6.99 a game for unlimited play or $3.49 for a month-long subscription.[6]

Verizon experienced some early success with V CAST, and the service earned strong reviews. Still, in the sports genre, Verizon could use new or additional marquee-branded sports content to offer a greater breadth of mobile content to entice users. Verizon had only scratched the surface of what it could start to support technologically.

From Mobile ESPN to ESPN MVP

The Entertainment and Sports Programming Network (ESPN) revolutionized television with the launch of its all-sports cable station in 1979. ESPN.com was launched in 1995, and it has since become one of the most visited websites in the world. In the early 2000s, continuing with its history of innovation, ESPN and its parent company, The Walt Disney Co., sought to establish a new standard when developing its mobile strategy.

Rather than offer its content through a mobile provider, such as Verizon or AT&T, ESPN chose to become one. In a unique business venture, ESPN and Disney became a Mobile Virtual Network Operator (MVNO) known as Mobile ESPN. Launched in November 2005, the new MVNO leased from Sprint the right to use its EV-DO wireless network, the Sprint Vision Power Network. Users would purchase an ESPN-branded phone and have access to a plethora of ESPN-related content.

This content included virtually every article that was on ESPN.com, real-time scores, favorite team updates, and a wide variety of highlights. In addition,

Mobile ESPN offered cutting-edge video and, on September 2, 2006, it broadcast the first live sporting event ever delivered to a cellular phone—a college football game between Michigan and Vanderbilt, won by the Wolverines 27-7.

Mobile ESPN had high hopes for its new technology, as it received strong reviews for its new and innovative user experience. Yet sports fans did not buy the service, and it was generally considered to be lacking for a number of reasons. Due to the markup from the Sprint EV-DO network, the service was fairly expensive, costing $64.95 a month for four hundred minutes; plans that included all of the data services cost in excess of $200 a month.[7] The handsets also retailed for as much as $500 because they needed the ability support the high-quality video streams they received.[8] In addition, the Sprint Vision Power Network was not as widespread as Verizon's BroadbandAccess Network, limiting the number of markets and areas that could take advantage of Mobile ESPN. Distribution was similarly limited as the service was only available at Best Buy until June 2006, when it was introduced at Sprint stores. Further, sports fans could still receive scores in some form on many mobile devices, and were able to watch ESPN at home or log on to ESPN.com. Many were also simply unwilling to abandon their existing wireless plans for a more expensive service that may not have offered an extraordinary upgrade in their daily sports routine. Ultimately, even significant price reductions failed to spur sales.

ESPN projected to have 240,000 subscribers within the first year, but reportedly had only 10,000.[9] Badly missing its revenue projections, Mobile ESPN was discontinued in December 2006, barely more than a year after its launch.

"ESPN is a special product," says Terry Denson, Verizon vice president for content strategy and acquisition. "But the mere fact that it was ESPN, and ESPN had a passionate consumer base, was not enough to entice or compel people to make unwise economic decisions for themselves."[10]

After its setback with mobile, ESPN adjusted its mobile strategy and opted to focus on its strength of offering comprehensive and in-depth sports content. The network looked to find a wireless provider with the technology to support high-quality video, as well as a wide-reaching network to maximize the number of subscribers who could have access to ESPN material. Verizon appeared to be a natural partner.

In May 2007, ESPN MVP was launched on all mobile devices that were V CAST-enabled. ESPN MVP offered many of the same services that were on the former Mobile ESPN. Fans could receive real-time scores, watch highlights from *SportsCenter*, or even update their fantasy sports teams. Verizon would later offer an ESPN Radio simulcast as well. Users only needed to pay $15 a month for all V CAST services which, in addition to ESPN, included numerous other sports channels, as well as mainstream television broadcast channels. Denson noted, "Once we had determined the core audience for the product, then partnering with ESPN was logical."[11]

The service worked well for both ESPN and Verizon. Once Verizon determined the best mix of content, the service saw a 15 percent increase in subscribers. Despite rapid changes in the mobile sector with the improvements to the iPhone and other devices, ESPN still chose to extend its deal with Verizon in 2009, promising to offer even more content on V CAST-enabled phones.

Those offerings included over one hundred live sporting events, as Verizon discovered that users preferred longer-form episodes and live events to short clips. In the fall of 2009, Verizon, in conjunction with ESPN mobile TV, broadcast live NCAA college football games every Saturday through phones enabled with its V Cast service.[12] Denson points out that the "opportunity to consume" on a mobile device tends to occur during idle periods or less engaging events. During those opportunities, users would prefer to watch a live sporting event that they might be missing and could not see otherwise, or they would enjoy watching one of their favorite shows, even if it's on a small screen.[13] In addition to the live events, Verizon was able to increase inventory across all channels to over a thousand full-length episodes for over two hundred series, including those from television and the Internet.

"In the mobile space, it's pretty easy to have a hypothesis, and test a hypothesis quickly," Denson said. "During these 'opportunities to consume' we asked, 'What are the competitive elements for entertainment in that opportunity?' Some carry a book. Some play a game. Well, why not fill it with content? We can provide you familiar, desirable content to watch."[14]

Changes in Mobile Technology

As Verizon moves into the future with mobile technology, it continues to face even greater challenges. While its 3G EV-DO network has been the envy of every wireless provider in the United States, AT&T, Sprint, and T-Mobile continue to narrow its advantage. V CAST faced its biggest competition with the June 2007 release of Apple's iPhone, which has seen several updates since. In a partnership with AT&T, the iPhone became the first mobile device to both display full web pages and be compatible with iTunes for music. It also has video-playing capabilities, and it continues to improve with the addition of new applications that are being released almost daily. Many of these applications are sports-related, including the *MLB At Bat* app (discussed in the previous chapter) from Major League Baseball. Still, Verizon continues to improve the quality of its phones, as many of them now offer full web pages, music-playing capabilities, e-mail access, and, of course, V CAST.

"We look to improve that holistic experience, and create that special relationship with the phone," Denson says. "We are doing a better job of refashioning V CAST as an entertainment experience."[15]

Verizon continues to find ways to expand its offerings to sports fans. In addition to ESPN MVP, V CAST also offers channels for CBS Sports, Fox Sports, the NHL, the Big East Conference, several action sports channels, and numerous other local channels for various teams. Verizon has also partnered with Qualcomm to use its MediaFLO technology to broadcast live TV on several advanced phones, such as the LG Voyager. Part of the goal is to add the widest variety of content possible so that Verizon users with a V CAST-enabled device will subscribe to the service. The same concept holds true with Verizon's forays into non-sports programming, where it continues to acquire the rights to show popular television and news programs.

"You need to have a ubiquity of familiar content to compete, and that's what we'll do," Denson says. "We've refashioned V CAST so it reflects consumer behavior and improves the user experience. We're getting the right content onto the phone."[16]

Despite the advances in technology, only a small percentage of all U.S. wireless subscribers actually watch mobile video, so there are plenty of opportunities that Verizon continues to explore.[17] Of those wireless subscribers who do watch mobile video in a given month, only a modest percentage are watching sports-related content.[18] Wireless providers see a tremendous future with mobile video, though, as nearly half of all mobile TV subscribers are under the age of thirty-five.[19] Moreover, because 65 percent of mobile TV subscribers are male, a compelling business opportunity exists, as this demographic group is highly attractive to advertisers and sponsors.[20]

The relative success of ESPN MVP on the Verizon V CAST, followed by the failure of Mobile ESPN, suggests that content providers are better off remaining in the content business and working with wireless providers to extend access to their brand and their services. Wireless providers now know that there is a market for sports video content on mobile devices. However, as the numbers above indicate, they have only scratched the surface of what is likely to be a rapidly growing and potentially profitable market. This is evidenced by Verizon continuing to expand its offerings through the V Cast "app store" beginning in 2010, a direct challenge to Apple's highly successful "app store."

MOBILE TECHNOLOGY: AN OVERVIEW

The increasingly rapid evolution of mobile technology and devices has fundamentally altered the consumption of information while away from home. Given fans' insatiable desire to be "in touch" with their favorite athletes and teams, as well as to have instantaneous access to sports information, this evolution has greatly benefitted the sports industry. Mobile technology generally dates back to the introduction of the transistor radio and the pager to the general public in 1954 and 1958, respectively. These inventions were vehicles for information mobility, and spawned the seemingly endless mobile technology options we have at our disposal today.

Though pagers were approved for public use by the FCC in 1958, it was not until 1986 that their application to sports became apparent. Among the early entrants into this space was the SportsPage Score Pager, which provided up-to-the-minute sports scores and updates. With the emergence of sports content delivered via pager, sports fans for the first time were able to access sports content while on the go. By 1994, there were over sixty-one million pagers in use, and competition among sports content providers intensified as sports betting lines, player injuries, and game schedules became readily accessible.

The introduction of satellite radio in the 1990s broadened and extended sports entertainment options for fans well beyond what could ever have been imagined forty years earlier when the transistor radio debuted. Fans now listen to baseball and motor sports through Sirius XM satellite radio's MLB and NASCAR stations. Likewise, college football fans follow their favorite teams through conference stations heard on Sirius XM satellite radio. These targeted channels exist in addition to the various ESPN, Fox Sports, and *The Sporting News* stations, allowing fans to tune in to their favorite team or sport at all hours of the day, anywhere in North America. Never before had sports fans been afforded the luxury of tuning in to sports with such ease while away from home.

Not until the rise of the short message service (SMS), otherwise known as text messaging, did cell phones provide an additional way for the sports industry to reach information-obsessed fans. Unbeknownst to those sending the first text message in 1992, demand for up-to-the-minute sports news and information delivered through this medium would soar. Ten years later, wireless providers established text messaging interoperability amongst carriers, which caused the number of monthly worldwide text messages to grow dramatically, into the tens of millions. Today, the number of monthly text messages exceeds several billion, further illustrating the ubiquity of text messaging.[21] As the popularity of text messaging increased, online companies such as Sportsalert.com emerged. Sportsalert.com allowed fans to subscribe to free text message alerts about their favorite team or sport. In addition to this service, sports fans were also able to text "search terms" (for example, Los Angeles Lakers) to companies such as 4INFO and receive schedules and game times in return, further enhancing the ability to obtain information while mobile.

The sports industry is uniquely positioned to utilize mobile content due to the immediacy of live sporting events. Fan demand for continuously updated and current information has fostered programming tailored to meet this demand. The evolution to 3G phones and the introduction of the ESPN Mobile Phone illustrated this, albeit with mixed results.

In 2001, the Japanese company NTT DoCoMo sought to meet this demand by introducing the first 3G phone. In successfully blending mobile technology with sports-related content, the company struck one of the first video content deals with the English Premier League during the 2002 season to show exclusive soccer highlights on its phones.[22]

The increasing demand for advances in mobile technology and accompanying content has driven companies to further develop this burgeoning market. Companies such as Sling Media, makers of the Sling Box, and Nike, given its Nike+ product line, are capitalizing on the consumer demand and related expectations.

SLING MEDIA

Frustrated by their inability to watch their favorite team on TV while traveling in 2002, diehard San Francisco Giants fans Blake and Jason Krikorian began crafting what would eventually become the Slingbox. By 2004, the brothers had received funding from investors including Goldman Sachs and Allen & Company, each of which believed Slingbox, a device that allows fans and consumers to access and control their televisions from remote locations using their PCs, would transform mobile technology and extend the concept of "placeshifting" technology.

Originally costing about $250 when launched in July 2005, the retroactively named "Slingbox Classic" allowed viewers to perform any of the functions found on their home television sets—such as changing channels, using programming menus, and so on—whether or not the TV was in use; all it required was a broadband Internet connection. This included programs that were saved on a television through digital video recording (DVR). Once purchased and installed, there were no additional monthly subscription fees or other costs. It did not matter whether the customer used digital cable or satellite as their home entertainment provider.

"Our entire goal was to connect consumers to the content they love—regardless," Blake Krikorian said. "When I say regardless, it's regardless of the display they're watching, regardless of their location, regardless of the source of the content, meaning where it's coming from, and regardless of the format. It was an overarching goal of reducing friction between the consumer and the content, and clearly that's what consumers want. But clearly it's what the content providers want and need, even though many times their actions are anything but resembling one trying to reduce friction between this consumer and that consumer."[23]

Slingbox's launch was met with intrigue in technology circles, while causing concern in legal circles. The Slingbox's appearance, described by some as looking like a "foil-wrapped chocolate bar," garnered a tremendous amount of trade media attention, while the legal community rather quickly questioned the legality of such transmissions. On one end of the argument were those that believed accessing sports programming remotely was nothing short of stealing from satellite and cable operators who paid for transmission rights. Entities such as MLB believed that the ability to circumvent geographical boundaries included in broadcast rights deals would harm the league's ability to increase rights fees over time. Conversely, others argued that since consumers had already paid a programmer for the content in their home market that it was their prerogative to watch the programming as they saw fit. Moreover, Sling Media believed that by providing its service, demand for such sports packages as MLB's *Extra Innings* would actually increase, as consumers would be deriving greater value given the ability to watch games while "away from home."

"A lot of people would say that our biggest feat of all was that we were able to make it through without being sued," Krikorian noted. "In fact, we even had deals with some of the leagues. The first guy to really get it was [NBA commissioner] David Stern," Krikorian added. "After we presented to him, he told us 'We follow our fans. This is something our fans will love. So we need to find a way to work together.'"[24]

Constant product improvements and innovation in the years that followed, including the development of additional software that enabled viewing on mobile devices, allowed consumers to more easily watch their favorite sports programming while away from home. In January 2007, the company announced its new Clip + Sling service, which allowed Slingbox owners to create video clips from programming viewed on their Slingbox and e-mail links to the user-generated clips to anyone, regardless of whether they owned a Slingbox. By mid-year, the company had reached an agreement with the National Hockey League to make the league's content available for such distribution. In doing so, the two agreed to share revenue generated from advertisements imbedded in the clips. The company reached a similar deal with the National Football League in August 2007. In September 2007, Sling Media contracted with DIRECTV to allow the satellite company to stream NFL games on its Supercast streaming service.

Through 2006, the company had attracted $46.6 million in venture capital funding, building on the initial 2004 investment of $10.5 million.[25] On September 24, 2007, Sling Media was acquired by EchoStar for approximately $380 million. EchoStar, which was already quite familiar with Sling Media following its January 2006 investment in the company, saw an opportunity to enhance its position in television entertainment, as it already manufactured many of the leading set-top boxes and DVR devices, and owned numerous satellites.

In October 2008, the company released the SlingCatcher, one of its most intriguing devices. Purchasers of this device can watch any content from their computer on a television screen, creating a full TV viewing experience. This includes movies or television shows downloaded through applications such as iTunes or Hulu, as well as videos from YouTube and other video providers. In addition, owners of both a SlingCatcher and a Slingbox can use both technologies to effectively watch their home television content on any television in the world.

"Our generation is still stuck with this notion that there is a separation between watching content on YouTube or on TV and cable. We kind of divide that in our head, but the younger generation doesn't. As consumers, we shouldn't focus on where content is coming from," Krikorian said. "So the real trick is getting this high-quality content from the Internet, off your laptop and seamlessly fit onto the TV in the family room to the point where you don't ever care where it's coming from."[26]

Sling Media has also continued to innovate with its core product, by releasing the Slingbox Pro-HD in September 2008. This device, which retailed for $300, provided the highest picture quality yet on the Slingbox, and it continued to improve users' ability to view home television content on smartphones and other mobile devices.

EchoStar's ownership of Sling Media should enable it to continue to innovate, provided the company's culture and progressive approach to new technology flourish. Proving able to capitalize on prior relationships, in 2010 the company announced the upcoming release of the Slingbox 700U. This device, only offered through service providers, is the smallest Slingbox available on the market.[27] Utilizing the ongoing close association with its former subsidiary, EchoStar came to an agreement with Dish Network to be the first provider to offer the sets.[28] Continued innovation such as this will enable Sling Media to further penetrate the sports-viewing landscape by crafting more comprehensive relationships with sports leagues and properties and, in the process, have a considerable impact on the sports industry.

NIKE+

While Sling Media focused on making the sports-viewing process more mobile, Nike found a way to tap into the mobile athlete market. Nike CEO Mark Parker wanted the company's running shoes to communicate real-time performance data to athletes. Accordingly, he contacted Apple CEO Steve Jobs with the idea of partnering to create such a product. Given that approximately 50 percent of iPod nano owners used their iPods during workouts, Jobs immediately saw an opportunity to leverage the iPod platform, especially since each iPod owner typically purchased three or four additional accessories.[29] In 2006, with the intent of bringing the sports and entertainment worlds together, Parker and Jobs announced a partnership between their two companies.

The initial product to be launched following this alliance was the Nike+ iPod Sport Kit, a wireless system allowing footwear enabled with Nike+ to communicate with an iPod nano and connect to a new Nike website, creating a synthesis of sport and entertainment. Upon its mid-2006 release, the Nike+ iPod Sport Kit, which took eighteen months to develop, initially retailed for $29 and was sold online through Nike and Apple, as well as through their brick and mortar stores and other select retail outlets in the United States. The Sport Kit relied on a small sensor that fit in the sole of running shoes enabled with Nike+ that allowed it to communicate with the iPod nano. With every stride, and via a second sensor attached to the nano, Nike+ provided real-time feedback while tracking distance, time, pace, and calories burned as the consumer ran. If, during a workout, the runner felt his energy level taper off, he could press and hold the center button of the nano to play a "PowerSong." The PowerSong was a pre-selected, motivational track that played when the athlete needed an emotional boost.

In addition to the in-workout support, prerecorded congratulatory messages were provided when athletes achieved new personal bests—whether in terms of reduced elapsed time or distance covered. Words of encouragement were delivered by such inspirational athletes as seven-time Tour de France winner and cancer survivor Lance Armstrong and three-time New York City Marathon winner Paula Radcliffe.

Following a workout, runners could send their data and statistics to nikeplus.com, a website that allows users to set goals for themselves, challenge friends, map runs, track workouts, and receive coaching advice, among other benefits. At nikeplus.com the runner could select from music playlists recommended by celebrity athletes and view celebrity athlete PowerSongs. These features further engaged the athlete in the technology, encouraged him or her to "do it like the pros," and reinforced Nike's "Just Do It" philosophy. Then Nike+ general manager Michael Tchao noted as much, indicating that "Nike+ is all about motivation and leveraging the power of community to motivate runners to run more. The social aspects of the nikeplus.com website have extended the experience beyond the simple tracking of runs. What keeps people coming back is the social interaction, the challenges, and the goals."[30]

The Nike+ iPod Sport Kit became an instant success in the months following its retail release. During Nike's Q2'07 earnings call in December 2006, less than six months after the introduction of Nike+, Parker announced that Nike+ users had logged more than three million miles.[31] According to Parker, Nike+ developed a whole new connection between the physical world of running and the digital world of content.[32]

Nike had once again revolutionized the way people run, as evidenced by its amassing the world's largest online running destination at nikeplus.com.[33] With more than twenty-two million miles logged on nikeplus.com within the first year, Nike+ had struck a chord with weekend warriors and elite runners alike; the number of miles logged is now measured in the hundreds of millions.

As the nikeplus.com community has grown, the site has added additional features including sports mixes, events, and other entertainment elements to further deepen the connection with the athlete and the Nike+ technology. One such feature Nike has added allows runners the ability to participate in races— *virtually*. For example, the 2008 Nike+ Human Race 10K brought together nearly eight hundred thousand runners from around the globe to participate in the largest one-day race event ever.[34] The Nike+ Human Race was staged at twenty-six physical race sites around the globe, including Los Angeles, New York, London, Paris, Rome, Tokyo, Shanghai, and Sao Paulo. Those who weren't able to attend the race in person at one of the twenty-six race sites raced virtually. Virtual runners tracked their time and distance with Nike+ technology and then logged their race results online at nikeplus.com. Those who attended the race in person were able to run alongside celebrity athletes such as Lance Armstrong in Austin or Paula Radcliffe in London, watch live race feeds from around the world, and attend post-race concerts featuring entertainers including hip-hop superstar Kanye West in Los Angeles. In all, nearly four million miles were logged on a single day for the Nike+ Human Race. The technology created opportunities to run against anyone in the world on any given day, while simultaneously blending sports and entertainment.

The Nike+ SportBand, a complementary product to the Nike+ iPod Sport Kit, was released in April 2008. The SportBand, a wristband that works in conjunction with the Nike+ shoe sensor, retailed for $59. It allows athletes to track distance, pace, time, and calories burned, and does so without requiring an iPod. When evaluating such opportunities, Tchao says one of the things Nike considers is "Whether the technology is easy to use, fills a need, and connects with the consumer in a meaningful way."[35] The introduction of the SportBand fit Nike's criteria and continues to build upon the overall success of the Nike+ brand while allowing runners to take advantage of the Nike+ mobile technology while on the go.

In addition, Nike has utilized the Nike+ brand to further expand revenue in its primary channels—footwear and apparel. Nike+ compatible shirts, jackets, shorts, and armbands have all been developed by Nike to protect the iPod or to conceal headphone wires while running. The company continues to build upon the success of Nike+ by extending its appeal to as many consumers as possible. Tchao believes "Nike+ has become one of the reasons consumers choose Nike" and that "Nike+ helps keep the consumer engaged and connected to Nike."[36]

In September 2008, Nike and Apple integrated the Nike+ capabilities into the second-generation iPod Touch, followed soon after by the iPhone 3GS, eliminating the need for an external receiver to be connected to the iPod. In addition, in June of 2010, Nike released the Nike+ iPod-compatible heart-rate monitor in the United States.[37] These advancements continue to push the envelope regarding the ability to congruently connect the consumer to sports and entertainment through the use of mobile technology, whether it be through virtual races, online competitions, or the consumer's need to consolidate while consuming sport and entertainment on the go.

The majority of Nike running shoes are now Nike+ compatible, which affords the company the opportunity to develop myriad compatible products in the future, further cementing its leadership in the area of convergence.

MOBILE TECHNOLOGY: THE BOTTOM LINE

The Verizon V CAST, the family of products and services offered by Sling Media, and Nike+ all underscore the rapid advancement of mobile technology. Each has accelerated the evolution of content targeting consumers, especially (traveling) sports fans and enthusiasts. Services and devices such as these have become and will remain increasingly viable platforms for those that produce, consume, and finance sports. As mobile technology continues to grow and enjoys the benefits of mass adoption and scale, industry stakeholders will be provided numerous opportunities. They will be able to market with precision, utilizing traditional and emerging trends in sports and athlete marketing. Stakeholders will also benefit from the ability to profit from the explosive growth in third-party applications, even if these applications lack the robust texture and detail that many sports fans seek. Throughout, stakeholders will always feel as if they are on the defensive, never fully satisfying consumer demand for next-generation mobile technology.

Reaching the Avid Fan

Many tech-savvy sports fans have an insatiable appetite for programming, particularly news and information about their favorite teams and athletes. These fans are also increasingly desirous of watching live content, especially games and special events. This consumer and fan demand creates enormous market opportunities for stakeholders that can satisfy it. Those that develop and deliver third-party applications for the mobile technology space are playing an increasingly important role throughout the sports business industry. Third-party application developers write programs that work within operating systems beyond their own. These technology developers, and those that distribute related content, most notably telecom companies, are poised to redirect the sports industry's flow of funds, affecting leagues and teams, sponsors and advertisers, and athletes at all levels of competition, as well as those that represent them.

To further monetize fan interest, sports leagues and teams will work closely with the third-party developers, so much so that, over time, the transition between in-home and away-from-home consumption will become seamless. This eventuality will be accelerated by the increasing availability of non-cellular-based mobile Internet access. As this seamlessness takes hold, leagues and teams will be able to generate incremental revenue from their media partners, sponsors, and advertisers, as engaged viewership and enhanced interactivity will be at hand. More fully immersing fans with their favorite sports content allows leagues and teams to extend their brands, provided consumers have more consistent and compelling experiences with them. No longer limited by location or constrained by time, fans will have access to exceedingly close relationships with their preferred sports and athletes—even if this connection is more perception than reality. With this in mind, Verizon's V CAST and MLB-AM's iPhone and iPad applications have been instrumental in the evolution of content designed to improve the fan experience.

Given the eighteen- to thirty-four-year-old male demographic that is the most interested in—and capable of—following sports on an ongoing basis, sponsors and advertisers will continue to rely on sports-related content to market their products and services. Over time, and as efficiencies are gained, the relationship between the sports industry and "traditional" media, such as television, will morph. Because the revenue generated by television will continue to finance the sports industry, it will remain incumbent upon leagues and teams to work with their media partners as these partners extend their offerings more deeply into new media. A failure to do so may inhibit the sports industry's ability to take full advantage of emerging revenue streams while simultaneously compromising vital strategic partnerships. Leagues and media partners may be well served to not only jointly develop third-party applications but also build or acquire technology companies demonstrating both revenue and branding opportunities.

Athletes, along with their agents and managers, as well as union leaders, will pay close attention as the flow of funds continues to evolve and include new sources of revenue. In addition to the marketing opportunities made available to athletes through mobile technology (see Chapter 3), athletes and their representatives will want to make sure they share in the incremental revenue generated given the closer connection between fans and their favorite players. Increasingly closer and tighter-knit relationships between athletes and fans are beneficial to industry stakeholders. However, should leagues (management) and athletes (labor) fail to properly structure or adequately negotiate collective bargaining agreements addressing developments in mobile technology, all involved will compromise this important revenue source.

Accommodating the Engaged Traveler

While many avid sports fans travel for leisure and business, the needs associated with accommodating the captivated traveler are slightly different. Unlike avid fans relying on mobile technology for a quick and oftentimes frequent "sports fix" while on the go, travelers require more inviting and complete mobile technology solutions that offer robust viewing experiences, such as Sling Media's family of products. As Terry Denson mentioned, these and other products and services that enable fans to conveniently consume sports while simultaneously providing an engaging viewing experience make it easier for sports business stakeholders to market their wares. In addition to the technology and content developers and distributors, those stakeholders with the most to gain in this regard are sports franchises, including their sponsors, local businesses that seek to reach travelers through customized advertising, and traditional forms of media.

The tactical use of mobile technology permits sports franchises to reach out-of-town visitors. Whether these visitors are in town for a college football game or a sales conference, local franchises that gain access to data and information about these fans are able to bundle products such as tickets to a game and discounts at local establishments owned and operated by team sponsors. Related sports and entertainment attractions also can be featured, as many such fans are interested in exploring and visiting another city's sports attractions, including museums and historic facilities.

In the process, local businesses, such as sports bars and themed restaurants, will advertise their proximity in order to capture the tourist dollar. Working together, sports teams, tourism authorities, and chambers of commerce stand to generate incremental revenue while enhancing the affiliated brands—each of which contributes to repeat business.

Travelers may not measurably influence television ratings. In fact, it can be argued that the only meaningful difference is the location from which they are following their favorite teams and players. Yet as mobile technology, as exemplified by Sling Media's offerings, allows fans to watch sporting events as if they are at home (that is, the hometown team on the hometown network), the ripple effect can be far more pronounced. As such viewing platforms continue to gain traction and become mainstream, they will have an impact on the negotiations between teams and television networks over rights fees. Sports leagues and teams have become concerned about the influence this type of mobile technology has on viewing patterns. This influence also leads to concerns from advertisers and sponsors who have relied on more traditional telecasts. Notably, migration to new media platforms supplies opportunities for nimble sports marketers that can craft campaigns to traveling fans. Further, any change in the sports broadcasting landscape to include emerging media platforms will draw the attention of players' unions and athletes who will seek to have their opinions heard regarding how best to share (affected) revenue streams.

Connecting with the "Serious Athlete"

In the era of rapidly advancing mobile technology, those nonprofessionals who consider themselves serious athletes are a marketer's dream. Many of these athletes possess strong attachments to the products and services they believe help them excel or reinforce their athletic lifestyle. Whether weekend warriors hoping to make a statement about their athletic prowess by accessorizing with the latest technology or hardcore athletes for whom mobile technology is a mandatory element of their competitive training regime, these athletes feel a compelling connection to the products and services they rely on. It is exactly this connection that enables the sports business industry to capitalize on this important market by improving its mobile experience. To the extent these athletes can be reached with targeted marketing techniques and campaigns, and communicated with in a credible fashion, measurable upside exists. This upside, while captured by content developers and distributors, brands, (local) businesses, professional athletes, and the public sector, also brings with it areas of concern.

Strategically positioned, content developers and distributors will complement other media distribution platforms by affording sponsors and advertisers an additional outlet to get consumers' attention. As they assist in providing vertical and horizontal market opportunities and deliver coveted audiences in the process, content developers and distributors may actually increase the amount of (sports) marketing taking place rather than simply siphoning dollars away from traditional media outlets. Traditional media must acknowledge and address the fact that any inability to demonstrate value in their own marketing platforms will lead to decreased revenue. Those that not only successfully communicate the benefits associated with their own platforms but also tactically and proactively address where new media options may prove additive will thrive. Working collaboratively, new and traditional forms of media can assist one another through the sharing of consumer- or fan-oriented statistical data and analyses that will allow each to make more compelling arguments for the sports marketing dollar. For example, the Nike+ Human Race provides a level of collaboration resulting in more targeted sponsorship and promotion supported by local businesses and embraced by communities.

Carefully developed to reduce consumer and fan backlash, similar collaboration is possible for those hoping to reach athletes. Because mobile devices already track distances covered and routes taken, these data can be further analyzed in an effort for nearby businesses to reach sought-after consumers with precision. The ability to contact athletes to make them aware of the nearby nutrition store or orthopedist may motivate local businesses to advertise, given the accuracy of the demographic reached.

Professional athletes are able to extend their personal brands and position themselves for new or extended endorsement opportunities by involving themselves with mobile services that enable serious athletes "to train with a pro." Professional athletes who detail their training regimes and serve in a mentorship capacity of sorts by providing training tips, advice, and words of encouragement, will prosper. Fostering these relationships over time creates an even deeper bond between serious athletes.

For this connection with serious athletes to flourish, privacy issues must be carefully monitored and accounted for. Should serious athletes feel as though their actions, both as athletes and as consumers, are being too closely watched and catered to, substantial backlash may occur.

MOBILE TECHNOLOGY AND CONVERGENCE: FINAL THOUGHTS FROM TICKETS.COM'S LARRY WITHERSPOON[38]

Larry Witherspoon was the CEO of Tickets.com. Tickets.com is owned by Major League Baseball Advanced Media, and at the time of the interview handled sales of tickets for fourteen major league teams. Witherspoon shared his perspective on convergence and mobile technology with the SBI.

SBI: How have convergence and mobile technology affected the area of sports entertainment overall?

WITHERSPOON: The biggest development in terms of sports has been the iPhone and the streaming applications. For example, with the MLB.com application, the sheer number of people that have purchased that app and are watching games on their iPhone has been striking. The improvements in bandwidth and the computing power on the phones have also been very impressive. So many people are utilizing this and related technologies that everyone in our industry must occasionally step back and figure out how to monetize it. When I worked for the Seattle Mariners as their chief information officer, we allowed people to order food with their cell phone but we never made money with it even though it was a cool idea and the sponsor liked it. Now with handheld devices fans can watch everything, including replays. This convergence on the technology side has rapidly elevated the importance and influence of tech-savvy executives in non-technology-specific companies and organizations.

SBI: How have technology executives taken to these increasingly important roles?

WITHERSPOON: They are now making decisions and driving not just business but entire businesses. On the mobile side, it's making it even more important because you can't undertake these initiatives without strategically attuned IT people. You have to have colleagues that can talk to a cellular provider like Verizon to understand what they are talking about instead of simply allowing a sponsorship sales guy to sell them something that you'll never monetize. If you don't have that, in the worst-case scenario, you'll have signed up for something that requires a substantial amount of support yet is lacking in return on investment.

SBI: Are there any areas of sports where fans have driven the demand for new technology?

WITHERSPOON: Fans are requiring the changes. For instance, the MLB.com app on the iPhone is tremendous. The feedback from the fans has generated ideas like the possibility of buying a ticket through the application. Also, fans have asked, "If I've already paid you to watch on the Internet, why can't I just stream the game on the phone?" This type of information helped MLB.com tier the product to premium and basic levels. All of this is important because fans like me use the mobile device as a primary source of information these days, specifically around sports. We'll even sit around a hotel while traveling and watch a game streaming on the device.

SBI: How has your relationship with MLBAM affected Tickets.com and the industry as a whole?

WITHERSPOON: By acquiring Tickets.com in 2005, MLBAM has forced technology to change in the ticketing space. Now, Ticketmaster has to compete in order to stay in baseball. MLB was tired of having somewhat stagnant technology so they bought a ticketing company to help in this regard. Now you've raised the bar across the board because these guys have to make changes to compete. As far as the mobile side is concerned, we've already launched a few initiatives. We were the first company to deliver a bar code to your cell phone. You can go online and instead of printing at home you can just have it sent to your phone. We also launched a mobile website where you can buy a ticket, go through the whole buying process, and have it delivered to your cell phone. So in essence, we closed the mobile loop. We are mobilizing all our client websites as well by putting their websites in the mobile world. For us it's a fairly simple approach because it's another available channel for our clients. You have to make things available through all the available channels to drive customer satisfaction.

SBI: Where is the most upside in terms of applying mobile technology in other sports sectors?

WITHERSPOON: You'll see the sports industry focusing on all the applications. Where we see the biggest advantage is in having all the channels available and growing your mobile base. In the ticketing world we see an enormous upside for teams with distressed inventory. With this mobile technology you can enable the secondary market and take primary sales on the device right up to game time. Now you have a window of opportunity prior to the game to send someone a text, point them to a web page where they have a special offer to buy the tickets immediately, and then get them into the stadium. Once the game has started you can send fans a text message with a link that they can click to buy tickets up to the fifth inning for $5. So there's an impressive upside on the distressed inventory component.

SBI: To what extent have sponsors begun to merge mobile technology with sponsorship?

WITHERSPOON: I haven't really seen it fully deployed yet. When I was with the Mariners we had mobile sponsors, but nowadays it is not as prevalent as it used to be. Cell phones are more of a commodity now, and they don't see as much value in that type of sponsorship. You have to innovate and give them fun and unique ways to activate. The problem is how do you make something available across all channels and do a sponsor deal? We as an organization cannot do that, but our clients can if they start to gain traction. For example, the San Francisco Giants had a pre-sale for Visa cardholders. A similar promotion or special offering can be done for cellular phone carrier clients. These clients need a compelling reason to be a customer. If you can actually give people an added benefit and an enhanced experience, they have that reason.

SBI: Where have you seen companies taking advantage of the marketing component?

WITHERSPOON: The cellular companies are not working together to move in the same direction on these types of initiatives. Not surprisingly, this forces everyone down their own narrow path even though the technology or idea is eventually going to be replicated a hundred different times to support each carrier. In the U.K., Orange has done a phenomenal job in their approach to marketing and using mobile. They have special areas you can go where there are massages, smoothies, or bathrooms for their customers.

SBI: Where will Tickets.com take advantage of what is going on in the marketplace in the years to come?

WITHERSPOON: With Tickets.com, we have changed our approach from a full-service model to one where we are a technology company that exists in a ticketing space. We were the first to do the bar code delivery, close the mobile loop, and allow our clients to have a presence in the mobile world to begin with. We are also adding stored value to Tickets.com products, allowing people to put money on their bar code to purchase a beer or coke, and thinking about content delivery. For content delivery, using video before the bar code comes up showing who your tickets are sponsored by is one concept. Additionally, and from a promotional standpoint, we can offer something where everyone that signs up through their mobile number or SMS gets a coupon for something like $5 per strikeout in every seventh inning of a baseball game. You can add this onto your ticket bar code so fans can use that money to spend at the stadium—and presumably stay longer and spend more.

SBI: What are the challenges and vulnerabilities going forward with mobile technology?

WITHERSPOON: I think the biggest challenge is how to credibly engage your partners going forward. I think the telephone companies who are facing the massive demand for bandwidth growth are going to have a hard time keeping up. Future innovation may be compromised until they get more value for what they are doing. Telephone companies have to continually replace much of what they have just spent money on to keep up with the demand. I think in the mobile world you have to properly develop products and services and truly engage your sponsor partner, your client, the fans, teams, and venues, while also making sure you cover all the financial bases. This is the best approach. Things need to be more collaborative on the mobile side, and the device itself dictates that. The variety of carriers and potential sponsorships dictate that as well. The Internet piece is also important in terms of viewers watching that way and how it affects your radio and television partners.

6 GAMBLING

THE WORLD SERIES OF POKER

The 2003 World Series of Poker (WSOP) is being played at Binion's Horseshoe and Casino in Las Vegas, Nevada, and the field of 839 players has now been reduced to two very different finalists. Sam Farha is a seasoned pro, a forty-four-year old Lebanese-American from Houston, Texas, and he looks and sounds like an experienced poker player. Chris Moneymaker is a twenty-seven-year old accountant from Spring Hill, Tennessee, playing in his first live poker tournament. He only qualified for this $10,000 buy-in event by winning a satellite tournament on PokerStars.com.

Moneymaker—which is his real last name—has led through much of the tournament and has the high stack. He's dealt a seven of hearts and a king of spades, while Farha is given a nine of hearts and queen of spades. On the flop, the dealer shows a nine of spades, two of diamonds, and six of spades. Those watching on ESPN (on tape delay) can see what each player has, and they know that Farha has an 82 percent chance of having the better hand. Both players check, and the dealer shows an eight of spades on the turn, decreasing Farha's odds to 61 percent. With a pair of nines, Farha puts $300,000 into the pot. Moneymaker hesitates slightly, calls Farha's bet, and then emphatically re-raises an additional $500,000. Farha calls.

On the river, the dealer shows a three of hearts, and Farha, with a pair of nines, has a better hand than Moneymaker's king-high. Moneymaker looks at the cards on the table, then looks at Farha, and says confidently, "I'm all in."

The crowd cheers wildly for Moneymaker, who's wearing sunglasses and a baseball cap. Farha, with his slicked-back hair, tries to hide the frustration he feels in this predicament. If he calls he could be out of the tournament should Moneymaker have a flush or a straight. If he folds, then Moneymaker will have taken $900,000 from Farha and will be poised to win the title. Farha shuffles his chips, trying to appear loose and confident. "You must have missed your flush, huh?" the accented Farha asks with some wry bravado.

Farha takes his time making a decision, hoping to draw some kind of reaction from Moneymaker and find out if he's bluffing. But the heavy-set Moneymaker sits still, with his right hand resting on his chin, not daring to move a muscle as he stares Farha down. Moving only his right hand, Farha tries to hide his annoyance, and folds. Moneymaker breathes an enormous sigh of relief.

"Considering the situation, I know it's early in the century, but that's the Bluff of the Century," ESPN's Norman Chad says. "What a play from Chris Moneymaker." At that moment, the poker world changed forever. Millions of viewers who watched this broadcast, seemingly aired on ESPN hundreds of times, probably said to themselves, "If Chris Moneymaker can do that, then maybe I can too." With all of the momentum on his side, Moneymaker would soon finish off Farha and claim the $2.5 million prize and the WSOP gold bracelet—the most prestigious prize in the game.

"I was a little underestimated because no one knew who I was," Moneymaker said after his win. "If I can win it, anybody can."

World Series of Poker—History

The origins of poker have been debated, but it's generally accepted that versions of the game existed in Europe and the Middle East as early as the fifteenth century. French colonialists introduced the game of "poque" to the U.S. in New Orleans, and it gradually spread from the Mississippi Delta through the South and the West in the nineteenth century.[1] Legendary Old West figure Wild Bill Hickok famously was shot dead while playing poker in Deadwood, South Dakota, with a hand of aces over eights, which is now known as a "dead man's hand."

Historically, poker carried a seedy reputation, in large part due to its association with gambling, and therefore held a somewhat minor place at Nevada card tables until the late 1960s. In 1969, Tom Moore bought the Holiday Hotel in Reno and held "The Texas Gamblers Reunion," which was a who's who of the more famous card players in the country, including casino owner Benny Binion.[2] The following year, Binion moved the event to his casino in Las Vegas and dubbed it the "World Series of Poker." With seven top gamblers participating, the WSOP maintained a very low profile, and few people outside of the casino walls cared about the result. Instead of holding a "Main Event," the "World

Series" featured just a few variations of poker and the competitors voted on a winner, Johnny Moss.

Los Angeles Times reporter Ted Thackery Jr. covered this initial event and was quick to offer some suggestions. "You got to have a winner, a real winner," Thackery said. "You need to find some way to make it a contest. If you want to get the press involved and turn the World Series into a real sporting event, you need to give it some structure, create some drama, and make it like a real tournament."[3]

Binion took the advice, and in 1971 the WSOP consisted of multiple events, including a "Main Event," which was a $5,000 freeze-out no-limit Texas Hold 'em competition. The following year, the buy-in was increased to $10,000 (where it remains today), and in 1973 the WSOP was aired on CBS with Jimmy "The Greek" Snyder providing commentary. Over the years, the WSOP gradually saw an increase in participants, and it was broadcast on television in most years by CBS, the Discovery Channel, and ESPN. These broadcasts routinely lasted one or two hours, and were simply a recap of the entire tournament.

Television coverage of poker changed dramatically in 2003 with the launch of the World Poker Tour (WPT) on the Travel Channel. Steven Lipscomb founded the series and felt there was a large market for televised poker that could be realized with improved technology. The WPT broadcasts featured lipstick-sized hole cameras that indicated which cards each player held. A variation of this had been used on the British TV program *Late Night Poker* in 1999. The WPT quickly became the top-rated program on the cable network, averaging nearly twice the viewers of any other Travel Channel program.[4]

ESPN improved its broadcast quality for its coverage of the 2003 WSOP. Rather than air just one recap show, the network chose to air seven episodes, which included multiple tables leading up to the finals of the Main Event. All of the coverage was tape-delayed, but the small cameras allowed viewers at home to not only see each player's cards but also see the odds each player had of winning the hand.

These new features that allowed viewers to delve deeply into the strategy of a poker game, coupled with the first-class broadcast quality and experience from ESPN, led to spectacular television ratings. The championships of the WSOP earned a 1.9 Nielsen rating, but many millions more watched the coverage as it replayed numerous times on the ESPN family of networks, and as word of mouth spread.[5]

The Poker Boom

Simultaneous to improved television coverage, another phenomenon was emerging. As more Americans gained Internet access, many poker websites were launched, such as PokerStars.com and PartyPoker.net. Participants on these sites could play poker and win real money. Several of these sites bought $10,000 entries into the WSOP Main Event and gave them to winners of satellite tournaments. Chris Moneymaker was one of these winners and, after his 2003 title at the WSOP, interest in poker soared.

Participation in the WSOP's Main Event increased dramatically from 839 in 2003 to 2,576 in 2004 and then to an all-time high of 8,773 in 2006. The 2009 WSOP featured fifty-seven separate events with over 60,000 participants from 115 different countries competing for a prize pool of over $180 million. By the end of the decade, poker accounted for more than $160 million in annual gaming revenue in Nevada, an increase of more than $100 million from the prior decade.[6] On the Internet, poker accounted for the largest portion of the online gambling market, accumulating nearly $20 billion in revenue in 2007.[7] The two most popular poker websites, PokerStars and Full Tilt Poker, regularly saw tens of thousands of players a day, and sometimes that number exceeded 100,000.[8] It is estimated that there were 1.8 million online poker players each month, wagering $200 million a day.[9] There were an estimated 60 to 80 million poker players in the United States, and another 80 to 100 million outside the U.S.[10]

As the market for poker grew, ESPN continued to expand its coverage of the WSOP. The 2004 WSOP featured twenty-two episodes and averaged a 1.7 Nielsen rating, with many broadcasts rating above 3.0.[11] In addition to the Main Event, ESPN also broadcast other events at the WSOP, which included more Texas Hold 'em games, as well as a wide variety of other poker card games in which the winner took home a coveted WSOP gold bracelet. The episodes allowed ESPN to fill its summer months with higher-rated programming, but WSOP ratings remained consistent into football season. Holding to form, the 2004 World Series was won by Greg Raymer, another unknown Internet player.

The popularity of the WSOP led to an abundance of other poker programming on TV, such as *Celebrity Poker Showdown* on Bravo, *Poker After Dark* on NBC, and *Poker Superstars* on Fox Sports Net. The WPT eventually moved from the Travel Channel to the Game Show Network, becoming that network's highest-rated program, but it also aired occasional specials on NBC.

Celebrities also helped further the poker boom, as many paid the $10,000 to enter the WSOP Main Event. After being tutored by professional poker player Annie Duke, actor Ben Affleck won the California State Poker Championship in 2004, winning $356,000. Other celebrities who have competed in the WSOP include Tobey Maguire, James Garner, and Adam Sandler. Oscar-nominated actress Jennifer Tilly won a bracelet at the 2005 WSOP, and talk-show host Montel Williams briefly held the chip lead in the 2007 Main Event. The 2009 WSOP featured the ESPN-televised "Ante up for Africa" celebrity poker tournament with such notable participants as Matt Damon, Nelly, and Charles Barkley. While 2009 was the third year of the tournament to raise money for the Darfur region of Africa, it was the first year ESPN had televised it.[12]

While the opportunity for any person to become a poker star has contributed to the sport's appeal, there are millions of poker players in the U.S. who do not desire such stardom. Some enjoy poker simply for the game experience and challenge, and televised poker helped bring winning strategies and tactics to life, while others are simply in it for the money and the thrill associated with gambling.

Setbacks for Poker

On October 13, 2006, President George W. Bush signed into law the Unlawful Internet Gambling Enforcement Act of 2006, which was an add-on amendment to the SAFE Port Act, a Homeland Security measure. The act was intended to improve security at U.S. ports, but congressmen who were concerned about the spread of Internet gambling added the amendment just before a vote was held.[13] After passage of the bill, many online poker sites, which were predominately based outside the U.S. and off-shore, ceased U.S. operations.

At the time, PartyPoker was one of the top two poker sites for U.S. citizens, and its Gibraltar-based parent company, PartyGaming, lost 60 percent of its stock value in a single day after suspending U.S. operations.[14] The WSOP subsequently prohibited Internet sites from buying seats at their events. As a result, the WSOP saw a drop from 8,773 participants in the 2006 Main Event to 6,358 in 2007.

However, some sites continued U.S. operations, such as PokerStars. The wording of the bill has been widely debated, and the law has not yet been strictly enforced.[15] In addition, it has led to several legal disputes with the U.S. and the World Trade Organization, and Congress has considered legislation to allow for legal online poker gaming.[16]

Still, the threat of legal action led to a considerable drop in online poker play. In addition, the televised poker market had become so saturated with programming that ratings began to dip. Although some poker shows were cancelled, ESPN continued its strong ratings, as the 2009 WSOP was up 11 percent from 2008.[17]

The World Series of Poker Moves Forward

In recent years, the WSOP's business side has witnessed considerable change. Binion's Horseshoe and Casino, which continued to own the WSOP (and related intellectual-property rights) after Benny's death in 1989, was sold to Harrah's for about $50 million in 2004. Harrah's subsequently sold the casino for $20 million to MTR Gaming, but kept the WSOP and moved it to the Harrah's-owned Rio All Suite Hotel and Casino in Las Vegas. Harrah's immediately saw a benefit for the Rio, as an estimated 125,000 poker fans visited the hotel during the seven-week tournament.[18]

In 2005, Harrah's hired former NBA and NASCAR executive Jeffrey Pollack to be the first commissioner of the WSOP. Pollack's mission was to realize the WSOP's potential as a legitimate entity in the sports marketplace. He said that the WSOP had two eras—the first thirty-six years, in which it saw very steady and organic growth, and then the current era, which he termed "WSOP 2.0."[19] Like most poker tournaments, the WSOP keeps 6 to 10 percent of the buy-in fee, but Pollack successfully sought additional revenue streams, particularly those linked to the licensing of intellectual property rights, sponsorship sales, product licensing, and international expansion.

The tournament now has over twenty corporate sponsors and is officially known as the "World Series of Poker Presented by Jack Link's Beef Jerky." Other partners have included Miller Brewing, Hershey's, Planters, Corum, Red Bull, Verizon, Hertz Rent-a-Car, Betfair, Everest Poker, and U.S. Playing Card Company. In addition, WSOP players are free to negotiate their own sponsorship deals, although they must adhere to twelve rules established by Pollack, one being Miller Brewing's exclusivity in the beer category. While specific sponsorship terms are not released to the public, Pollack's success in this area was impressive, considering that just years earlier many companies shied away from being associated with a gambling-related entity.

"Our business plan is to position the World Series of Poker as a sports league, and have the elements in place that make it a sports league," said Pollack, who ended his tenure as commissioner following the 2009 event. "We're not a startup, but we may act like a startup in terms of being aggressive, proactive, and lean."[20]

In 2006, Pollack worked to extend WSOP's agreement with ESPN through 2010, which was subsequently renewed through 2017. While the terms were not disclosed, it was a considerable increase from the $55,000 a year ESPN had previously been paying Harrah's.[21] Normally, ESPN's broadcasts had been edited and shown on tape delay due to the length of many poker matches. However, the new contract called for a second live WSOP broadcast to air on ESPN on pay-per-view for $24.95 for the final table, which, in 2007, lasted fourteen hours.

"ESPN has been absolutely critical to our success," Pollack said. "We're considered a sport, in part, because we're on ESPN. We're a sport because we are what sports fans like to watch—and ESPN embraces us with the same spirit as any other sports programming."[22]

In 2008, Pollack decided to change the format of the WSOP Main Event. While the Main Event normally takes place in the summer, it now stops in July with nine players left at the final table. Coverage resumes again in November, providing players three months to establish their own sponsorship deals. In addition, the WSOP uses the intermission to promote the "November Nine" and generate buzz heading into the final. ESPN can also do a quick turnaround on the tape-delayed coverage, decreasing the number of people who are aware of the final result ahead of its airing.

The result of moving the final table to November paid dividends for both ESPN and the WSOP. The ratings for the 2008 tournament were up 15 percent over 2007, but the final drew nearly 2.4 million television viewers, up 52 percent from the previous year.[23] The final was held at the Penn & Teller Theater at the Rio, and long lines spread through the hotel for a chance to fill one of the 1,065 seats. It is believed to have been the largest live audience ever for a poker game.[24]

In 2009, total prize money over the history of the WSOP surpassed $1 billion.[25] Further cementing the WSOP's stature as a major sports and entertainment property was ESPN's decision that same year to extend its contract with the WSOP. Doing so delivered immediate dividends for both as the 2010 WSOP exceeded several all-time figures, including a record 72,966 participants and a prize pool of $187 million.[26]

While part of the event's appeal is that anyone can win, Pollack also under-stands the value of athlete brands and building recognizable stars in the game. As a result, he worked to host several WSOP events for some of poker's bigger names, such as the $50,000 H.O.R.S.E. competition and the Tournament of Champions. Even so, some of the game's biggest stars, such as Phil Hellmuth, Johnny Chan, Phil Ivey, and Chris Ferguson, are considered successes if they can simply win a bracelet or have a reasonably high finish at the crowded six-thousand-plus-person Main Event.

Yet Pollack still points to the openness of the sport that has been impor-tant to its appeal. "What separates the World Series of Poker from anything on ESPN is the accessibility of hope. Anyone can enter and anyone can win. This is our credo. You can't buy your way onto an NBA court or NHL rink, but you can watch the WSOP Final Table from your home in November, decide to enter our event the following year, and have a pretty good shot at sitting at a table with a top professional and appearing on ESPN's coverage."[27]

Pollack also worked to expand the offerings for the WSOP. There is now a WSOP Circuit that includes about a dozen regional tournaments held at differ-ent sites throughout the U.S., all of them owned by Harrah's. In addition, there is a WSOP Academy that offers instruction from some of the most recognizable names in the game.

"The World Series of Poker is the single-biggest publicity generator for Harrah's," noted Pollack. "And, when a WSOP event is held, there is a lift in food, lodging, and gaming at our properties."[28]

The WSOP has also expanded internationally. Harrah's would like to extend the WSOP to all corners of the globe and has started in Europe. The inaugural WSOP Europe (WSOPE) was held in 2007 in London and won by Annette Obrestad, one day prior to her nineteenth birthday.

The young Norwegian is symbolic of the game's dramatic growth over the years, and its "anyone can win" mantra. She started her poker career online in Norway, when she was known only by her screen name, "Annette_15," to reflect her age, and won over $800,000 over the next three years through the Internet. She won £1 million at the WSOPE. Obrestad represents a dramatic departure from the Wild Bill Hickok days of poker in the Old American West. She was not even eligible to compete in the U.S. WSOP until 2010, when she turned twenty-one. Yet it's players like Obrestad who continue to usher in a new era of sports stars through this unique convergence of sports and entertainment.

GAMBLING: AN OVERVIEW

Long before the days of Internet wagering and televised poker stars, gambling existed as one of the world's oldest pastimes. Evidenced by the fact that dice were among the artifacts discovered inside the Egyptian Pyramids, gambling dates back several thousand years.[29] Moreover, the Bible includes numerous references to gambling, even suggesting that Roman soldiers cast lots as a way to distribute Jesus' clothing following his crucifixion.[30]

Catering to Romans visiting resorts, versions of modern-day casinos also appeared in ancient times and, by the nineteenth century, casinos dotted the European landscape, most notably in Monte Carlo, Monaco. Closer to home and at about the same time, gambling began to take hold on the East Coast of the United States and, by 1931, Nevada became the first state to legalize casinos, a development that enabled the state to become the global leader in gambling in the decades that followed.

Despite this rich history and tradition, gambling remains controversial, with staunch supporters and opponents making equally compelling arguments as to its societal value. What all parties agree on, however, is the fact that gambling appeals to our inherent interest in risk-taking. When the thrill associated with risk-taking was combined with sports, historically horse racing, boxing, and baseball, a booming industry emerged. Proponents of sports gambling suggest that it stokes interest in attending and watching games on television, which, in turn, generates revenue for sports leagues, individual teams, and the athletes themselves. Conversely, opponents staunchly argue that gambling threatens the integrity of sports, both at the amateur and professional levels, and can lead to the fixing of games. For example, two of the most infamous sports-betting scandals of the twentieth century occurred in professional baseball and collegiate basketball.

Eight members of Major League Baseball's Chicago White Sox conspired to lose the 1919 World Series to the Cincinnati Reds. Dubbed the "Black Sox" scandal, the fixing of the World Series resulted from these players, most notably Shoeless Joe Jackson, accepting money from gamblers in exchange for their commitment to allow the Reds to prevail. Commissioner Kenesaw Mountain Landis banned the players for life, a move that underscored the seriousness with which organized sports take gambling.

Decades later, in 1951, thirty-five active and former college basketball players were accused of point shaving in at least eighty-six games dating back to 1947. Of these, twenty were eventually convicted, as were fourteen gamblers who had persuaded the players to artificially manipulate the point spread. As many as seven colleges and universities were eventually embroiled in the scandal, including four from New York State: City College of New York (CCNY), Manhattan College, New York University, and Long Island University. So devastating was this scandal that, in 1999, *New York Newsday* listed it as the worst event in that state's sports history.[31]

Because of these and more recent infractions, the government's role in regulating sports gambling has become more stringent. Congress passed the Professional and Amateur Sports Protection Act of 1992, which made it illegal to conduct betting, gambling, or wagering operations on sports with a few exceptions. These exceptions were made for Delaware, Oregon, and Nevada; Nevada exists as the only state currently allowing sports gambling, while Delaware passed legislation to legalize sports betting in 2009. However, on May 4, 2010, following a challenge to the law brought by the four major professional sports leagues and the NCAA, the U.S. Supreme Court ultimately denied Delaware's appeal to legalize a sports betting lottery, thus ending its protracted legal battle on the issue. Years after the Sports Protection Act, and with the proliferation of the Internet, online sports wagering flourished. However, because so many gambling-related websites were located in foreign countries, regulating them largely proved fruitless. In an effort to combat its inability to enforce gambling laws, Congress passed the Unlawful Internet Gambling Enforcement Act in 2006. This legislation made it illegal for banks and credit card companies to send payments to Internet gambling sites. The law led those offshore firms running gambling enterprises to stop accepting wagers from U.S. customers, severely crippling many of the firms' operations.

In addition to the aforementioned and more traditional forms of gambling, the rapid emergence of fantasy sports and related gaming leagues represents another variation of online gambling. As previously described, fantasy sports enable fans to create and manage virtual teams in a wide variety of sports. Websites offering these games either provide the service for free, hoping to capitalize on related revenue streams from advertising and sponsorship, or charge fees for hosting the activities, while still generating incremental revenue from marketing activities. Customers of these leagues compete against one another in virtual leagues, with winners routinely winning cash and other prizes, albeit indirectly, given the side wagers made between and among fantasy team owners. By decade's end, approximately thirty million people were playing fantasy sports in North America, generating $800 million in revenue.[32]

It is precisely because of the interest and growth in myriad forms of gambling that the World Series of Poker, Betfair.com, and the impact March Madness has on Las Vegas are analyzed here in greater detail.

BETFAIR.COM

The world's leading legal Internet gambling site does not have a bookmaker—that is, it has no employees charged with setting odds. Nor does anyone placing a wager through the site have to bet against the house. In much the same way eBay forever changed the online market for goods and services following its launch in 1995, the world's largest betting exchange, Betfair, empowers gamblers to both set and seek the best odds, and has revolutionized the gambling industry in the process.

Most casinos, bookmakers, and Internet gambling sites have an entity that establishes odds on sporting events. Gamblers subsequently bet against the odds in hopes of a payoff. However, Betfair's betting exchange is a marketplace that allows users to accept bets on offer or to request their own odds. In exchange, Betfair receives between 2 and 5 percent in commissions for each wager placed, effectively serving as the middle man between wagering parties—parties who remain unaware of one another's identity.

Founded in England in 2000, Betfair is the brainchild of Andrew Black and Edward Wray. Black was a former professional gambler who had been expelled from school for poor performance and eventually became a computer analyst who created pricing models for derivatives. Wray was a former JP Morgan debt capital markets expert. They both recognized that Betfair was a fairer and more realistic way of establishing odds for sporting events and viewed it as a true stock market of sports for sports betting.

Traditional bookmakers "mark up" the true odds to account for the expenses of having an in-house bookmaking service and for the risks they incur. But Betfair uses its technology to precisely offset opposing bets, thereby eliminating any counterparty risk, and thus its odds are usually 20 percent better than those found on most gambling sites, and up to 50 percent better on more speculative bets.

"We are very much a technology-driven business and a product-led business, and we've just chosen to apply our technology to the sports-betting domain," says Betfair CEO David Yu. "About one-third of our staff are product or technology employees. We're not much different than a financial exchange. Once an order is placed, we confirm that there is enough money in your account to cover the potential liability, and, if there is, we then match the order. We can get the money to the winner within about a hundred milliseconds after an event is settled."[33]

Customers from over a hundred different countries can bet on any kind of sporting event, or they can place novelty bets on outcomes such as the effects of climate change or how long a certain CEO will remain employed. It also allows users to place different kinds of sports bets, including if a team will lose a match—most other bookmakers only allow gamblers to bet on winning outcomes. It is important to note that by allowing bettors to wager on both outcomes, Betfair opened new betting opportunities, namely the ability to trade positions on event outcomes similar to how one would trade stocks as prices fluctuate.

In 2006, Softbank purchased 23 percent of Betfair for $600 million, implying a valuation of $2.6 billion. Today, some analysts estimate that the company is worth over $5 billion.[34] Due to its unique market juxtaposition Betfair has grown every year; it generated $372 million in revenue and $64 million in profits the year following Softbank's purchase, and by the end of 2009, annual revenues totaled $500 million.[35] The company handles nearly twenty million transactions a day, more than all of the European stock markets combined.[36] Betfair has more than 2.5 million clients and witnessed $5,000 per minute being deposited into the site.[37]

"Our advantages are that we have control over our software technology and our high rate of innovation, as well as our liquidity," Yu says. "We can outpace our competition because of our size, scale, and efficiency. When a customer comes in, they want to place a bet, but the worst thing for a bettor is if his bet is not matched."[38]

Betfair has continued to expand over the years. It offers a separate betting exchange in Australia and conducts some of its operations in Malta. The Malta operation is home to Betfair Poker, Betfair Casino, and a number of other exchange-enabled games. Betfair entered the poker business in 2005 by purchasing PokerChamps.com. Using PokerChamps.com's technology, Betfair rebranded the site as Betfair Poker and has since become a sponsorship partner of the World Series of Poker.

Presently, about half of Betfair's revenue comes from Britain, but it has made strides in other nations, particularly Australia.[39] While the company continuously seeks to increase its global reach, there are still numerous countries that make Internet gambling difficult, such as the U.S., which in 2006 passed the aforementioned Unlawful Internet Gambling Enforcement Act. Betfair has a strict policy of respecting local laws, so it has never accepted bank deposits on its exchange from banks dealing in the U.S.

Betfair has continued to be successful due to its ability to innovate and improve its service through emerging technology. The service now enables gamblers to continue betting on a sporting event while it is in progress, allowing for odds to change in real time as developments warrant. Betfair has also used its technology to address potential controversies and irregularities in sports wagering. Most prominently, it uncovered a scandal involving a 2007 tennis match in Poland between Russian Nikolay Davydenko, ranked number four in the world at the time, and eighty-seventh ranked Argentinean Martin Vassallo Arguello. Davydenko was heavily favored, and he won the first set. Yet as the likelihood of him winning the match increased, significantly more money suspiciously was bet in favor of Arguello. Davydenko lost the second set and then withdrew in the third set due to injury. Betfair reported all of its data to the ATP, professional tennis's governing body, and immediately voided over $7 million in bets. It was the first time Betfair had ever taken such a measure. It has since been revealed that nine people based in Russia had bet $1.5 million on Davydenko to lose, while two unknown people would gain $6 million from the loss.[40] Davydenko denied allegations of match fixing, and an ATP investigation found no conclusive evidence of improprieties.

Betfair has memorandums of understanding with approximately fifty sports governing bodies, including the ATP, to report such suspicious activity in an effort to maintain events' integrity. The International Olympic Committee, which initially resisted such a partnership for the 2004 Summer Games in Athens, changed its policy for the 2008 Summer Games in Beijing.

"Betfair is a very legitimate business in an industry where there are, unfortunately, some very unscrupulous and more questionable players. Our approach has always been to be the most regulated—to the most upstanding end," Yu says. "We obtain licenses wherever possible, and push integrity campaigns. We know every transaction and can monitor patterns in real time. And we have offered to share information with sporting bodies if there is any suspicious activity. We ultimately want to have sports as clean as possible."[41]

Betfair further extended its reach and industry clout with its 2009 acquisition of the U.S.-based horse racing network and betting platform TVG. The $50 million purchase afforded Betfair the opportunity to deeply penetrate the U.S. market, and do so by taking advantage of its technology to improve customer service and, by extension, drive revenue generated by the enhanced service.[42] In time, the acquisition may also carry significant value if and when gambling regulations in the U.S. are eased.

Over the years, Betfair has succeeded and thrived because it has not only understood people's insatiable appetite for gambling but also leveraged emerging technologies and thus enabled gamblers the freedom to wager how and when they want.

MARCH MADNESS

In the U.S., gambling and sports continue to have a dynamic yet tenuous relationship. Nonetheless, the ongoing discussion between sports leagues and the gambling industry has not lessened the impact gambling is having despite the very limited working relationship between the two. The NCAA's annual college basketball championship tournament, dubbed "March Madness," is a prime example of this, as it routinely attracts more than 140 million TV viewers during the course of the seventeen-day tournament, with an additional 8.3 million visitors following the action online.[43] While the primary attraction may be the compelling play of storied college programs and underdogs alike, a significant component of the tournament's popularity has been its attractiveness to gamblers, both legal and illegal. From the seemingly innocuous office pools (which are illegal but seldom discouraged) to the placing of bets at Las Vegas sports books, the tournament is one of the largest gambling events of the year, with an estimated $7 billion wagered annually.[44] This amount, which includes both legal and illegal gambling activities, surpasses the estimated $6 billion gambled on the Super Bowl.[45]

Intense interest in the tournament begins in mid-March when the NCAA selection committee announces the sixty-eight-team field on "selection Sunday." The field comprises teams that have earned automatic bids due to winning their respective conference, or that otherwise were selected on the basis of their overall performance throughout the season. These teams face each other in four different regional brackets in a single elimination format, with each regional winner earning a spot in the "Final Four."

This format is ideal for those interested in wagering on the tournament's games, and their interest has been stoked by those offering compelling gambling options. Gamblers that choose to partake in legalized gambling flock to Las Vegas on the eve of the tournament. Not surprisingly, Las Vegas Convention and Visitors Authority (LVCVA) Senior Vice President of Operations Terry Jicinsky states that March Madness is "One of the most important sports-specific events that occur in Las Vegas every year."[46] The uptick in gambling activity that the tournament creates can be seen in the month-over-month increases from February to March; it is not uncommon for the amount of bets placed on basketball to double, approaching $200 million.[47] The tournament-driven tourism is annually and directly reflected in hotel occupancy rates. For instance, despite the fact that March had the third highest monthly convention attendance in 2009, figures indicated that Las Vegas hotels were at 89.7 percent occupancy during March, the second-highest monthly occupancy rate of the year.[48] In addition, in excess of 3.6 million people flew into and out of Las Vegas during March of 2009, which stands as the highest monthly number of visitors for the year.[49] Among the economic impacts these visitors provided the city during the period was $34 million in hotel room taxes, 40 percent of which flowed directly to the LVCVA.[50]

Las Vegas presents an attractive option for college basketball fans hoping to wager on their favorite team. With vast sports books equipped with multiple big-screen and plasma televisions, comfortable seating, wait service, numerous dining alternatives, and the option to bet on any number of upcoming games, the Las Vegas sports book has become the preferred destination for tournament fans. The unique nature of the opening rounds of the tournament, when as many as four games are played simultaneously, makes the sports book a natural place for fans and bettors to congregate. According to Jicinsky, "The diverse group of fans that come as a result of March Madness is attractive from a marketing standpoint because it builds brand loyalty amongst a diverse group of people and attracts travel from regions across America."[51] Many hotels, such as the Hard Rock Hotel and Casino, have established special viewing theaters for the tournament. At the Hard Rock, the six-thousand-square-foot meeting room, Festival Hall, provides up to six hundred fans multiple big-screen televisions, betting stations and kiosks, and food and beverage service.[52] Casinos that offer these separate viewing areas tend to monetize the process by charging a $20 daily entry fee.

Although the NCAA tournament drives a great deal of traffic to Las Vegas, with the sports books being the main destination for these basketball-crazed fans, the sports books only generate about 3 percent of overall casino revenue.[53] Casinos primarily benefit from persuading visitors to spend money on other activities such as slots, table games, restaurants, shopping, and shows. Events such as the Super Bowl and March Madness serve as a "loss leader" of sorts in that they help create additional non-gaming revenue that measurably contributes to the casino's bottom line. For the 2009 NCAA Men's Basketball tournament, the Wynn Hotel found another way to capitalize on the popularity of March Madness. Long-time college basketball announcer Billy Packer and legendary college basketball coach Bobby Knight hosted *Survive and Advance*, a series of five one-hour television programs that were filmed at the Wynn Las Vegas Resort throughout the men's tournament. Televised by the Fox Sports network, the shows included live commentary from the hosts, guest coaches, former players, and well-known personalities. The addition of this show to the Wynn Hotel served as another draw for fans interested in seeing and interacting with a show hosted by two of college basketball's mainstays. Casinos have also capitalized on these captive audiences by creating additional revenue opportunities associated with proposition betting on major sporting events. These wagers, which allow gamblers to bet on such outcomes as whether a huge underdog will ever have the lead on a top-seeded team, or whether a very low-seeded team will ever win the tournament, help leverage the hype around March Madness to boost incremental business at the sports books.[54] Proposition betting, viewed by many as a fun way to stay engaged with the action, helps attract fans that want something more than the traditional "cover the spread" and "over-under bets."

The confluence of events surrounding March Madness has resulted in the tournament's serving as an extraordinary example of the convergence of sports, gambling, and tourism. Casual fan interest in the tournament can be created and extended via the office pool; even if a fan's favorite team is eliminated, the tournament's format provides him or her the impetus to remain interested. For fans seeking an even more engrossing and immersive March Madness experience, Las

Vegas casinos have positioned their sports books as the ultimate game-watching experience. As Jicinsky indicates, "Las Vegas is positioned as a sports betting travel destination that allows fans to connect with friends and family."[55] This is of great importance during events like March Madness, when Las Vegas provides a differentiated experience and competitive advantage that trumps other gambling outlets. The Las Vegas experience and the prevalence of office pools have both solidified March Madness as one of the biggest sporting and gambling events of the year. As a result, the popularity of both continues to not only drive the tournament's success but also measurably contribute to that of Las Vegas.

GAMBLING: THE BOTTOM LINE

Globally, the casino and gaming sector is forecast to have a value in excess of $400 billion by 2013, a projected increase of more than 30 percent from 2008.[56] Estimates further suggest that by 2015 Internet gambling could become the largest ecommerce industry, generating in excess of $500 billion annually.[57] The World Series of Poker, Betfair.com, and the impact March Madness has on Las Vegas demonstrate gaming's diversity, acceptance, and potential for growth. Whether designed to assist a parent corporation with marketing and branding, enable gamblers to wager on their own terms, or drive tourism, gambling's impact on the sports business industry will remain profound. This impact reaches all corners of the sports industry, occasionally with unintended consequences. As the industry continues to grow, the ability for a wide cross-section of industry stakeholders to profit from gambling will grow. This, in turn, will elicit ongoing government interest, if not interaction and additional oversight.

Wager Anytime and Anyplace

Significant advances in technology not only facilitate instantaneous online wagering by gamblers and sports fans but also position this form of gambling to grow dramatically. This real-time opportunity empowers gamblers and sports fans to be sure, enabling them the flexibility to participate at their convenience rather than be constrained by less immediate alternatives. While this may add to their enjoyment of and connection to sports, as well as generate revenue—both directly and indirectly—for those throughout the sports industry, it has also led to stakeholder concern. Whether from one's personal computer or mobile device, or even from a seat at a sporting event, the ability to wager on sports with such immediacy has an impact not only on the gambling industry, those that facilitate it, and those that wager, but also on sports leagues, teams and athletes, their sponsors and advertisers, and those that televise sports. The government, law enforcement, and advocacy groups are also keenly following the evolution of instantaneous wagering.

Casinos are both harmed by this and afforded a marketing opportunity. While there is a potential impact as gamblers migrate from bricks-and-mortar casinos to online wagering, casinos simultaneously have the chance to work with sports leagues and franchises to market the overall entertainment experience they deliver to patrons and tourists. After all, the casinos in Las Vegas are quick to promote the fact that they are a destination for those that enjoy sports and entertainment, and cater to those that want a more complete sports gambling and entertainment experience. Much in the way that TV historically has driven attendance at sporting events rather than cannibalizing it, the same opening exists for casinos when it comes to online wagering.

Responsibly utilizing sports leagues and teams to reinforce this message not only blunts a portion of the competition but also extends the marketplace to advertise their services. Significantly, this is occurring at a time when the relationship between sports and gambling, once taboo, is strengthening.

In time, casinos may have the ability to participate in Internet wagering by establishing their own online presence. Doing so, especially when delivering trusted brand names to consumers seeking a safe and secure gambling environment, would allow them to extend their business offerings and even eliminate the narrowing gap between gambling and fantasy sports. Any failure to aggressively pursue online gambling and the marketing possibilities it yields (to the extent permitted if or when domestic laws change) will place them at a decided disadvantage, because gamblers seeking continuously updated betting lines will look elsewhere. For example, should lines not be updated between periods (or even timeouts) of the Stanley Cup, gamblers that want a continuous, immersive wagering experience will seek out alternatives.

Significantly, the prospect of instantaneous wagering in the U.S. must be addressed. Land-based casinos, recognizing the chance to extend their brands online, will use their influence to have the 2006 Unlawful Internet Gambling Enforcement Act overturned, with the intention of narrowing the global online advantage enjoyed by such companies as Betfair.com. As technology provides efficiencies, including ease of access and security, "bookies" will become as scarce as ticket scalpers became with the onset and acceptance of the secondary ticketing market.

Sports leagues, organizations, teams, and athletes (including those at collegiate and amateur levels) must, above all else, protect the integrity of their games. The once tenuous relationship between sports and gambling will return should a perceived coziness between the two industries exist, undermining fan confidence and, over time, interest. The mere implication of impropriety between the two industries, whether institutionalized or the result of individual, rogue behavior, will rapidly lead to a decline in perceived integrity. The sports business industry must continue to avoid this at all costs as advertisers, sponsors, and TV networks will be intolerant of such developments.

Since it is in the financial interest of all stakeholders to ensure, and even promote, aboveboard gambling, the industry will redouble its efforts with the use of technology to make certain that event outcomes are on the level. Provided safeguards are squarely in place, such as those employed by Betfair.com, advertisers, sponsors, and TV networks stand to benefit from a stronger relationship between sports and gambling. The expanding of advertising inventory, the extending of sponsor categories, and the ability to further refine TV broadcasts to meet the needs of fans seeking gambling-related data will benefit not only these parties but the leagues, teams, and athletes as well, as they will lead to increased revenue over time.

Increases in revenue will require those charged with monitoring and enforcing instantaneous wagering, from those that enable it, such as content developers, to those that facilitate the financial transactions, to work closely with the sports industry to create and maintain a level playing field. Law enforcement agencies and advocacy groups will play a high-profile role to ensure that the relationship between gambling and sports is legal while mitigating any negative social consequences such as potential upticks in gambling addiction. Finally, as described in detail further on, governments will look to both regulate and profit from the enhanced relationship between sports and gambling, likely by taxing it to fund the oversight sought by both law enforcement agencies and advocacy groups.

Sports Gambling and Business Development

The growing acceptance of and access to gambling, as evidenced by the expansion of land-based casinos, riverboat gambling, and tribal casinos, afford those that own and operate such properties the opportunity to generate substantial incremental revenue from gamblers and sports fans. Although legalized, state-sanctioned sports gambling is available only in New Jersey and Nevada, the keen interest from local, state, and federal governments in generating increased tax revenue may lead to fewer restrictions in the years to come. At the same time, the proliferation of online gambling sites will continue, resulting in gambling becoming a commodity of sorts, far more available and convenient to access than ever before.

These developments will permit land-based hotels and casinos that offer a complete entertainment experience, especially those in Las Vegas and Atlantic City, the opportunity to thrive. By offering a compelling, differentiated product that includes sports, entertainment, and the ability to vacation, these destinations have the chance to leverage this experience to attract visitors. For example, the Las Vegas Convention and Visitors Authority, noting that tourists arrive from geographically dispersed domestic and international markets to wager on major sporting events, has the opportunity to parlay these tourist experiences into repeat business, whether linked to family vacations or conventions. By using sports-related gambling to differentiate the experience, provided they do so credibly and authentically, casinos have the ability to generate incremental, non-sports-related revenue from activities ranging from the playing of poker to the upselling of weekend packages.

This will become even easier as the barriers between the sports and gambling industries continue to fall. The ongoing trend toward sports sponsorship by gambling-related organizations will allow them to market their relationship with professional sports leagues, teams, and retired athletes more extensively. Reinforcing and stoking the inherent relationship between the two, while simultaneously promoting one another's business interests, will lead to professional sports franchises moving to destination cities that offer gambling.

Further, tourist destinations that offer gambling can promote their locations and sports-related services by utilizing the online gambling sites as marketing vehicles. Properly structured, such strategic alliances can prove symbiotic and can lead to additional cross-promotional opportunities for such products and services as live shows and upscale dining experiences.

Gambler and fan interest in sports will continue to grow, and those poised to parlay this interest to drive additional spending, such as Harrah's with the WSOP and the LVCVA, will prosper.

The Fed's Evolving Role

Given the aforementioned dynamics associated with the ability to gamble on sports at any time and from nearly any location, additional government scrutiny, if not regulation, will accompany the advancing ease now provided gamblers. This especially will be the case should online gambling become legal in the U.S. It must be noted, in no uncertain terms, that legislation will ultimately be the driver that extends or constrains legal gambling activity, and the possibility exists that gambling advocates will fall short in their efforts to extend gambling's reach.

Regardless of the rapidity with which gambling is legalized, ensuring that all gambling-related regulations are adhered to and protecting the integrity of sporting event outcomes will be of paramount importance to those that produce and consume sports. This includes leagues, franchises, and athletes at the professional and amateur levels, TV networks, sponsors and advertisers, and of course gamblers and fans.

While on the one hand providing the optimal amount of oversight, governments, especially local or regional municipalities, will also become inclined to work even more closely with those entities that promote sports-related gambling, whether they do so directly or not. More extensive partnerships with chambers of commerce, tourism boards, and visitors' centers will be crafted as cities not only recognize the opportunity to seize on the growing interest in gambling but do so at a time when their budgets are tight. Doing so will bring with it both support and opposition from elected officials and advocacy groups who will debate the balance between the need for incremental (tax) revenue and the sensitive social and ethical issues related to gambling. Professional sports will be keenly interested in, and aware of, the impact associated with indirectly generating incremental tax revenue for all levels of government. For instance, the federal government may become less likely to pursue antitrust litigation against certain sports as it sees the material financial impact brought about by gambling. Alternatively, should the sports industry disagree with (or otherwise lobby against) government policies regarding gambling, it is possible that its business practices will draw added scrutiny. Further, the government would then be positioned to either rescind current or restrict future gambling initiatives. Any of these possibilities will have an impact on the industry's ability to generate revenue through TV contracts, through advertising and sponsorships, and at the turnstile, affecting athletes' salaries in the process.

Should the appropriate balance between the sports and gambling industries not be struck, TV networks, advertisers, sponsors, and fans will lose confidence in the integrity of the games they are producing, financing, or watching. This development would no doubt have dire consequences to all those that anticipated monetizing the emerging closer relationship between the two.

GAMBLING AND CONVERGENCE: FINAL THOUGHTS FROM THE AGA'S FRANK FAHRENKOPF[58]

Frank Fahrenkopf is the president and CEO of the American Gaming Association (AGA). The AGA represents the commercial casino entertainment industry regarding federal legislative and regulatory issues. Fahrenkopf shared his perspective on convergence and gambling with the SBI.

SBI: How has convergence affected the relationship between sports and gambling?

FAHRENKOPF: I don't think there has been much convergence because of the professional and amateur sports protection act of 1992 (PASPA). The act fundamentally states that it is illegal to bet on sports in the United States with a number of narrow exceptions. One of these exceptions is that you must be within the borders of Nevada, you have to be twenty-one years of age, and you have to visit a casino's sports book to place your bets. This exception was grandfathered specifically because Nevada had a long history of tight regulation and control. However, in the early 1990s there were a number of other states—Oregon, Montana, and Delaware—that offered lottery games linked to NFL scores. The state of New Jersey was also given one year to decide whether it wanted to pass legislation to allow sports books in the state. Other than these outlets, the only place you could bet legally in the U.S. was at horse racing tracks. As a result, legal sports betting hasn't converged with sports much at all; illegal sports gambling, on the other hand, is a different story.

SBI: Is there a strong interrelationship between legal and illegal sports wagering and those that offer it?

FAHRENKOPF: The interrelationship between sports and gambling, legal or otherwise, is strong—and continues to grow. I think the great success and popularity of sports in this country is directly correlated to gambling. The widespread illegal gambling in the U.S. has helped drive sports interest. The legal gaming industry has also become integral in rooting out illegal activity in sports. The Arizona State basketball fixing scandal was uncovered by the legal sports books that noticed an unusual betting line on the game. They reached out to the NCAA and the FBI, which resulted in the players being interviewed at halftime. As a result, they found out that the games were being fixed. We recognized it because we were able to identify betting patterns and realize something was amiss. Now we work with the NCAA in installing the appropriate computer software and training NCAA employees about what to look for in terms of irregularities. We were once seen as the bad guys; now we are regarded as the people that do more to insure the integrity of sporting events than anyone else.

SBI: What position does sports-related gambling currently hold in the U.S.?

FAHRENKOPF: There was a federal commission created by Congress that worked between 1996 and 1999 that studied the extent and spread of gambling in America. The testimony by law enforcement during the hearings was that every year, upward of $360 billion was bet on sports. Of that $360 billion, less than 1 percent was legally being bet in Nevada and at race tracks. So, from a legal standpoint, sports gambling is very limited in the U.S. Nonetheless, it remains very important as estimates during Final Four or Super Bowl weekends have shown that upward of $90 million is brought into Las Vegas during those events. Outside of the United States, sports wagering is incredibly popular and much more a way of everyday life. Seemingly on every street corner prior to soccer games you can place your bets, as well as buy your tickets.

SBI: What are your thoughts and observations about offshore gambling and its proposed legality in the U.S.?

FAHRENKOPF: In 2009, there were two pieces of legislation being considered by Congress. The first, introduced by Congressman Barney Frank, would have legalized Internet gambling in the U.S. The second, by Senator Menendez of New Jersey, was termed the "poker carve out" and stated that the prohibition on Internet gambling wouldn't apply to games of skill such as poker, mahjong, chess, etc. Neither of the pieces of legislation attempted to overrule PASPA in order to make sports wagering in the U.S. legal over the Internet. I think that eventually some form of legislation to legalize online gambling in the U.S. will be enacted, but what form it will take is still up for much debate. I do *not* think we will see the legalization of online sports betting in the U.S. any time soon.

Ultimately, we do not specifically know the breadth of Internet gambling, but estimates place the annual worldwide market at approximately $20 to $25 billion dollars, of which around $5.5 billion is estimated to be wagered by U.S. residents. According to gaming analysis firm H2 Gaming Capital, in 2009, approximately 26 percent of the $5.5 billion was wagered on poker, 29 percent on other casino-type games, while nearly 32 percent was wagered on sports. The remainder was wagered on online bingo, skill games, and the online lottery.

SBI: Do you see the potential for additional "carve outs"?

FAHRENKOPF: I know the inclination of legislators on both the federal and state levels. Those on the far right of the Republican Party view gambling as a sin, while those on the far left of the Democratic Party believe government should be there to protect the public at large. These two groups come together whenever there is a move to change gaming in any state. For example, ministers and church groups align to fight gaming "carve outs," which makes it more difficult for politicians in state legislatures and the U.S. Congress to pass gambling-related legislation. Poker is different because the courts view it simultaneously as a game of skill and a game of chance. It doesn't have the social negativity that regular types of casino games have and, as a result, it is most likely that if any "carve outs" do indeed pass, it will be the one highlighting poker.

SBI: To what extent can the casino industry in the U.S. take advantage of Internet gambling?

FAHRENKOPF: Our industry is deeply divided on Internet gambling. Companies led by Harrah's, which owns the World Series of Poker, were very supportive of the bills introduced in 2009. Under both of those bills, a federal regulatory regime would have been established instead of the current situation where gambling is under state regulation. Other gaming companies support Internet gambling with a state regime of regulation. Still other operators, including many smaller casino companies, are against Internet gambling altogether. While I don't believe either of the current bills will pass in this Congress, there may be inevitability to some type of bill eventually passing. I think the best argument for these bills is that we know that U.S. citizens are gambling on the Internet anyway. From my perspective this creates a consumer protection concern that should be recognized and addressed because this arena currently is unregulated and uncontrolled. If it ultimately becomes federally (or state) licensed and controlled, then it can be regulated—and taxes can be generated from it. I do think Internet gambling will eventually be legalized in some form, but, because of PASPA and the stance of professional and amateur sports, I don't see online sports wagering ever passing.

SBI: Do you see the leagues ever embracing gambling?

FAHRENKOPF: I anticipate the leagues continuing a slow dance around the gambling issue. For example, the situation with the NBA referee [Tim Donaghy] shows how the leagues approach the issue of gambling. Leagues have to take and project a strong position against gambling because they must staunchly protect their reputation and image in terms of the integrity of their game. The integrity of the game is very important and has to remain sacrosanct. Individuals that violate it have to be expelled.

SBI: What kind of impact do fantasy sports have with respect to gambling?

FAHRENKOPF: Fantasy is very popular. In terms of the leagues such as the NFL, they make a lot of money from advertising and fantasy sports. One of the reasons the NFL and other leagues don't want everyone else to bet on their games is because they might lose a portion of the income from fantasy sports because legal wagering would likely serve as a substitute for gambling. However, I do not see fantasy sports as a gateway to going to casinos or gambling on sports. Although each stokes interest in the sport, they are totally separate in that regard. From my experience, personal wagering amongst friends through fantasy sports does not increase a sports fan's likelihood to gamble on other casino games.

SBI: Where do you feel the sports and casino industries can find common ground concerning the public's interest in gambling while also protecting the integrity of athletic competitions?

FAHRENKOPF: In order to protect the integrity of sports, and from both the league and casino perspective, I would make sure that nothing was promoted that contributed in any way to illegal activity. Any suggestion of impropriety concerning organized sporting events potentially threatens not only the league it occurred in but also the trust of the gambling public at large. Both stakeholders must protect the sanctity of the game in order to remain relevant and above corruption in the eyes of the consumer; failing to do so could have substantial financial ramifications.

Part III

AT-VENUE CONVERGENCE

Over time, "at-venue" convergence has proven to be one of the most difficult areas in sports to profit from, yet it has become, and is poised to remain, among the most important revenue drivers in the sports industry.

Historically, stadiums and arenas were built solely so fans could attend sporting and entertainment events, by providing them "a place to go and watch a game." However, in our modern technological world, this is not enough, as fans demand an experiential outing, a convenient and complete game-day experience that transforms mere games into memorable sporting events. By enhancing the fan experience with just the right mix of sports and entertainment, and delivering the optimal blend of marketing and promotion, those that invest in, manage, or own venues can prosper.

The history of the sports venue development originated in ancient Greece with the emergence of venues including the Stadium of Athens in 331 B.C., which was constructed for the ancient Olympics. Built by hollowing out a slope and constructing rows of seats in a traditional u-shape, semi-circular at one end while open at the other, the stadium had a seating capacity of about fifty thousand.

However, because they lacked a ticketing system, the Greeks missed the opportunity to fully monetize the events—an opportunity the Romans would take advantage of four hundred years later with their famed Coliseum and Circus Maximus. These venues were used for a broader set of contests and featured various levels of seating arrangements, including placing the emperor and his entourage in the best seats, a precursor to today's luxury suites. In addition to this preferred seating, these wide-ranging contests brought with them diverse audiences that created a market for myriad merchants who sold crafts and souvenirs in the Coliseum concourses.

By the late nineteenth and early twentieth centuries, and during a period when college football and professional baseball were the preeminent sports in America, the stadium experience was focused almost entirely on the specific sport being played at the venue. Franklin Field at the University of Pennsylvania (1895, football), Crosley Field in Cincinnati (1912, baseball), Fenway Park in Boston (1912, baseball), and Memorial Stadium at the University of Illinois (1923, football) were among the classic stadiums of the era.

While many of these stadiums were financed by team owners, a few pioneering structures were publicly financed, owned, operated, or some combination thereof, and were built to serve the expanding needs of growing urban centers. These stadiums, including the Los Angeles Memorial Coliseum (1923), Chicago's Soldier Field (1924), and Cleveland's Municipal Stadium (1931), were all designed with multi-use in mind. Hosting such events as boxing matches, concerts, and religious convocations, these venues foreshadowed the later movement toward maximizing revenue through venue flexibility. Because politicians and local businesses believed the fans and consumers at such stadiums would frequent the many shops and restaurants in the surrounding area on event days, these venues served as examples of how local stakeholders attempted to benefit from at-venue convergence by hosting a variety of events that attracted consumers throughout the year.

By the 1950s, and with the emergence of television as a compelling medium, the popularity of sports grew rapidly. As sports' fan base grew, franchise owners were well positioned to convince local governments to help finance these stadiums. Doing so greatly reduced and in some cases eliminated a franchise owner's up-front capital costs and dramatically increased the economic viability of the sports franchises.

Many of the publicly financed sports facilities of the 1960s and 1970s, such as Pittsburgh's Three Rivers Stadium (1970), Cincinnati's Riverfront Stadium (1970), and Philadelphia's Veterans Stadium (1971), were designed as multipurpose stadiums, with multiple professional sports franchises serving as anchor tenants. Although numerous tenants helped reduce a city's economic risk, over time, these stadiums became obsolete because they lacked emerging revenue-generating capabilities, such as luxury suites and private clubs, which hindered franchise owners' ability to monetize the venues in which their teams played. In addition, multipurpose venues also lacked the sightlines and amenities fans and consumers were growing accustomed to, making these venues obsolete.

More recently, and as public sector interest in financing stadiums waned, modern athletic venues created other forms of entertainment in order to maximize revenue. Marketing and promotion played an enormous role in the creation of these new venues and contributed to their becoming places "to see and be seen," especially with the advent of the luxury suite and other exclusive areas where affluent fans and corporate customers gathered.

By extracting value from scarce in-venue real estate, the luxury suite revolutionized the way venues were both designed and funded. The joining of smart real estate development with a compelling sports experience generated considerable additional revenues for venue owners, much of which came from corporate clientele who sought to use their suites for business development purposes. In addition to the luxury suite, the adding of private stadium clubs was yet another method venue owners and operators relied on to extract revenue from attendees who wanted a more upscale and complete sports experience.

An early example of this trend was Baltimore's Oriole Park at Camden Yards. Opened in 1992, it inspired a new era in venue design—the retro ballpark. Hailed as an important venue because of its success in revitalizing an urban area, the primary determinant that contributed most significantly to increased and sustainable revenues for the franchise was not simply the intimacy of the design but also the fact that the stadium delivered amenities corporate customers and fans alike sought. Discussed in further detail in Chapter 7, Oriole Park was the example from which a generation of other stadiums, including Denver's Coors Field, Pittsburgh's Heinz Field, and San Diego's PETCO Park, soon followed.

Corporations, sensing the opportunity to market their products and services to fans and consumers through signage; on-site promotion to include product sampling; and other sports marketing activities, especially venue naming rights, quickly increased their spending. This spending was not limited to activities intended to reach end users, as companies appreciated the business-to-business marketing opportunities afforded them at the venues, most notably through entertaining (potential) clients in luxury suites.

By 2000, the convergence of sports, real estate, and technology was on full display, particularly at AT&T Park in San Francisco, home of Major League Baseball's Giants. Prior to games, fans routinely take advantage of the numerous fine dining opportunities within a short walk of the stadium and, as games get under way, these same fans can easily check in with the office by accessing the Internet courtesy of the stadium's Wi-Fi network. During games, fans are able to have a drink at one of the club-level bars or on the centerfield patio overlooking the San Francisco Bay. AT&T Park also offers an entertainment experience for children, as they are able to play video games and enjoy other interactive games and experiences in a designated area behind the outfield seating.

All of these activities ensure that the fans, whether corporate or traditional, will have a great game-day experience and, more important, will extend the amount of time they spend in the area, spending more freely in the process.

It wasn't just franchise owners and municipalities that sought to integrate sports and entertainment in an effort to increase venue usage. Promoters, witnessing the need for additional venue usage and appreciating the demand for captivating events targeting youth, created special events that had both scripted and unscripted elements. For example, the Warped Tour, created in 1993, consists of a combination of action sports competitions, live music on numerous stages venue-wide, and an impressive display of vendors selling a wide variety of sports and music-related merchandise. Title sponsored by Van's, a skateboarding shoe manufacturer and well-respected brand among the target audience, the Warped Tour reinforces just how compelling and profitable at-venue convergence can be.

As we look toward the future, venues and events—such as AT&T Park and the Van's Warped Tour—that deliver a well-rounded entertainment experience will continue to thrive. Those that deliver on this count and also take advantage of technology that further enhances the fan and consumer experience will excel. When the at-venue experience is supported by technological advances that fans and consumers embrace, the ability to further monetize the at-venue experience is readily apparent.

Much like sightline improvements, increased merchandising opportunities, and improved dining options, integrated communications that continuously stream information to and from patrons throughout the venue are now the norm. Sprint's FanView is one such product that illustrates the power of this trend by offering race fans customized, portable entertainment and information. FanView provides viewers live in-car TV cameras and radio feeds, data and statistics, and video content from ESPN and the Speed Network.

This continued emphasis on integrated communications will force venues and the sports and entertainment events held there to be aggressive in meeting fan and consumer demand or otherwise face losing fans and consumers to the more convenient and technologically improved in-home viewing experience.

Industry stakeholders must think through every aspect of how the game-day experience captures and maintains fan attention and, by extension, fan and consumer spending.

The origins of at-venue convergence illustrate the importance of enhancing the experience and creating value for all the stakeholders involved in and around the venue. Spectators not only expect but also increasingly are willing to pay for all-encompassing game-day experiences. Venue financiers and developers, as well as municipalities and franchise owners, must develop flexible arenas and stadiums if they are to extract incremental revenue from the merging of sports, real estate, technology, and marketing—thus the focus of this final section.

In Chapter 7, we delve into sports-anchored real estate. Included will be a discussion of the evolutionary process by which multiple types of real estate development became integral parts of venues. We will examine how these factors contribute toward owners and developers establishing day-long sports entertainment experiences for both corporate and casual fans that include retail businesses, commercial real estate opportunities, entertainment complexes, and residential living. Highlighted examples include Dubai Sports City, Coors Field, and L.A. LIVE. As has been true throughout each chapter, analysis is provided by engaged principals, in this case Malcolm Thorpe—the marketing director of sports business at Dubai Sports City, who now works at the U.K.-based investment company Blenheim Chalcot; Ray Baker—Chairman, Denver Metropolitan Major League Baseball District; Tim Leiweke—President, AEG; and Matt Rossetti—President, Rossetti.

Compelling developments in venue technology are the basis for Chapter 8. Analyzed in this chapter are emerging technologies that exist today which are then used to gauge what will be necessary in future venue development. How these technologies can be maximized for profit and ultimately affect each stakeholder's bottom line will be illustrated. Examples include the University of Phoenix Stadium, Sprint's FanView, and Cisco's sports-related technology prowess. Within these examples are select observations from industry stakeholders Mike Bidwill—President, Arizona Cardinals; JP Brocket—General Manager, Wireless Consumer Applications, Sprint Product Management; Ron Ricci—VP, Corporate Positioning, Cisco; and Jack Hill—General Manager, Cowboys Stadium.

Last, in Chapter 9, we will explore how targeted corporate marketing is changing the fan experience. We will present an overview of in- or near-venue sports marketing and sponsorship and inspect strategies for brand integration in or near venue, as well as tactics for reaching fans through cross-branding and marketing alternatives. Especially compelling in this regard are ESPN's Wide World of Sports, The O_2 in London, and Red Bull's sports marketing and branding initiatives. Additional commentary from executives in this chapter is provided by Ken Potrock—SVP, Global Sports Enterprises, Walt Disney Parks Resorts; David Campbell—CEO, The O_2; Robert Hollander—Managing Director, Amalfi Ventures and CEO of the IBeam Group, LLC; and Arturo "Arte" Moreno—Owner, Angels Baseball.

7 SPORTS-ANCHORED DEVELOPMENT

DUBAI SPORTS CITY

Malcolm Thorpe was enjoying lunch on the second floor of the Els Club's temporary clubhouse in Dubai. With plenty on his plate, both literally and figuratively, the director of marketing for sports business at Dubai Sports City (DSC) appeared both focused and tired. Behind him was a clear view of a five-hundred-yard, two-sided driving range, standing out like a luscious green meadow in the middle of a bustling construction site. Visible through the sandy desert air was a sea of cranes coming together to build one of the most ambitious sports developments the world had ever seen. Glowing from amidst the cranes was a nearly finished cricket stadium that a month later would host the venue's first major event, a Pakistan-Australia match. Although the match had already been scheduled prior to a terrorism incident that took place in Lahore, DSC would effectively serve as the temporary de facto home for the Pakistani cricket team during 2009 due to the attacks.

To Thorpe's left, flanking an Ernie Els–designed golf course, stood the shells of a series of sprawling villas that were 80 percent sold despite the global financial crisis of 2008–10. Large residential towers were sprouting up further to his left, which were intended to be surrounded by a canal, two retail complexes, and a variety of sports facilities that would rival those from any large American city. The *temporary* clubhouse itself was as luxurious and modern as any upscale U.S. country club. The setting truly gave meaning to DSC's slogan of "Live Sport." Thorpe had plenty to be concerned about though. The economic climate had delayed the opening of many of DSC's venues. There had been general governmental pressure on developers throughout Dubai to build many of the world's most grandiose projects as quickly as possible. But in 2009, credit was tight, and some projects would have to wait.

In the meantime, DSC officials were concerned about the logistics for the upcoming cricket match, and needed to get everything from concessions to parking up to acceptable standards. Academies for thousands of young athletes were set to open just a few months later, and a long wait-list already existed for several of them. At the time, the International Cricket Council (ICC) was eager to move across town into its new offices at DSC but was awaiting electricity for the building. Construction on a new ten-thousand-seat indoor arena had momentarily stopped while architects revised plans so the facility could seat fifteen thousand and support a retractable roof that could be opened for outdoor tennis. Thorpe himself was looking to find partners and sponsors who would become stakeholders in the complex and, in turn, help fund the construction that was needed for DSC to reach completion. A veteran sports executive from International Management Group (IMG), Thorpe had the sports industry experience and relationships around the globe that were crucial to DSC becoming a success.

"When we finish this," Thorpe said with smile, "then we're just at the beginning."[1]

The Rise of Dubai

After being controlled by the British for more than a century, the United Arab Emirates (UAE) was formed in 1971, incorporating seven different emirates that were located north of Oman, southwest of the Persian Gulf, and east of Saudi Arabia. Each emirate has considerable autonomy over its governance, with Abu Dhabi (the capital) and Dubai (the most populated emirate) maintaining veto power over national decisions. The president of the UAE is the ruler of Abu Dhabi and comes from the Al Nahyan family, while the nation's prime minister and vice president is the ruler of Dubai and is from the Al Maktoum family. These leaders, along with their families, are regarded as avid sports fans.

Although approximately 10 percent of the world's known oil reserves are located in Abu Dhabi, it is believed that Dubai's oil supply may be exhausted within the next few decades.[2] Recognizing this possibility, the Al Maktoum family sought to diversify the Dubai economy by engaging in real estate development, creating a global financial center, and positioning the emirate as a tourist destination. This effort was effectively kick-started after the Persian Gulf War of 1990, during which time the UAE was an ally of the United States and Dubai provided refueling bases for allied forces.

Using its oil monies, Dubai actively recruited businesses, tourists, and immigrants who were lured by friendly tax policies and the promise of new economic opportunities, as well as the warm weather and white sandy beaches. This business development included the construction of a series of gleaming skyscrapers, corporate headquarters, and tourist centers. The population of Dubai rose from 370,000 in 1985 to 675,000 in 1995 and to 1.4 million by 2009 as the city became a Middle Eastern headquarters for many financial firms and media entities.[3] Major American oil firm Halliburton moved its headquarters to Dubai, and companies opening offices in Dubai included Goldman Sachs, Credit Suisse, Deutsche Bank, Morgan Stanley, Microsoft, Oracle, CNN, and Reuters.

The city witnessed the beginning of construction of some of the world's most architecturally unique structures, ranging from the tallest building in the world to a series of man-made islands, many complete with luxurious restaurants operated by top-name chefs. The city also became extremely diverse, as UAE nationals make up less than 20 percent of the population, while over 40 percent of the population is from India, nearly 15 percent is from Pakistan, and only about one-quarter are ethnically Arab.[4] By 2007, Dubai's economy had become considerably more diversified, as oil represented just 6 percent of the emirates' revenues.[5] Tourism also boomed in Dubai, as six million people stayed in Dubai hotels annually by 2008, nearly triple the number from a decade earlier.[6]

As sports enthusiasts, the Al Maktoum family sought to attract high-profile sporting events to Dubai. Sheikh Mohammed bin Rashid Al Maktoum is the prime minister of UAE and ruler of Dubai, and is a very influential figure in horse racing. He owns a multitude of top thoroughbreds that have won races all over the world, including Bernardini, which won the 2006 Preakness Stakes. Sheikh Mohammed is also a noted endurance rider, and his children have won several international equestrian competitions. In 1996, Sheikh Mohammed established the Dubai World Cup, which became the world's richest horse race with recent purses in excess of $6 million. In addition, Sheikh Mohammed has created a slew of prominent camel racing and falconry events, both of which are exceedingly popular among UAE nationals.

Dubai also holds some of the world's most prestigious tennis and golf events. The Barclays Dubai Tennis Championships have been won by superstars Roger Federer and Rafael Nadal on the men's side, and Venus Williams and Justine Henin on the women's side. Tiger Woods and Ernie Els have won the Dubai

Desert Classic golf tournament on several occasions. These top athletes have all been lured by generous appearance fees, reportedly as high as $3 million for Woods.[7]

In addition to these sports, and fueled by the emirates' cultural diversity, soccer, rugby, and cricket are very popular in Dubai. The UAE hosts international events in each of these sports and has a small professional soccer league. The Dubai Autodrome has hosted numerous auto races. As if this collection of sports venues and events isn't enough, Dubai has also earned fame for housing an indoor snow skiing facility at the Mall of the Emirates.

Roughly a decade after making a splash on the sports scene with well-known names competing in Dubai-based events, the emirate was ready to enhance its sports status and secure even higher-profile competitions. Intent on establishing itself as a global sports leader, the emirate set out to establish the world's most impressive collection of sports-related offerings, and sought to do so on a scale imaginable only in Dubai.

Building a Sports City

In September 2003, developers Abdul Rahim Al-Zarooni, Abdulrahman Bukhatir, and Abdul Rahman Falaknaz envisioned a "sports city" in Dubai. The venue would house myriad sports facilities, as well as retail and residential developments. This "sports city" could be a catalyst for elevating Dubai's sports status, especially once numerous, high-profile international competitions were successfully held. Falaknaz pitched the idea to Sheikh Mohammed and, after just two questions about the expense and timing, the Dubai leader turned to an aide and said, "Do it."[8] Two days later, Sheikh Muhammad approached Falaknaz at an event and immediately asked him, "Have you done it yet?"[9]

DSC will cost over $4 billion to build and will cover fifty million square feet on the western end of Dubai.[10] Once completed, DSC will include four major stadiums: a sixty-thousand-seat stadium for soccer, rugby, track and field, and other events; a twenty-five-thousand-seat cricket ground; a ten-thousand-seat arena for indoor sports such as basketball or ice hockey, as well as ATP tennis matches (it should also serve as a much-needed entertainment and concert venue in Dubai); and a five-thousand-seat field hockey stadium with a surrounding track. Significantly, DSC also contains the aforementioned Ernie Els–designed golf course as part of its expansive facilities.

DSC is also home to several academies, including those run by famed golf coach Butch Harmon and British Davis Cup captain and tennis aficionado David Lloyd. In addition, ICC and the International (field) Hockey Federation (FIH) are also involved with operating academies, and programs exist for swimming and rugby. Bradenton Prep, a K–12 school that was started in Florida to allow prospective elite athletes to fit an academic curriculum around their sports training, opened a satellite campus at DSC in fall 2009. Recognizing DSC's potential, and hoping to leverage it to extend their own brand, Manchester United has established a soccer school.

DSC eventually sees opportunities in hosting youth sporting events, and academy management envisions a "festival of sport," whereby youth teams from around the globe stay in one of the three planned DSC hotels and compete in on-site tournaments. This idea of youth sports tourism is similar to what Disney officials have found success with at the ESPN Wide World of Sports Complex in Orlando (to be discussed in greater detail in Chapter 9), as Dubai is one of the favorite tourist destinations for European and Asian children.

DSC also plans to create a first-class sports medicine facility and a high-performance training center, allowing the complex to host team training camps for all kinds of sports clubs, as well as offer surgical procedures, injury rehabilitation, and intensive training for any of the world's elite athletes.

The cricket practice grounds are quite unique, in that they have turf available from the United Kingdom, Pakistan, India, and Australia, allowing a national team to come through Dubai on a trip east or west, while simultaneously becoming acclimated to the playing surface of the country they plan to visit.

Among DSC's biggest early successes was its ability, in 2005, to persuade the ICC to relocate its headquarters from Lord's Cricket Grounds in London, where it had been for nearly a century. For the ICC, the move allowed the federation not only to be closer to cricket-playing nations in South Asia, particularly India and Pakistan, but also to conduct its operations tax free. Dubai is a short flight from both India and Pakistan, and has even been mentioned as a possible site for an expansion team in the new and very popular Indian Premier League for cricket. However, given the desires stated by new ICC president Sharad Pawar, the ICC headquarters may be on the move yet again, this time either to Mumbai or back to the United Kingdom.[11]

DSC is truly its own city, as the property is home to a wide variety of residential units with prices running the gamut. Although many are apartments, there are hundreds of villas and townhouses, many of which are adjacent to the golf course. In total, DSC is expected to have a population of sixty thousand once completed.[12]

"'Live sport' is what we're all about," Thorpe said. "People will live here, spend time here, send their kids to programs here, and be immersed in sport."[13]

A wide variety of retail and commercial enterprises will also be included in and around the property. An Arena Mall is planned to be adjacent to the ten-thousand-seat arena, but there are also commercial and retail hubs at the northern and southern ends of the man-made canal within DSC. Health clubs and other community facilities will be available for DSC residents, and families may very well send their children to one of the on-site schools, or otherwise have them participate in one of the other sports academies. The first phase of the project—consisting of the golf course, cricket stadium, and several academies—was completed in 2009, while the entire project is slated to be fully finished post-2012.

"I think every new sports facility will have some other element to it in the future to drive revenue," Thorpe said. "You can't put more and more use on the sports element. You need to have the opportunity to create revenue. Selling real estate or leasing shop space is a great way to do that."[14]

All of this is part of the much greater Dubailand development, which was announced in 2003 to contain forty-five "mega projects" in a three-billion-square-foot, 107-square-mile development. To date, about half of those projects are in development. Eventually, Dubailand will have the largest collection of amusement parks in the world, with an astonishing list that tentatively includes Warner Brothers Movie World, Six Flags Dubai, Universal Studios Dubai, Fantasia, Legoland Dubai, Falcon City of Wonders, and a Dreamworks theme park, among others. Several luxury and eco-tourism hotels are planned for Dubailand, including the Asia Asia, a 6,500-room hotel that will be the world's largest. The development's Mall of Arabia will be the largest mall in the world, and will be situated next to an amusement park called The Restless Planet that will feature life-size robotic dinosaurs. Dubailand already is the home to Dubai Motor City, which includes the Autodrome and will contain a Formula One amusement park for families. Tiger Woods Dubai plans to offer a 580-acre facility that would be Woods's first golf resort and academy. This is just one of nine golf courses in all of Dubailand as, in addition to the Els course, there will be a Dubai Golf City with five courses of its own. Other golf courses are for the residential complexes in Dubailand. In total, 2.5 million people are projected to live in Dubailand alone.

Dubailand is being developed by Tatweer, which is a subsidiary of Dubai Holding. Founded in 2004, the company is 99.67 percent owned by Sheikh Mohammed.[15] As with DSC, Tatweer has sold land plots within Dubailand to several private entities for them to create these projects. DSC's three owners—Al Zarooni, Bukhatir, and Falaknaz—are trying to operate the complex as a for-profit venture, expecting the revenues from DSC to eventually exceed its enormous costs. However, since the government owns the land and has subsidized much of the development, the Al-Maktoum royal family will receive approximately 10 percent of the profits.[16] The rationale behind Dubailand and DSC is that they will further develop tourism in the emirate and continue to diversify the region's economy. DSC hopes that its state-of-the-art facilities and built-in residences will attract major international sporting competitions. To a great extent, Dubailand is seen as having the potential to turn Dubai into a massive Las Vegas without the gambling (wagering is against Muslim law), or a family tourist destination like Orlando, only on a far more substantial scale.

Challenges in a New Economic Climate

The ambitious DSC faces numerous challenges in the years ahead, as does the city of Dubai in general. It has been estimated that Dubai requires another 800,000 new residents and businesspeople to populate its newly constructed infrastructure—a considerable increase to its 1.4 million population.[17] The worldwide economic downturn that began in 2008 had a significant impact on Dubai, slowing construction and creating vacancies. Dubai has been particularly susceptible due to the drop in oil prices and the setbacks of the financial services industry. As a result, Abu Dhabi stepped in to assist Dubai with its mounting debt in late 2009. Abu Dhabi's more conservative approach could have an impact going forward, not only on Dubai's rapid development but also its cultural sensibilities.

"The key is getting people to understand what this is going to be, and how they can benefit from it in the long term," Thorpe said in 2009. "The best way to do that is to come from the inside. If we can get people involved from the beginning, then ultimately the real value to them will not just be as the sponsor of a sports facility, but being the sponsor of a community."[18] DSC also faces several challenges with its own infrastructure. Thorpe acknowledged that the complex does not have enough on-site parking to accommodate all patrons should the main sixty-thousand-seat stadium be at full capacity, but was hopeful that a new metro would be completed in time to mitigate those fears. The power grid and sewage lines in Dubai are still being developed as well, but DSC's owners did not want to wait for those necessities to reach the complex, so they constructed their own on-site power distribution network and sewage treatment plant.

Due to the changing economic climate, DSC is being forced to adjust its plan and will open the development gradually. Some areas will be redesigned (like the arena to accommodate the Dubai Tennis Championships), while others will need to wait until capital is more readily available as part of an economic rebound. DSC was also ready to face competition within the region, as plans for similar sports cities have been announced within Saudi Arabia and Tunisia, and have been discussed in several major cities in Europe and Asia. Doha in Qatar has a much smaller sports city that was used for the 2006 Asian Games, which government officials have explored expanding.

In terms of its size and scope, DSC has the potential to be as impressive as any sports facility in the world. With its stadiums, schools, academies, training centers, retail complexes, residential units, and hotels, it represents the very essence of sports-anchored development. "There's so much going on here. As and when this is fully finished, it's going to be busy, it's going to be great," Thorpe said.[19]

SPORTS-ANCHORED DEVELOPMENT: AN OVERVIEW

DSC presents both the challenges in undertaking sports-anchored development and the potential that exists if stakeholders can successfully complete the vision. The evolution of the sports venue has reached a point at which the consumer is no longer seen as a single-purpose visitor to a destination. Increasingly, sports venues are being positioned simultaneously as a draw for a particular event and as a gateway to consumer entertainment in the surrounding area. History indicates that the concept, referred to as sports-anchored development (SAD), dates back about fifty years.

The idea that a sports venue could serve as the anchor of a multifaceted destination became a reality with the 1962 development of the Suzuka Circuit,

Japan's first full-fledged racing course.[20] Aside from designing a race course that surpassed the international standard, the Suzuka Circuit was also positioned to provide consumers with a bevy of entertainment options. One year after the circuit was built, the Techniland Company added an amusement park, Motopia, to complement its race course. Centered on the goal of cultivating "future fans" and promoting car culture in Japan, Motopia added to the unique character of the development.[21] Staying in line with the motorsports experience, Motopia provided visitors the opportunity to experience the physical sensations and skills required to operate a wide range of vehicles. Along with Motopia, the complex contains a resort featuring a full service hotel, gourmet restaurants, and natural hot springs. In addition to the entertainment options, the complex offers a traffic development center that focuses on the mind-set and operational skills of each driver and rider.

The current era of SAD began with the opening of Baltimore's Oriole Park at Camden Yards in 1992. Home to MLB's Orioles, the stadium not only was the first in what would become a wave of "retro" stadiums underscoring baseball's rich history and tradition but simultaneously offered fans enhanced amenities, provided new revenue opportunities for owners, and enabled businesses surrounding the stadium to flourish. Among the features of the Oriole Park at Camden Yards development was Eutaw Street, which sits between the ballpark and the B&O Warehouse. The Eutaw thoroughfare was turned into a pedestrian plaza consisting of shops and eateries, including former Orioles first baseman Boog Powell's outdoor barbecue stand.

Oriole Park at Camden Yards has become the model for how sports venues can anchor downtown redevelopment and growth. The surrounding area flourished to the extent of $166.9 million in increased state gross product in 2006 as the vision of the development was brought to fruition.[22] The area now includes M&T Bank Stadium, where the NFL's Baltimore Ravens play; the Hilton Baltimore Hotel and Convention Center; the Camden Yards Sports Complex; the National Aquarium and Science Center; and Camden Station, which holds the Sports Legends Museum.

Developments surrounding the Olympic Games have also served as an example of SAD. The 2000 Sydney Olympics development was planned not only to host the worldwide event but also to upgrade the sporting, entertainment, and general urban infrastructure of Sydney for worldwide business opportunities, including tourism.[23] The economic impact of the Games was enormous, as Sydney, New South Wales, and Australia saw $600 million in new business investment, $288 million in new business under the Australian Technology Showcase, and almost $2 billion in post-Games sports infrastructure and service contracts.[24] Incorporated in this were twelve new hotels completed in the year before the Games, providing 2,567 rooms; thirty-three residential projects completed prior to the Games, such as Stamford Plaza and Finger Warf, that included 3,055 new units; and a number of other restaurants and retail establishments that came as a result of the development.[25] Besides these benefits, Sydney has continued to enjoy the structures built for the games, including the Olympic Center; the athlete and media villages, which have been retrofitted for residential use; the Sydney SuperDome; and Sydney aquatic centers.[26]

Four years after the Sydney Olympics, PETCO Park, home to MLB's San Diego Padres, opened in the Gaslamp Quarter of downtown San Diego. At an approximate cost of $450 million, the forty-two-thousand-seat stadium serves as the Quarter's sports and entertainment anchor and was instrumental to the broader revitalization of the downtown area. Funded by the Center City Development Corporation and the San Diego Redevelopment Agency, as well as the team itself, PETCO Park has been the driving force for residential, retail, and commercial growth in the area. As a result of the minimum $311 million investment the city of San Diego stipulated the Padres and their private partners contribute, the Quarter has now become one of the jewels of the city.[27]

What made the PETCO Park development unique was the aforementioned required investment into the surrounding area. This investment led to a 500 percent property value increase in the decade following the project's approval in 1988 along with at least $1.5 billion invested into the community by private developers.[28] The success of this development plan will likely encourage other municipalities in reinvigorating some of their urban areas. Included in the PETCO development plans were the 512-room Omni Hotel. In addition to having luxury condominiums on top of the hotel, it offers a pedestrian overpass that allows hotel patrons direct access into the stadium. Moreover, the four-block area around the stadium includes a wide range of housing options, restaurants, and bars. The bars and restaurants that have been flexible enough to adapt to the dramatic ebbs and flows of traffic have seen the most success in capitalizing from this development. To put the overall PETCO development in perspective, from 2003 to 2009 PETCO Park and ancillary development created 19,200 jobs, while generating $5.25 in private investment for every $1 in public funding.[29]

SAD will continue to be a focal point for real estate developers and sports franchise owners. The opportunity for incremental revenue generation is compelling, and such development can aid the redevelopment efforts of cities while simultaneously increasing sports and entertainment offerings for consumers, as evidenced by DSC, Coors Field, and L.A. LIVE.

COORS FIELD

The Lower Downtown Historic District in Denver, Colorado, more commonly known as "LoDo," is home to a multitude of sports facilities, office and commercial space, residential units, retail and restaurant outlets, and, critically, transportation hubs. Coors Field, home to Major League Baseball's Colorado Rockies, is located at the heart of this historic, formerly neglected part of the city. Opened in April of 1995, Coors Field, which is owned by the Denver Metropolitan Major League Baseball Stadium District, was the first major new stadium built in LoDo. Costing $215 million to construct ($38.5 million of which was paid by the franchise to expand the originally envisioned seating capacity from 45,000 to the actual capacity of 50,249), the stadium occupies seventy-six acres of land and pays tribute to traditional ballparks with its exposed steel trusses, architectural detailing reflecting its historic neighborhood, and asymmetrical field.[30] As a result of the project's success, Coors Field now anchors one of the busiest dining and entertainment areas in Denver.

In anticipation of Colorado being awarded its own professional baseball team, and in support of funding for a new baseball stadium, a 0.1 percent sales tax was approved by the voters of the six counties in the greater Denver area.[31] This 1990 sales tax ultimately raised $168 million, which was then applied to the overall cost of the stadium. The remaining cost of the stadium was provided by the (originally named) Denver Rockies baseball team and the Coors Brewing Company, which paid $15 million for the venue's naming rights.[32] Ray Baker, chairman of the Denver Metropolitan Major League Baseball Stadium District, highlighted the importance of the public-private partnership when noting, "The key ingredient to gaining support for both the ballpark and franchise was having a strong and supportive political base, one that included the mayor and governor."[33]

Understanding the importance of the surrounding areas when developing Coors Field and its place in the LoDo neighborhood, project planners did not include a great deal of parking. This was not an oversight; rather they did so purposely. The idea was to have substantially fewer than fifty thousand parking spaces around the ballpark in order to create an intimate setting, much like Fenway Park, where people are more likely to enjoy walking to a venue nestled right in the city.[34] In fact, the stadium only has parking for approximately four thousand vehicles. The effect on the businesses in the area was immediately felt, as one neighboring bar, the Wynkoop Brewing Company, saw its sales increase 50 percent the year following the opening of Coors Field.[35]

Since the initial sales tax was approved in 1990, more than $6 billion has been invested in the LoDo area, including over $2 billion that came from public investment on projects including viaducts in the area.[36] The magnitude of the investment, both private and public, demanded a fairly immediate and measurable return in order to satisfy the numerous investors and stakeholders, particularly taxpayers. Thankfully for these stakeholders, their investment began to pay off quickly. From 1994 to 1995, sales tax revenue in LoDo increased by 86 percent.[37] Further, LoDo properties adjacent to Coors Field went from being assessed at less than $2 per square foot to $27 per square foot.[38] This enhanced the reputation of LoDo in terms of residential development and contributed to the downtown population growing by 45 percent while the metro area grew by only 18 percent. According to Baker, "The new ballpark's national exposure, as well as that of the team, generated a tremendous amount of interest and drew a great deal of people to downtown Denver that wouldn't have otherwise visited. Ultimately, these initial visitors were exposed to what Denver offered, and this created repeat tourism that didn't exist prior to the construction of Coors Field."[39]

Additional economic highlights and growth resulting from the Coors Field and LoDo development included thirty new or renovated office buildings totaling approximately $820 million between 1991 and 2001 and food and beverage sales tax collections for LoDo increasing 651 percent from 1991 to 1998.[40] In terms of actual impact on the Rockies, franchise ownership has seen the team's value increase from the $95 million expansion fee to an estimated $384 million by the end of the 2009 season.[41]

From its successful beginning, Coors Field became the anchor for a number of establishments along LoDo's twenty-five blocks. Among the bigger attractions are the Denver Center for the Performing Arts and Opera Colorado. With over twenty bars and restaurants also located in the district, sports fans before and after the game are able to choose between name-brand eateries or more locally styled pubs and lounges such as the aforementioned Wynkoop Brewing Company or the 9th Door Restaurant and Lounge.

The successful public-private partnership that resulted in the building of Coors Field and the revitalization of LoDo contributed to the community's ability to undertake additional venue development, including INVESCO Field at Mile High Stadium (home to the NFL's Denver Broncos) and the Pepsi Center (where the NBA's Denver Nuggets and NHL's Colorado Avalanche play). Although these venues encountered their own development hurdles, they ultimately have made positive contributions to the immediate area, as have the Rockies. Baker reinforces this point when mentioning the fact that "[t]he Colorado Rockies management, personnel, and offices are located in Coors Field within the district—and this provides an important benefit to that area. Their presence was substantial in terms of ensuring there's a tenant that has a vested interest in the success of the surrounding area."[42]

By capitalizing on the surrounding areas of a new ballpark, the city of Denver has revitalized an area by attracting patrons year round. Sports fans and casual consumers alike have flocked to Coors Field and the LoDo district, thus reviving what was once a deteriorating yet historic part of the city. By maximizing the amount of year-round traffic, the city has found a way to build value both for itself through the generation of taxes and for its private businesses, which benefitted from the increase in consumers. As such, Coors Field and its surrounding LoDo district have successfully joined the key elements of SAD.

L.A. LIVE

Utilizing many of the elements that made Coors Field and LoDo successful, Anschutz Entertainment Group (AEG) elevated sports-anchored development to a new level in 2008 with the official grand opening of L.A. LIVE, a four-million-square-foot, $2.5 billion downtown Los Angeles sports, residential, and entertainment district.[43] Anchored by the AEG-developed and operated STAPLES Center, the only sports venue in the world to have four professional sports teams as tenants, including the NBA's Los Angeles Lakers and Los Angeles Clippers, as well as the NHL's Los Angeles Kings and the WNBA's Sparks, L.A. LIVE is the cornerstone of a new Los Angeles skyline and reinvigorated downtown.

AEG has reached this market leadership position as a result of leveraging the experience gained while establishing its place as one of the leading sports and entertainment providers in the world. AEG has nearly a hundred domestic and international holdings, including Minneapolis's Target Center (as operators), home of the NBA's Timberwolves and the U.S. Bank Theater, an entertainment venue that can be configured to range from 2,500 to 7,500 seats, and The Home Depot Center in Carson, California, which serves as an official Olympic Training site and home to Major League Soccer's L.A. Galaxy and Chivas USA franchises. The Home Depot Center complex also contains an 8,000-seat tennis stadium, a 10,000-seat track-and-field facility, a 2,300-seat indoor velodrome, and other athletic venues. Internationally, AEG controls London's O_2, which includes the 20,000-seat O_2 arena for sports and entertainment; a more personal 2,350-capacity club; an eleven-screen multiplex cinema; and a music museum; along with restaurants, bars, and clubs (see also Chapter 9).[44] Due to the integration of sports and entertainment found at the O_2, it will play a prominent role in the hosting of the 2012 Summer Olympics.

L.A. LIVE's first phase opened in October 2007 and instantaneously showcased the fusion of sports and entertainment. Phase one included a large plaza that covers nearly two acres spanning the open space directly outside of STAPLES Center across the street to the foot of the newly built, 7,100-seat Nokia Theatre, which has hosted the Emmy Awards and American Idol Finals. To commemorate the theatre's grand opening, the Eagles and the Dixie Chicks performed in concert for six nights, reinforcing L.A. LIVE's unique mix of sports and entertainment.

Phase two, which rolled out in December of 2008, featured a staggered debut of numerous sports and entertainment offerings, such as an ESPN Zone restaurant and sports bar; Fleming's Prime Steakhouse & Wine Bar; the Farm of Beverly Hills; the Yard House; Rock'N Fish; The Conga Room (with owners including NBA players Baron Davis and Trevor Ariza, and celebrities such as Jimmy Smits and Jennifer Lopez); Lucky Strike Lanes & Lounge; the Grammy Museum; and the 2,300-seat Club Nokia, which provides a more intimate venue than its Nokia Theatre and STAPLES Center neighbors. Following these openings was a newly established restaurant by celebrity chef Wolfgang Puck, as well as the legendary Trader Vic's, a long-standing institution among the rich and famous of Beverly Hills, and other well-known restaurants such as Katsuya and Rosa Mexicano.

Consumers living in the area, including neighboring University of Southern California students, are now provided a multitude of options besides visiting STAPLES Center for a game or event. As a result of the variety of choices, more than 13.5 million visitors are expected to visit the site annually for dining and entertainment purposes. Speaking to the entertainment district's impact, AEG president Tim Leiweke stated, "L.A. LIVE is at the center of bringing Los Angeles back to its roots as a point of destination, a tourism mecca which exists in an event-driven city and economy."[45] Realizing the potential impact of the additional $18 million in annual tax revenue and the benefit the proposed L.A. LIVE hotel development would have on the existing Los Angeles Convention Center, the city's Community Redevelopment Agency agreed to commit a $16 million loan for the project, while city government agreed to waive upward of $270 million in hotel bed taxes and $4 million in fees for the project.[46]

Opened in 2010, L.A. LIVE's third and final phase included a Regal Cinema with fourteen screens and a fifty-four-floor JW Marriott and Ritz-Carlton Hotel with 878 Marriott guest rooms and 123 Ritz-Carlton rooms. The hotels' anticipated effect on the Los Angeles Convention Center was felt long before they opened. Los Angeles had long suffered as a forgotten destination for large convention events because it lacked both the quality and quantity of convenient hotel rooms sought by convention planners. As Leiweke indicated in 2009, "The publicly controlled Convention Center has stagnated in terms of signage, advertising, facilities, and resources—thus the key to the rejuvenation of the area is the opening of the JW Marriott and Ritz-Carlton."[47] The addition of the JW Marriott and Ritz-Carlton hotels alleviated that problem, as evidenced by the fact the convention center booked an additional fifty conventions in the time leading up to the hotels' opening.[48] This rejuvenation was acknowledged by NBA Commissioner David Stern when awarding STAPLES Center the 2011 All-Star Game in large part because "it's getting more difficult to find cities with the kinds of amenities, close hotel accommodations, the convention center and the like, and L.A. has been a popular destination."[49]

Further enhancing the downtown area, the hotel tower has 224 luxury condominiums on its top floors, complete with Ritz-Carlton amenities and services. Many of these residences have been purchased by well-know businessmen along with sports and entertainment superstars.

A separate, 12,300-square-foot building located along Nokia Plaza on one side and Figueroa St. on the other contains a full-fledged broadcast facility directly across from STAPLES Center. Its inclusion in the entertainment district also demonstrates the convergence of sports and entertainment. The five-story ESPN building houses the ESPN Zone on the first two floors, while two television production studios with digital control rooms constitute the upper floors. One of these studios is home to ESPN's late-night production of its famed sports news program, *SportsCenter*, along with local ESPN radio affiliate ESPN Radio 710-AM. The presence of ESPN's production studios is important because it solidifies Los Angeles's standing as a global hub of sports entertainment, a designation traditionally afforded New York City. To further strengthen the bond between L.A. LIVE and ESPN, the network's annual sports awards event, The ESPY's, was moved to the Nokia Theatre. Leiweke believes that "the economics of the L.A. LIVE campus are driven by the hundreds of predictable nights from the concerts, sporting events, and other planned events on an annual basis."[50] As such, the ability to monetize the location was not lost on those owning and operating The Conga Room. When choosing the club's specific location, the potential to attract sports fans, high-profile visitors, tourists, and affluent downtown dwellers was evident. The owners even anticipated a potential windfall from developing special events held in recognition of the district's sports franchises should they win championships as teams like the Lakers routinely do.[51] In between special events, visitors, tourists, and residents drawn to the entertainment district also provide a continual base of business to the club and its surrounding establishments.

As L.A. LIVE grows to symbolize the Southern California sports and entertainment scene, it becomes the hub for a new downtown Los Angeles. What started with AEG's building of STAPLES Center in 1999 has turned into an entertainment district that brings all the elements of sports, entertainment, and real estate together to help drive business in a revitalized downtown.

SPORTS-ANCHORED DEVELOPMENT:
THE BOTTOM LINE

Until relatively recently, SAD was nothing more than an unsophisticated attempt to generate modest incremental revenue from those on their way to or from sporting events. As evidenced by DSC's ambitious undertaking, along with the demonstrated success of Coors Field and the emergence of L.A. LIVE as a global hub for sports and entertainment, SAD has become complex and is now an integral part of the sports business. Going forward, those intending to leverage retail, commercial, and residential real estate holdings to attract sports-related spending on a year-round basis will have to be mindful of several issues, including the consumers' overall "street to seat" experience. They will also need to analyze the prudence associated with constructing large, all-encompassing complexes such as "sports cities." In both cases, the need for sports business stakeholders to tactically partner with the public sector in order to secure funding and mutually beneficial outcomes will continue.

Expanding the Game-Day Experience

The game-day experience starts when fans begin working their way to the venue, and it is on full display by the time they arrive. The game-day experience was once framed by accessible parking, how courteous the ticket takers were, and whether the team had the specific piece of merchandise you wanted in stock. However, in an era of technological innovation and brand immersion, the game-day experience has morphed into an extra-sensory one designed by architects and urban planners, delivered by media companies, and funded by corporate sponsors. Those involved in planning and implementing the expanded game-day experience must strike a careful balance between business development opportunities and over-commercialization. In short, seamless, optimally intrusive integration is a must in order for fans to embrace it. Successfully accomplished, game-day business can be extended, enabling franchise owners, local businesses and communities surrounding the venue, and municipalities to prosper.

Providing fans with a more interactive and complete experience development-wide can be powerful and profitable, provided it is accomplished without inundating the consumer. For instance, providing real-time access to news and information about parking availability and cross-promotions with businesses surrounding the venue may serve the dual purposes of customer service and revenue generation. In addition, when a complete and coherent game-day experience is promoted—and delivered—fans are more inclined to arrive earlier and stay longer, a key goal of those seeking to profit from SAD. Coors Field exemplifies such a relationship and has done so consistently since the beginning of the modern era of SAD. Longer, engaged stays allow franchise owners, especially those with a financial stake in the development, the chance to significantly increase revenue, the metric by which overall franchise value is measured. The franchises' (potential) sponsors and media partners welcome well-thought-out developments as they provide each additional mechanisms to market and promote; such sports-anchored developments also assuage the concerns of the finance community because the teams have increased the diversity of their holdings. In addition, the majority of the revenue generated throughout the development that is earmarked for the franchise owner is not subject to revenue sharing, either with other franchises or the players. Over time, and during collective bargaining, players' associations no doubt will attempt to capture some of this revenue, as they will argue that without the game itself, related real estate holdings would suffer—if they could exist at all. In the interim, athletes may still benefit, as successful developments lead to incremental revenue generation that the owner may reinvest into payroll.

Surrounding (residential) communities are also affected by SAD. For these communities to benefit from the development—let alone invest in it—they must feel as if they are part of the process. This includes the ability to utilize such surrounding amenities as parking and neighboring green space within the development for their own purposes and causes, particularly on non-game days. Ensuring that sports-anchored developments become hubs of activity on non-game days, while simultaneously enhancing the community and its residents on non-game days, reinforces the franchise's commitment to the community and squarely positions it as a strong community and corporate citizen. This is particularly important at a time when many view athletes as out of touch with fans, while others believe franchise owners are solely interested in their own bottom lines, even if this involves (further) disenfranchising or even displacing residents.

Should a community fail to embrace the sports-anchored development's many attributes, a rapid decline in the development's viability will occur, leading to reduced retail and commercial activity on non-game days, activity which routinely determines the long-term fate of such developments. Lacking cohesion and buy-in from all stakeholders not only will result in a drop in business and a reduction in real estate values but also will compromise the municipality, given the fact that it, through its taxpayers, remains financially liable for the development. Compounding matters, the anchor tenant—the sports franchise—may relocate, cementing a long-term crisis.

Self-Contained Sports and Entertainment Complexes

While not entirely prompted by Dubai's desire to enhance its global reputation by building a sports city, many cities and regions have since considered the possibility of extravagant, self-contained sports complexes. Cities or regions looking to boost their brands and drive tourism by developing large, self-contained sports and entertainment offerings, such as DSC or ESPN's Wide World of Sports (see Chapter 9), recognize the universal appeal of sports and believe this appeal can be monetized through advertising and sponsorship as well as tourism. Due to cultural issues, acreage limitations, and expense, among other concerns, similar mega sports-anchored developments are unlikely to become the norm. Nonetheless, they represent among the most interesting examples of the convergence of sports and real estate. Because sport transcends cultures and has a rich history of bringing disparate groups together under the banner of competition, myriad stakeholders are affected by it: the host city or region, event organizers, (amateur) sports leagues and governing bodies, sponsors and advertisers, and fans.

Host cities or regions where these self-contained sports complexes exist are taking enormous risks, especially if they lack the fundamental infrastructure, financial resources, and region-wide commitment to success. The amount of time it takes to develop comprehensive developments, when considered alongside routinely occurring cost overruns, exacerbates the potential risk to municipalities. Cities or regions that have developable real estate, access to capable labor, and financial backing from both public and private sources, and that combine these attributes with a keen sense of marketing and promotion, can flourish. Whether successful or not, these mega sports and entertainment experiences will have a measurable impact on the host city or region's reputation and significantly contribute to its brand.

For instance, inadequate infrastructure, ranging from poor ingress and egress and insufficient parking, to a lack of entertainment alternatives, such as dining and shopping, will severely inhibit repeat business. The loss of repeat business—especially if it is from groups such as amateur sports leagues hosting (inter) national tournaments or sports academies hosting extended training and instructional camps, will have dire consequences. Chief among them is compromising the city, both financially and from a branding perspective, as well as the region at large; a development certain to have an impact on tourism.

Alternatively, meticulously planned, developed, and serviced, these complexes can create an extraordinary sense of (sports) culture, bridging cultural differences in the process. As this occurs, these self-contained entities, such as L.A. LIVE, build, reinforce, and extend a brand based on competition, convenience, and stellar customer service. This enables these complexes to generate revenue on site while simultaneously driving tourism throughout the region. Event and (amateur) league organizers welcome the diversity of offerings and convenience and can themselves evangelize the merits of the complex, persuading families and friends to also take part in the experience. As their ability to promote the complex becomes evident and is embraced by the city or region, their influence over future large-scale events to be hosted and amenities to be added may ensue.

By developing a symbiotic relationship with patrons who have a vested interest in and a connection to the facilities, self-contained sports complexes and sports-anchored developments are in the enviable position of attracting incremental advertisers and sponsors—advertisers and sponsors that are particularly interested in aligning with properties and patrons that have strong brand allegiances.

Leaving a Legacy

The relationship between sports and the public sector, especially when public financing is involved, will remain a delicate one. While profitable, mutually beneficial relationships certainly can be established, so too can relationships easily become strained due to poor planning.

For years, smartly constructed or renovated venues have been trumpeted as centerpieces for redevelopment and revitalization of urban areas, providing meaningful short- and medium-term benefits and advantages to the community. But failing to craft long-term strategies to address sports facilities and the potential they have as sports-anchored developments can harm the municipality and the franchise, as well as those that fund them. In short, without a compelling exit strategy once venues become obsolete, municipalities and their taxpayers, both individual and corporate, are vulnerable—and the likelihood of further municipal investment in sports-related development is greatly reduced.

Adaptive reuse, the concept of converting old or obsolete structures for new purposes, has thus far been sparingly applied to sports venues. In essence, it is the opposite of expanding the game-day experience because adaptive reuse converts venues that were designed for a single purpose into a venue utilized for multiple functions; essentially, "expanding the *everyday* experience." Sports-venue-related adaptive reuse typically takes one of two forms. First, residential living can be built into the shell of the stadium, with the stadium's field being converted to park space for residents. For example, Arsenal, the English Premier League soccer team located in North London, is converting its old Highbury Stadium to have hundreds of apartments and anticipates turning a substantial profit on the conversion. By maintaining the venue's historical significance, Arsenal is demonstrating the financial and community upside associated with adaptive reuse. Second, venerable old venues can be transformed into restaurant and retail districts, to include hotels. Such is the case in Prague, Czech Republic, where Strahov Stadium, which seated 220,000, is planning a massive transformation in order to maintain the area's vitality and relevance.

For such adaptive reuse to be feasible in the U.S., venues must possess preservation value, in terms of historical significance, and deliver an economic return that surpasses alternative uses. Venues that do not have storied pasts or otherwise do not resonate with fans and communities alike may not be as compelling candidates for adaptive reuse because the opportunity costs, financial and environmental, may prove too high relative to other redevelopment options. Taking these aspects into account, franchise owners, developers and environmentalists, surrounding businesses and communities, and municipalities will shape, if not dictate, the interest in and feasibility of adaptive reuse.

Franchise owners are presented with the unique opportunity to generate profits while simultaneously extending their personal and franchise brands. Depending on the ownership and operating structure of the venue, franchise owners, working closely with the aforementioned stakeholders, can reinforce their commitment to the communities in which their teams play, as well as use any proceeds raised to offset the costs associated with new venue construction. Further, by considering adaptive reuse during initial venue design phases, franchise owners have the opportunity to plan well into the future, ensuring that today's optimally developed venue will remain an economically viable and valuable one tomorrow. By tactically including residents and taxpayers in the process, franchise owners and municipalities become advocates, committed to the financial and community interests of many.

SPORTS-ANCHORED DEVELOPMENT AND CONVERGENCE: FINAL THOUGHTS FROM ROSSETTI'S MATT ROSSETTI[52]

Matt Rossetti is the president of Rossetti. Rossetti is one of the world's leading architectural, planning, and design firms, with completed projects such as Ford Field, home of the NFL's Detroit Lions; MLS's New York Red Bulls Arena; and the USTA's National Tennis Center, home of tennis's U.S. Open. Rossetti shared his perspective on convergence and sports-anchored development with the SBI.

SBI: Where has convergence impacted sports-anchored development the most?

ROSSETTI: It really comes down to providing the opportunity to live the sports and entertainment experience, as opposed to merely visiting it. First off, sports-anchored developments are not for the past thinkers—it's all about the new breed of urban dwellers as a result of rapidly changing demographics in the U.S. The impact will be substantial in the ability to accommodate this growing appetite for an urban experience based on a full immersion of entertainment 24/7. This approach has tremendous implications for public transit and sustainable planning, as it has little use for the automobile and traditional zoning governance on parking. Also of importance is how the sports and entertainment cache can be leveraged to highlight the attributes of the complete development surrounding the performance venue.

SBI: Can you give an example of where an entity has taken advantage of sports-anchored development?

ROSSETTI: The LoDo district of Denver is an excellent example of a sports-anchored development that occurred due to organic growth based on the power and draw of a major sports venue. Coors Field provided the catalyst for hundreds of bars, restaurants, and housing units that sprang up to take advantage of a new district being created for the new urban dweller seeking the sports and entertainment experience. Sungui Arena Complex, in Inchon, Korea, is a perfect example of a master planned sports-anchored development that incorporates a major transit station within the complex, eliminating the need for any significant parking structures. In this case, the development is carefully planned and implemented all at once, according to a master vision set out by the design team for Hyundai, the developer of the complex.

SBI: How has Rossetti changed along with the style and type of convergence you have described?

ROSSETTI: Our plan for the arena and surrounding entertainment district in downtown Edmonton is a great example of how our firm is changing to help shape the convergence of the future. Rossetti's strength is that we have an equal expertise in mixed-use commercial development along with sports development. We knit the two together through design and master planning, while looking at the economic impact and considering the final details relating to environmental graphics, branding, and interior design. Historically, there has been very little or no communication between the entities that understood the commercial language and the sports and entertainment language. We've been successfully bridging both aspects by understanding and capitalizing on the important opportunities on both the commercial and sports fronts.

SBI: Can you give a specific example of where you worked with a potential client that wanted to take advantage of the convergence of sports and real estate?

ROSSETTI: The mixed-use project I mentioned in Inchon, South Korea, where we utilized a developer's mentality in order to convince our client on the potential success of the convergence. A request was issued seeking proposals that optimized the best use of this downtown, twenty-five-acre site to maximize density and return on investment, including a twenty-five-thousand-seat soccer stadium. We worked closely with our client to determine the right mix and density of uses to provide a substantial asset to the neighboring communities, sustainable operating revenue for the life of the project, and significant return for the stakeholders.

SBI: How did Rossetti approach the Inchon development, given these conditions?

ROSSETTI: We analyzed the market and the zoning requirements, and then created an economic engine based primarily on three fifty-story condo towers and a substantial amount of retail integrated throughout the site. There was a square footage limitation based on a predetermined floor area ratio from the zoning restrictions. As a result, we had to develop a concept that fit within those limitations, which yielded the massing and density for the condo towers. The complex also has a continuous public plaza connecting the transit station at the north to the public park on the south end, allowing for retail to locate adjacent to the concourse of the building. On event days, the retail is closed off from the public side and accessible only by the concourse and the inside of the building and vice versa during non-event times.

SBI: Where will convergence have an impact on sports-anchored development the most going forward, and what challenges exist?

ROSSETTI: Technology, demographics, and sustainable design are the three areas I see having the most significant impacts on convergence with respect to developments of the future. The challenge is that all three require great vision and some optimism which, given the economic environment, is a bit challenging. Predicting how rapidly changing technology will continue to enhance communication, combined with a new breed of living habits in a sustainable environment, all point toward a convergence of uses within an integrated physical experience.

SBI: How have changes in venue technology affected sports-anchored developments?

ROSSETTI: From our perspective, technology is wedded to infrastructure and therefore the backbone of any successful new development. Understanding how technology will be used for functional and entertainment purposes is a critical consideration from the onset of the planning and design. In addition to the functional and entertainment aspects, the other major component in terms of the successful implementation of technology is the return on investment. From day one, consideration must be given to how it will pay off in the long term, quite possibly through advertising and sponsorship, or comprehensive partnerships among sports franchises, venues, and technology firms.

SBI: What are the critical success factors for sports-anchored development, and where is it vulnerable going forward?

ROSSETTI: Density and multimodal public transportation are key to any successful future sports-anchored development due to the enormous flow of people to the events and the ability to create an environment capable of drawing crowds and entertaining them. *Density* and *public transportation* have been historically negative terms for the Ozzie and Harriet optic. Zoning regulations across the country have been based on suburban sprawl and need to change overnight to promote and not fight the new urban dweller demographic. This is something we don't see happening nearly at the pace it needs to be and will cause extra costs and time to these projects—and in some cases, keep them from happening altogether.

SBI: What does Rossetti need to be cognizant of to maintain its leadership position?

ROSSETTI: In addition to remaining savvy on the politics of zoning, transit, and other development obstacles, we continue to focus on the place-making aspects of sports-anchored developments. While iconic architecture can create a buzz about a place, true mixed-use developments (with or without a sports anchor) are not only about the architecture, but especially the spaces between buildings. I think of these components theatrically like the set of a stage. The buildings themselves create the backdrop in order to support the acting and performance, which are the patrons, shoppers, fans, neighbors—how they hang out, people watch, stroll, and shop in the area. Utilizing the DNA of the surrounding area, district, or city, there is an opportunity to design something wedded to the culture and the specific site which creates places of significance and memory.

SBI: How will those attending sporting events feel the impact of such convergence?

ROSSETTI: I think people will start to live the events instead of just showing up for them. The new experience will be a total immersion into a densely packed environment of living, shopping, working, and dining, intermingled with the play aspects of sports and entertainment. The pedestrian and alternative modes of transportation will have the same priority as the automobile to the arteries of circulation. Parking will be limited and restricted to specific areas, allowing more greening of the streets and sidewalks with increased uses such as cafes and shops that spill out of the physical enclosure. The atmosphere will be one in which people will invest there, live there, and visit to play there again and again.

VENUE TECHNOLOGY

UNIVERSITY OF PHOENIX STADIUM

It's February 3, 2008, and the New York Giants have their backs against the wall in Super Bowl XLII. For nearly fifty-nine minutes of football, the Giants have put forth a remarkable effort against the undefeated and heavily favored New England Patriots at University of Phoenix Stadium in Glendale, Arizona. But now the Giants find themselves trailing 14-10 with 1:15 left, and facing a crucial third down and five with the ball at their own forty-four-yard line.

Giants quarterback Eli Manning takes the snap out of the shotgun and immediately feels pressure from the Patriots defensive front. Manning steps forward, but finds more blue jerseys, and suddenly he's firmly in the grasp of lineman Jarvis Green. Just when it appears as though Manning is destined to be sacked, he somehow spins and slips through the rush, backtracks five yards, and heaves the ball deep downfield. Waiting for it at the twenty-four-yard line is unheralded wide receiver David Tyree, who is covered closely by All-Pro safety Rodney Harrison.

Tyree leaps for the ball, and it's clear that Manning has thrown it in the only possible place where his receiver can catch it. In mid-air, Tyree extends his arms and barely has possession of the football. To hold on, he bends his right arm down and pins the ball against his helmet. Tyree falls on his back, but the ball stays between his hand and helmet, and miraculously never touches the field. Not long after, Steve Sabol of NFL Films would deem the catch, "The greatest play the Super Bowl has ever produced."

As Tyree caught the ball, many of the 71,101 fans in attendance were able to take cell phone pictures of the moment and immediately forward them to friends, loved ones, and even those with whom they had bet on the game. Members of the media instantly blogged and uploaded photos, thanks to the high-speed wireless connectivity available at the facility. Fox Sports, which had been broadcasting the game, had a plethora of cameras on hand and was able to seamlessly set up and replay Tyree's catch from nearly every conceivable angle to the 97.5 million fans watching at home in the United States. Due to the unique design of the stadium, fans sitting in the last few rows had a clearer and closer view of the play than they might have had elsewhere.

Playing on a field that literally had been rolled in just a few days earlier, and beneath a roof that had been closed due to the threat of rain, the Giants would only need four more plays to score the go-ahead touchdown and take a 17-14 lead with just thirty-five seconds left. New England failed to answer, and the Giants completed one of the great upsets in Super Bowl history.

And it all took place in one of the most advanced venues in all of sports.

Building a Desert Oasis

Since moving to Arizona from St. Louis in 1988, the Arizona Cardinals had been one of the least-successful teams in the National Football League (NFL). Part of this sub-par performance was due to the franchise's inadequate stadium situation. The Cardinals shared Sun Devil Stadium with Arizona State University on the school's campus in Tempe.

While the school was able to schedule night games in the hot desert climate during September and October, the Cardinals were subject to the NFL's television schedule and often had to play afternoon games in hundred-degree weather in the fall. The stifling heat kept fans away, and the Cardinals usually ranked toward the bottom of the NFL in attendance. Moreover, the aging stadium did not enable the franchise to generate much-needed incremental revenue. The organization knew it needed a new enclosed stadium not only to keep fans cool when the temperatures rose but also to deliver a fan experience that would facilitate increased spending by all those hoping to link their brands to the Cardinals, whether these be diehard football fans or corporate patrons.

After several attempts to obtain public assistance for a new stadium failed, Maricopa County voters approved a referendum in November 2000 to construct what would become University of Phoenix Stadium in Glendale, about twenty miles west of Phoenix. The cost would be $475 million, with the Arizona Sports and Tourism Authority (the stadium's owner) bearing $302 million of the cost, while the Cardinals contributed more than $165 million, and the city of Glendale added nearly $10 million.[1] The stadium was financed by a county-wide 1 percent hotel occupancy tax and a 3.25 percent car rental tax.[2] The Cardinals had to cover all cost overruns, but they receive all game-day revenue and all permanent stadium sponsorship revenue. The Tourism Authority receives all non-NFL event revenue.

Venue flexibility was vitally important to both the Cardinals and the Tourism Authority in determining the stadium's design. The Cardinals wanted a retractable roof so that fans could keep cool in September and October, but then enjoy the desert weather in November and December. They also wanted to play on natural grass, the preferred surface for both players and fans. The Tourism Authority also desired the retractable roof so that the venue could host conventions and other events beyond just football. But a natural grass surface would be difficult to maintain with the retractable roof and with convention-goers regularly stomping on the turf. So both parties, working together, chose a retractable field that could roll out to allow for flexible event space and easier maintenance given the weather. Leaving the grass outside most of the time also reduced humidity inside the stadium and saved $50 million in costs associated with maintaining the grass indoors.[3] At the time, the only retractable fields were in soccer stadiums in Amsterdam, Netherlands; Gelsenkirchen, Germany; and Sapporo, Japan.

The Cardinals approached numerous architects to design the stadium, ultimately selecting Peter Eisenman, who is a football fan and has designed structures in the U.S., Italy, Germany, and Spain. Eisenman worked with well-known sports architecture firm HOK+Sport (now known as Populous) to build one of the most advanced sports facilities in the world.

"We wanted to build a stadium with an iconic presence," said Cardinals president Michael Bidwill. "When people saw our stadium on Monday Night Football from a blimp shot, we wanted them to instantly recognize this was our home and a great place for football. We chose to hire a well-known architect because we wanted to build something unique that set us apart from other stadiums."[4]

The stadium was designed to look like a barrel cactus from the outside, with alternating metallic panels and recessed glass strips surrounding the exterior. The roof itself is quite unique, as it uses a translucent fabric made by BirdAir that allows sunlight streams to seep through the stadium, providing a brighter atmosphere than most domes. The asymmetrical roof weighs 18.5 million pounds and is supported by two seven-hundred-foot long trusses.[5] Eisenman and HOK worked with Uni-Systems to build the roof on an incline, making it more efficient to open and close, which it can do in twelve to fifteen minutes. The roof is closed any time the temperature is projected to be over seventy-five degrees for a game, or in the rare event of rain in the Arizona desert.

The field takes a bit longer to roll in—seventy-five minutes—and it is contained in an 18.9-million-pound, 234-foot-wide by 400-foot-long steel tray.[6] It's powered by seventy-six one-horsepower electric motors, and rolls in on thirteen rail tracks.[7] Typically, the field is rolled in on Friday for games that take place on Sunday. When the Cardinals aren't playing, the stadium has 160,000 square feet of contiguous convention space at its disposal.[8]

"The NFL is known for being forward looking and innovative. We really wanted our stadium to reflect that," Bidwill says. "Fans look at our building and see something that is asymmetrical and modern."[9]

The interior of University Phoenix Stadium is also more fan-friendly than many other new stadiums that have been built in recent years. The Cardinals had thirty-three of the stadium's eighty-eight suites placed on the club level, instead of building two floors exclusively for suites. The move took fifteen feet off the building's height, meaning fans in the upper levels could be closer to the field.[10] In addition, more than 50 percent of the seating is in the lower level. The eighty-eight suites are much fewer than in many other new NFL stadiums, such as the Cowboys Stadium in Arlington or Reliant Stadium in Houston, but the Cardinals did not want to overbuild and believed University of Phoenix Stadium was appropriate for its market. However, there is room for limited suite expansion should the Cardinals desire to increase the capacity.

The Cardinals hired Pentagram, an internationally renowned design firm, to handle much of the stadium's interior and graphic design elements. The firm, which had never worked in sports before, transformed the suites into stadium "lofts." Along with the two thirty-nine-thousand-square-foot club lounges, the lofts use open ceilings to reflect an urban industrial theme. The lofts also have cork floors, carpeted walls, chalkboards, huge metallic lamps suspended from the ceiling, swivel high-back chairs, and garage-style doors that roll up in front of the loft to provide a view to the inner bowl.[11] Outside the lofts, corrugated metal walls hide the premium experience to passersby. The design enables the Cardinals to differentiate their lofts from traditional luxury suites, which have become standard in sports stadiums.

Pentagram also designed the interior of the stadium with the intention of bringing the Cardinals brand to life, this being the first time the team ever controlled its own stadium. Red is the dominant color throughout University of Phoenix Stadium, with accents of black, gold, and white. In addition, there are nods to the Cardinals history, which goes as far back as 1898 when the team played in Chicago, making it the oldest football club in the United States. There is also Arizona branding throughout the stadium, showing off the state's natural wonders.

"We deliberately hired a design firm that had never worked in sports before, because we wanted something unique," Bidwill says. "The lofts and much of the interior design reflect that."[12]

The stadium's clubs are sponsored by computer technology company Insight Enterprises and the Gila River Indian Community. They can host a variety of non-football events, including high school proms and company functions. Plazas at both ends of the interior are sponsored by Budweiser and Coca-Cola, respectively. Still, despite numerous sponsorship opportunities, the Cardinals have held back somewhat. "We've taken a less is more approach," Bidwill says. "We want fewer partners with deeper relationships, and less clutter in the stadium. We wanted to have an authentic feel to the facility."[13]

For the Cardinals, the fan experience begins even before someone steps foot inside the stadium. Outside the structure are three eight-acre parcels of grass, one of which is known as the "Great Lawn," that provide an improved tailgate experience over parking lot asphalt in the Arizona desert heat. Also outside the stadium is the Pat Tillman Freedom Plaza, named for the former Cardinals defensive back who died while serving in the U.S. Army Rangers in Afghanistan. The stadium offers 14,000 on-site parking spaces, seats 63,400 fans, and is expandable to 72,200 seats for large events.

Wired for Everything

In addition to the stadium's architectural achievements, the Cardinals and the Tourism Authority wanted University of Phoenix Stadium to push the limits of venue technology. Together, they worked with both Cisco and Arizona-based Insight Enterprises to realize those goals by creating a cutting-edge communications infrastructure with a multimedia IP network. "We wanted to make this the most technologically advanced stadium in the world," Bidwill says. "Technology is one of the main, differentiating, pillars of our stadium."[14]

Typically, stadiums have multiple IP networks that can be difficult to manage and cause problems with cohesion between different parts of a sports facility. For example, there might be separate networks for security, ticketing systems, or merchandise sales. However, Cisco and Insight were able to wire University of Phoenix Stadium with one IP network. Using Cisco's Connected Sports solutions, the stadium combines data, voice, video, wireless, and social networking to create a single, secure network that essentially serves every stadium-related function. Cisco and Insight also wired the team's headquarters and training facility in Tempe on the same network. The stadium uses a "main data facility" or MDF that connects the infrastructure of all Cisco routers, reduces the amount of wiring needed and, critically, is easier to add functions to as technology advances.[15]

These efforts allowed Cardinals coaches and staff to send everything from game video to ticket data back and forth between Glendale and Tempe. In addition, fans in suites can use Cisco IP phones with touchscreens to order food, purchase merchandise, buy tickets to upcoming games, or check stats and scores from around the NFL. The network also streamlines security on game days, so that officials can view surveillance cameras, communicate with police officers about incidents around the venue, or report on traffic outside the stadium. The network can collect and aggregate data once a patron has a ticket bar code scanned or orders food; it also allows for replays to be shown on video boards. The stadium's concessionaire uses the network to swipe ID cards and monitor alcohol sales to fans.

University of Phoenix Stadium uses a mobile IP network, making it completely accessible for all wireless connections.[16] While this helps fans with connection speed on mobile devices, and coaches and game personnel with communications, it is also available for all the conventions and other events that the facility hosts.

"It's not just about football, either," stated Mark Feller, vice president of technology for the Cardinals, in an interview with Baselinemag.com. "This stadium is a multi-event facility that hosts concerts, other sporting events, car shows, food shows, and all kinds of expos. Anyone who comes in here can use this Cisco network connection on the floor in the expo or anywhere else in the facility."[17]

A Resounding Success

Before University of Phoenix Stadium even opened, it was named one of the ten "most impressive" sports facilities in the world by *Business Week*, and it was the only venue in the United States to receive that honor. It originally opened in August 2006 as Cardinals Stadium, but in a nod to corporate marketing was renamed soon thereafter when University of Phoenix purchased the naming rights for $154.5 million over twenty years[18] (University of Phoenix is a for-profit institution that specializes in adult education and does not have an intercollegiate athletics program).

The multipurpose nature of the facility allowed it to host 91 events in 110 event days between August 4, 2006, and January 8, 2007. Those included Cardinals games, concerts, conventions, trade shows, high school football state championship games, motor sports events, the Fiesta Bowl, and the BCS National Championship Game. As noted earlier, the stadium hosted Super Bowl XLII in February 2008 and, in 2009, it also played host to the West Regional semi-finals and finals of the NCAA Division Men's Basketball Tournament.

The facility actually can hold up to five events simultaneously, utilizing the main concrete floor, the concourses, and the two thirty-nine-thousand-square-foot clubs.[19] This represents considerable flexibility over traditional football venues, which often host few events beyond the home team's allotment of eight regular season games and two preseason games.

The people in the greater Phoenix area have clearly taken to the new stadium, as the Cardinals have sold out every home game since the venue opened. Buoyed by a visible fan base that can stay cool at 1:00 P.M., and playing in significantly better conditions, the Cardinals improved their performance on the field dramatically. It didn't hurt that the Cardinals' revenue increased by over $30 million in the first year at the new stadium, enabling the team to sign several quality free agents and offer contract extensions to their promising young players.[20] University of Phoenix Stadium hosted the NFC Championship Game in January 2009, and, as fans cheered the Cardinals on to their first Super Bowl appearance, there was little doubt the venue significantly contributed to the team's success.

VENUE TECHNOLOGY: AN OVERVIEW

The evolution to technically advanced venues such as University of Phoenix Stadium and the soon-to-be-discussed Cowboys Stadium did not happen overnight. In fact, at-venue technology was nonexistent in the early years of sports. Games took place during the day at stadiums that used manual scoreboards and offered exceedingly basic audio capabilities. Additional amenities and entertainment were largely an afterthought, and the fan experience centered on the game itself. As sports and entertainment merged, and as at-venue technology advanced, the overall fan experience improved.

This improved viewing experience began in 1929 when the NFL's Providence Steamrollers hosted the Chicago Cardinals under newly installed floodlights at Kinsley Park Stadium in Providence, Rhode Island. Six years later, and although minor league baseball had hosted night games, the business of baseball was forever changed as the Cincinnati Reds beat the Philadelphia Phillies under the lights at Crosley Field. While other teams were initially reluctant to schedule night games, the Reds, given their losing record, sagging attendance, and poor financial performance, had nothing to lose. By season's end, the Reds' total attendance had doubled from the prior season in large part due to the night games, which averaged 18,620 fans per game compared to 4,700 for day games.[21] The incremental revenue generated by the night games helped the team become a winner on the field, as evidenced by its winning the pennant in both 1939 and 1940, as well as the World Series that year. Fans embraced technological improvements and bolstered sports's bottom line in the process.

During the same era, scoreboards were manually adjusted as games progressed, but with the University of Michigan employing the first electronic scoreboard in 1930, the at-venue viewing experience began to change dramatically. In 1960, Bill Veeck, the owner of the Chicago White Sox and Old Comiskey Park, transformed the scoreboard into an entertainment platform by adding flashing bulbs and the ability to launch fireworks, as well as bellow sound effects following White Sox home runs.[22] Twenty years later another major shift in scoreboard technology ushered fans into the modern era of at-venue entertainment. During the 1980 MLB All-Star Game at Dodger Stadium, Japanese electronics manufacturer Mitsubishi introduced Diamond Vision, which transformed the static electronic scoreboard into a giant television.[23] Sony Electronics followed with the JumboTron, whose catchy name became synonymous for stadium scoreboards. The introduction of "giant television scoreboards" provided the home team the ability to better interact with and entertain its fans by displaying player likenesses, stats, highlights, and other facts such as the scores from other games. These scoreboards eventually became high definition (HD) LED video displays that further increased the fan's entertainment experience, particularly during timeouts and other stoppages in play.

Like the scoreboard, at-venue audio capabilities have drastically improved since the "horn on a pole" days of yesteryear. Sports venues have incorporated sophisticated and integrated audio systems to add to the fan's entertainment experience. 360-degree sound systems now complement the video clips on the HD video displays and encourage fan participation, such as the often deafening and synchronized chant of "DE-FENSE! DE-FENSE!" Industry experts refer to this paradigm shift in audio technology as "soundscape"—audio designed specifically to support what fans are expecting to experience when they scan their ticket and walk into a venue.[24]

Audio advancements and HD displays are no longer limited to over-sized scoreboards. Plasma screens, LCD screens, or both are now located throughout most sports venues to keep the fans both informed and entertained. Upon its opening in 2006, Emirates Stadium in the United Kingdom, home to the Arsenal Football Club, partnered with Sony to deliver next-generation entertainment by becoming the first venue in the world to have streaming HD throughout the stadium.[25]

Emerging technologies such as Wi-Fi afford consumers the ability to "be connected" to their laptops or PDAs wherever they may be. For the past decade this has included fans interested in staying in touch, whether this be with colleagues at the office, their family on the go, or stadium concessionaires. At-venue Wi-Fi networks are also intended to provide fans a richer, real-time entertainment experience by enabling them to check sports scores, watch instant replays, or follow the performances of the players on their fantasy league teams.

Significantly, these same fans demanded a more encompassing and complete entertainment experience with regard to the event they were attending. They increasingly required being closer to the action or, at the very least, much more in tune with the action taking place before them—and the requisite technology soon followed. Venues such as University of Phoenix Stadium, recent innovations such as Kangaroo TV, and in-venue technological advancements delivered by Cisco further immerse the fans in the event and make them feel as though they are on top of the action at all times.

KANGAROO TV

As auto racing became more technologically advanced, many in the industry saw an opportunity to enhance the viewing experience of fans at race tracks.

This opportunity presented itself most clearly in NASCAR, which has its primary series sponsored by Sprint Nextel. Marc Arseneau, a motor sports enthusiast and race car driver, was struck by the lack of modern technological devices available to fans trackside, especially given the enhancements available to fans viewing from home. To address this void in the marketplace, Arseneau founded Kangaroo Media in 2001, and it was not long after that he teamed with Nextel (now known as Sprint Nextel) on a multimillion-dollar project that would forever change the way fans watch races trackside.[26]

Kangaroo TV's wireless device, which received its name because it comes in a pouch designed to hang around the user's neck, weighs less than a pound and measures 6.25 inches high by 4.125 inches wide by 1.5 inches deep, and has a 3.5-inch diagonal screen. It delivers a full-color, high-resolution, no-glare screen image, allowing at-track, real-time delivery of video, audio, and data during race events.[27] The company believes that Kangaroo TV, with as many as ten live video feeds, as well as replays, highlights, statistics, and "behind-the-scenes" audio, provides a "never-before-seen freedom in shaping your sports fan experience."[28]

After initially being made available during a 2003 Champ Car race, Kangaroo TV entered into an agreement with NASCAR Digital Entertainment in 2004 that garnered Kangaroo TV large-scale exposure. In conjunction with SPEED Channel and NASCAR tracks, Kangaroo TV was made available at seven NASCAR Craftsman Truck Series events toward the conclusion of the 2004 racing season.[29] Parlaying this successful rollout, Kangaroo TV was able to expand its relationship with NASCAR in August 2005 by negotiating a five-year licensing and supplier agreement with Sprint Nextel. Kangaroo TV received at least $10 million in revenue in the first year of the agreement, and Sprint Nextel agreed to license and market the multimedia handset at NASCAR races, as well as lend its technological expertise to the company.[30]

"When you are considering how best to deliver a near real-time experience for thousands of fans, a pretty extensive architecture and technology is required. When you have a large number of people in one venue, bandwidth becomes critical," says JP Brocket, Sprint Product Management's GM for wireless consumer applications. "The solution that Kangaroo TV and Sprint came up with is very difficult to replicate in a traditional wireless environment. The multitask mash-up broadcast over broadband is a very beautiful, elegant design that supports an almost unlimited number of devices and really gets you close to that real-time solution. With the shared IP and resources, they make a great partner."[31]

Now branded the "NASCAR Sprint FanView®," the device can be rented trackside for a weekend rate of approximately $49.99. However, existing Sprint customers can rent the device for $29.99 for the entire weekend. In an effort to cross-promote its affiliation with NASCAR, Sprint offers fans the opportunity to reserve the FanView for an upcoming race or purchase the device for about $370 at the company's dedicated URL, www.sprintfanview.com. The device, which only works at tracks during NASCAR Sprint Cup Series events, provides fans with access to the aforementioned SPEED Channel programming, as well as ESPN programming.

"It is a tremendous proposition on delivery of the 'Now Network' of the speed and the brand and the technology. There's no question that's one of the big things around FanView," Brocket says. "It's also in support of delivering that ultimate fan experience with the Sprint name, the Sprint brand, and the Sprint partnership with NASCAR."[32]

To capitalize on its relationship with NASCAR, and to acquire additional in-venue broadcast rights, Kangaroo Media successfully closed $5 million (Canadian) in financing in the weeks following the NASCAR announcement and raised an additional $20 million (Canadian) in March 2006.[33] By November 2006, *Time* magazine was hailing Kangaroo TV's newest motor sports offering as one of the best inventions of the year.[34]

Among the most intriguing in-venue broadcast rights secured with the proceeds of its newly raised capital was that with DIRECTV in September 2006, in which Kangaroo TV was granted the right to rebroadcast DIRECTV's "Sunday Ticket" into NFL stadiums for the Miami and Washington, D.C. franchises.[35] As part of the agreement, DIRECTV became the primary sponsor of the new service, and it was branded "NFL SUNDAY TICKET(TM) In-Stadium by DIRECTV."[36] Not only did this licensing agreement and marketing partnership reinforce the principals' marketing messages to their precise demographic, but elements of the Kangaroo TV football offering also grew to deliver specific value-added content to those with the device. Fans attending Houston Texans, Seattle Seahawks, or Washington Redskins games could specifically request statistics on particular players, presumably those players making up the fan's fantasy team roster. In addition to the "My Fantasy Team" page, those with the device enjoyed numerous other "traditional" amenities, such as those associated with the NASCAR Sprint FanView. The rental fee for the NFL device was about $25 per game, or $150 per season—with an additional $30 discount afforded season ticket holders or DIRECTV subscribers.

By the end of 2007, Kangaroo Media's revenues had doubled from 2006 and totaled $14.27 million.[37] Of importance, and unlike 2006 when the company had but a single source of revenue from Sprint and NASCAR, Kangaroo Media had made good on its pledge to acquire new broadcast properties and generated nearly 20 percent of its revenue from its new agreements with Formula One Racing and the NFL. It must be noted that the pursuing of these additional agreements contributed to the company's net loss growing by $2.75 million to $15.97 million for 2007.[38]

Kangaroo's increased revenues spawned additional opportunities, as evidenced by the fact that the NFL's Miami Dolphins, seeking to extend and differentiate their game-day experience, furthered their partnership with Kangaroo TV in 2009. The team provided five thousand wireless handheld devices to those sitting in suites and club seats. Witnessing the improvement to the game-day experience, Miami Dolphins owner Stephen Ross acquired a controlling share in Kangaroo Media in late 2009 and made the device, which was renamed Game Day Vision, available during the 2010 Super Bowl held at Sun Life Stadium in Miami. Game Day Vision was subsequently made available on a season-long basis for $259.[39] Heading into the 2010 season, Ross anticipated providing an additional 20,000 units, which was enough to supply his season ticket holders with one device for every two seats purchased.[40] To further expand the game-day experience league-wide, it was Ross's desire to have the device available not just at each NFL stadium, but also at each Super Bowl.

While Kangaroo Media was seeing success in football, it was also seeing opportunities in golf, as it has partnered with the European PGA Tour to provide Kangaroo TVs at numerous events. The company rented its devices at the 2008 Players Championship at Ponte Vedra Beach, Florida, for $25 a day, $45 for the weekend, and $75 for the tournament. The device received a flurry of positive reviews in the media, as it allowed fans to keep track of live golf shots going on throughout the tournament, as opposed to just the two or three players that they might be following. Kangaroo does have some competition in this space however, as San Diego–based WiseDV sampled a similar device at the 2008 Buick Invitational at Torrey Pines in La Jolla, California, which was subsequently available at the 2008 PGA Championship. WiseDV has also developed a device for tennis, and it has been used at the U.S. Open in Flushing Meadows, New York. WiseDV's MyLeaderboard, which is more of a data-centric device, was also available at the 2008 PGA Championship and has a licensing agreement with the PGA Tour to be used at just under twenty golf tournaments. The PGA Tour followed this licensing agreement by entering into a four-year, non-exclusive agreement with Kangaroo TV in 2009 whereby its products would be available at approximately fifty tournaments.

Moving forward, Kangaroo and Sprint will work to continue to innovate in an effort to hold off competitors. Kangaroo also will look to expand into more events after its initial successful forays into auto racing, golf, and football. However, leagues and events have not yet determined a clear framework for content distribution rights fees. "The rights and the content distribution fees are going to be the biggest challenges for us going forward," Brocket said. "It's a very fragmented model right now."[41]

CISCO

In the fall of 2006, Cisco Systems, the worldwide leader in networking solutions, created Cisco Sports and Entertainment, a standalone sports-and-entertainment-focused business unit. Formed to take advantage of the growing global demand for at-venue technology, and in an effort to parlay its leadership position, Cisco Sports and Entertainment also began offering a family of technology solutions known as Cisco Connected Sports (CCS). CCS enables venue owners and operators to reach increasingly empowered and tech-savvy fan bases. CCS assists venues in delivering more compelling game-day experiences, while simultaneously reducing costs and generating meaningful incremental revenue, each of which are particularly important during periods of rapidly escalating venue renovation and construction costs.

Cisco products and services have been integrated into noteworthy venues worldwide. In Europe, Cisco has partnered with Santiago Bernabéu Stadium in Spain and Manchester City Football Stadium in the United Kingdom. At Santiago Bernabéu Stadium, home of Real Madrid Club de Fútbol, Cisco has incorporated a video, voice, data, and wireless network across the seven-site complex. This network allows stadium management to remotely control everything from the 256 turnstiles to the stadium's lighting and has resulted in savings in excess of 50 percent in implementation and maintenance costs.[42] Furthermore, the volume of each stadium speaker can be individually adjusted depending on overall levels of background noise, providing fans the optimal sound quality experience during games.[43] Ron Ricci, vice president of corporate positioning for Cisco, explains that, because of the benefits delivered, "a network suddenly has massive relevancy to sports stadiums, sports teams, and ultimately entertainment venues" in regard to how those venues will be managed.[44]

Manchester City Football Stadium, which houses one of the U.K.'s oldest soccer clubs, has deployed both smart-card services and RF-equipped devices across the wireless network built by Cisco. The Cisco-built infrastructure creates the backbone that allows the team to use smart-cards with RF microchips, rather than paper tickets for season ticketholders. Fans gain expedited entry simply by swiping their cards at the entrance gates, allowing the Manchester City Football Club to admit more than twelve hundred fans per minute.[45] These smart-cards track all fan transactions, enabling the team to directly offer merchandise specials or personalized services such as fan loyalty offerings to the cardholder. The data generated from the card have allowed the team to implement a ticket buy-back plan that returns partial credit to season ticketholders if they cancel their seat in advance of games they do not plan to attend. This has allowed the club to resell those seats, driving incremental revenue in excess of $500,000 in the first season of implementation.[46] This is exactly what Ricci had in mind when referencing the team's willingness to utilize technology within their venues, stating that the technology platform "has to affect their (sports teams) business model and their business practices in some better way than it has done before."[47]

Allianz Arena, home to Munich's top two soccer teams, FC Bayern and TSV 1860, was outfitted with Cisco's technology prior to the arena playing host to the 2006 World Cup. The arena, seating sixty-six thousand, has been dubbed a new type of sports venue, integrating automated building and access control systems, electronic payment at all catering and retail outlets, and a hundred wireless access points throughout the arena. With the worldwide attention the World Cup brought to the arena and the need for up-to-the-minute press updates and employee communication, Cisco built the network with 99.99 percent reliability—on the average just one crash in every ten thousand days. In addition, for security purposes, the staff at Allianz Arena needed to know how many people were in the venue at any given time, and the automated building and access control system allowed them to do so in real time. The access control system also uses RFID smart-cards, like Manchester City Football Club, allowing venue operators to check whether people have valid tickets and are at the correct gate. Stefan Leihard, chief executive at Allianz Arena, says that the IP network allows them "to manage a huge stadium with only a few employees."[48] Reinforcing this statement is the reality that a groundsman can check the state of the pitch from his home via the Internet, and can automatically make any necessary adjustments from his keyboard. Throughout the stadium, venue operators can access all the stadium's business controls from wireless handheld devices, further easing the ability to manage the stadium on game day.

Cisco products have also been integrated into approximately 70 percent of the venues in North America. The company's most comprehensive and sophisticated incorporation of venue technology is on display at two marquee venues that opened in 2009. Cisco partnered with the New York Yankees to integrate Cisco solutions within the franchise's new $1.3 billion stadium. Cisco CEO John Chambers claimed that the extensive technology integration called StadiumVision "will change all sports," presumably in reference to the creation of the ultimate fan experience.[49] More than one thousand centrally controlled flat-panel HDTV monitors have been installed throughout the stadium so that fans won't miss a moment as they walk from their seats to the restrooms, concessions stands, or in-stadium restaurants and bars. Video cameras have been placed around the field so that the fan can experience the game from multiple angles—the dugout, the outfield, or even their favorite player's view. The monitors are also used to provide real-time sports scores, Yankees trivia, news, and weather—all on the same screen. Following games, the monitors direct patrons to the nearest exits, as well as provide current traffic information. When the stadium is being utilized on non-game days, the monitors can be used to display customized content for special events and activities. The premium luxury suites, which cost as much as $850,000 per year, have been equipped with touch-screen Internet Protocol (IP) phones that allow fans to order concessions and Yankees merchandise for delivery in-suite, resulting in new and significant revenue streams.[50] Those in luxury suites can also choose which angles of the field they want to see on their own in-suite HDTV monitors. In addition, the Yankees can install Cisco's TelePresence video technology in not only the stadium but also a Bronx public library, so that the athletes can reach out to the kids and fans in the community.

Like the Yankees' new stadium, the new venue for the Dallas Cowboys has been outfitted for today but also has been equipped with the infrastructure necessary to remain relevant for years. "We wanted to future-proof it," recalls the Dallas Cowboys CIO, Pete Walsh. "We picked technology infrastructure that will take us to the next 15 to 20 years."[51] Within its 3.2 million square feet, the eighty-thousand-seat stadium (expandable to a hundred thousand seats) features an iconic, center-hung, seventy-foot tall HD videoboard, over fifteen cameras to capture live in-venue video content, and over 2,900 video screens networked by Cisco StadiumVision. Other technical features include RFID bracelets for children so that if they get lost parents can use technology to find them, as well as a web-based driving direction application so that fans can plan their routes from home directly into their specific parking space.

Cisco has primed these stadiums to support fans' future use of mobile technology, including ordering concessions, viewing instant replays, playing fantasy sports, and chatting real time with friends inside the stadium, all from one's own personal mobile device. As consumers continue to accept, gravitate toward, and demand more advanced technologies, sports venues will continue to more deftly integrate comprehensive technology offerings within venues to meet these fan expectations. Accordingly, venue operators and team owners will continue to look to Cisco in order to provide a more integrated fan experience. Cisco is in a favorable position to capitalize on this fan demand by delivering additional revenue opportunities for teams while also being more responsive to fans, as well as to advertisers and sponsors.

VENUE TECHNOLOGY: THE BOTTOM LINE

University of Phoenix Stadium, Sprint's FanView, and Cisco's comprehensive approach to technology integration all reinforce technology's rapidly advancing role in, around, and throughout sports venues. With products and services that run the gamut, one consistency exists among these three: all are dedicated to improving and enhancing the game-day experience for fans and do so in a manner that provides meaningful branding opportunities, as well as much-needed incremental revenue. As these and other industry stakeholders continue to shape and refine the technology-driven game-day presentation, they must remain mindful that patrons seek a total experience that allows them to enjoy technological capabilities on their own terms. When contemplating how best to accommodate this necessity, venue owners and operators, among others, must appreciate that venue flexibility is crucial, as is the requirement to balance the desire for environmentally friendly solutions with the realities of revenue generation.

It's About the Total Experience

In-venue creature comforts have evolved—a stadium seat with a back on it and traditional ballpark fare no longer constitute a "total experience." Instead, fans expect to be entertained—or at the very least have unfettered access to entertainment while at sporting events. This entertainment, which must involve the latest technology, can be delivered (pushed) directly by the team or venue, or can be accessed (pulled) by fans depending on their specific wants and needs. Technology companies, venue owners and operators, vendors, sponsors, local businesses, and municipalities are among those affected by rapidly advancing in-venue technology.

Even though most fans are unaware of a team's or venue's technology partner, this is less important to certain technology companies, such as Cisco, which consider their involvement in sports to be a uniquely powerful branding and business development platform in its own right. A company's ability to wire a stadium or otherwise be instrumental in the successful development of a venue affords it the opportunity to market its services to others, including suite holders, sponsors, and local municipalities. For technology-oriented companies such as Sprint seeking to market to fans, the ability to place its branded products and services literally in the hands of its (potential) consumers is a powerful way to build brand affinity, encourage trial usage and, ideally, secure long-term, brand-loyal consumers.

As fans consume in-venue technology, and often do so without regard to its origin or infrastructure, venue owners and operators have the opportunity to improve the game-day experience by improving venue efficiencies and converting economies of scale to revenue-generating activities. A single technology platform can ensure that a "smart" building can not only respond more quickly to staff and fan needs but also begin to anticipate them. Customized marketing and promotional campaigns, whether designed to sell more in-venue product such as concessions or merchandise, or promote a team's sponsors or charitable causes, will continue to be delivered with precision utilizing "find me, follow me" and on-demand technologies. Fans will embrace receiving ticket bar codes to their cell phones and the ability to order concessions from the comfort of their own seats provided it does not come across as too intrusive, or "Big Brotherish." Should fans deem these technological advancements an infringement, either to their privacy or to their ability to enjoy the game itself, the delivery of such technology and the marketing and financial benefits associated with it will be compromised. In addition, the game itself will be affected by this technology. Crowd noise and general aesthetics may vary greatly depending on how the venue operators integrate these new options.

In addition to sports franchises and leagues at both amateur and professional levels needing to be vigilant when determining appropriate levels of venue technology, so too must vendors and sponsors, whose brands may be adversely affected if consumers deem their presence as too invasive. In an era of measurable marketing and sales activation, technology that carries sophisticated patron tracking is not only available and utilized but relied on. Understanding patrons' buying patterns can result in customized messaging to the extent that a fan can be notified of purchase opportunities. For instance, a fan that has purchased numerous commemorative bobbleheads can be reminded that the one he appears to be missing to complete his collection is on sale at the merchandise kiosk located near his seat. While this will certainly motivate some sponsors and licensees to participate, others will be concerned about the intrusive nature of such opportunities.

Similar forms of technology can help moderate other game-day activities, such as tracking of fan consumption of alcohol and adjusting of concession prices based on game-day patterns and preferences, ultimately optimizing revenue generation while simultaneously improving the game-day experience for all.

Surrounding businesses may view improved in-venue technological improvements with ambivalence. A more efficient game-day experience, one that includes the use of technology to direct patrons into and out of the venue, will have an impact on adjacent businesses. To the extent it becomes easier to navigate venue ingress and egress, nearby retail establishments may be helped or harmed depending on their location and ability to take advantage of changing arrival and departure patterns. Accordingly, and in an effort to ensure that their interests and concerns are taken into consideration, local businesses must participate in the venue-development process.

Any decline in local business brought about by increased in-venue efficiencies could have a negative impact on local municipalities that generate tax revenue from nearby bars and restaurants, as well as on the employees of those businesses. While municipalities would certainly still generate taxes from in-venue sales, improved technology could result in fewer seasonal jobs for local workers and, over time, influence a city's interest in allocating public dollars to the pursuit of new or renovated venues.

Flexibility Is Key

Given the exorbitant costs associated with venue renovation and construction, (re)constructing venues with built-in flexibility is key in order to maximize long-term revenue potential. Agile venues capable of accommodating a wide variety of sports and entertainment events, as well as other business and community-oriented events, substantially improve a venue's ability to be profitable. It is crucial, however, that venue owners and operators be able to tailor the in-venue fan experiences for each event, even if some are occurring simultaneously. Owners and operators must also consider the potential for accelerated wear and tear on the venue, as well as the business needs of a diverse, and sometimes conflicting, array of sponsors. The adaptability of their staff must also be taken into account when considering certain events.

Extensively planned and well-thought-out venues also have a stronger chance of securing increasingly scarce public investment because these venues are positioned to contribute to the local communities and related public sectors on non-game days. Such an approach is displayed at University of Phoenix Stadium, which considered the eventual needs of major sporting events, such as the Super Bowl, when originally devising its venue and associated technological needs and related scalability, as well as the ability to add more luxury suites. In such scenarios, franchise owners, local municipalities and (business) communities, and sponsors are deeply affected, as are venue and architectural design firms.

Venue flexibility affords franchise owners the opportunity to extend their brands and generate incremental revenue through the hosting of a wider range of events. Added diversity in turn exposes (casual) fans and non-fans alike to the venue and, provided they have a satisfying experience, leads to enhanced affinity among many stakeholder groups. Venues lacking agility will see their primary tenants seek improvements in order to capture additional revenue or relocate should the venue not allow them to be competitive; this was the case for the Arizona Cardinals at Sun Devil Stadium in Tempe, Arizona.

Venues offering comprehensive sports, business, and entertainment options are invaluable to surrounding sports-anchored developments, as well as the (business) community at large. Increases in tourism brought about by the hosting of a diverse number of events serve as a catalyst for economic impact, and bring with them wide-ranging support from elected officials, local businesses, and taxpayers alike. Properly devised and implemented, flexible venues are able to make strong arguments for (additional) public sector investment. This in turn not only stabilizes the sports franchise tenant, but also enables it to extend the franchise value over time by securing more committed fans that appreciate the role the franchise plays community-wide.

Architectural and venue design firms that take sponsor activation into account when planning flexible facilities position franchise owners to make compelling cases when securing marketing partnerships. When combining customized activation with the sense of community presence afforded flexible venues, sponsors are more inclined to align their marketing strategies with those of the venue and franchise. This is even more pronounced when those sponsors seek to reach the demographics represented by the wide range of events hosted. This ultimately enhances the sponsor's brand value, as well as that of the franchise and the community.

Balancing the Green

Among the biggest challenges facing those who incorporate cutting-edge venue technology into venues is balancing the need to become and remain more environmentally sound without hampering the fan experience or compromising revenue generation. In venue renovation and construction, there is a strong motivation to become LEED (Leadership in Energy & Environmental Design) certified. LEED certification is the recognized standard for measuring building sustainability and generally serves to recognize facilities that are "green." While notable on a variety of levels ranging from natural resource conservation to increased cost efficiencies, "going green" can also pose risks to certain stakeholders. Because of this dynamic, many industry stakeholders are affected by the future of venue technology, including venue owners and operators, franchises, municipalities, sponsors, and those that develop and provide the technology and related infrastructure necessary to implement such initiatives.

Self-sustaining and energy-efficient venues, such as those that generate their own power, recycle water and other products, incorporate biodegradable materials into the venue development and management process, or some combination thereof are certainly poised to enjoy long-term cost savings. But they are also uniquely positioned to enjoy substantial marketing and branding benefits as well. For example, Cowboys Stadium became the first venue in the United States to join the Environmental Protection Agency's National Environmental Performance Track System. In achieving this recognition, the venue's efforts (along with those of the primary tenant, the NFL's Dallas Cowboys) to meet and sustain recognized green goals will be monitored. This achievement permits the team to market itself as a noteworthy community citizen, reinforcing this leadership position with game-day promotions designed to generate environmental awareness and boost positive publicity about the venue and the team. Besides the environmental benefits, these two developments will also enable each to extend their brand reach.

However, fan backlash may arise if fans believe they are being asked to finance, through increased ticket prices and so on, the cost of going green. Such a sentiment would be exacerbated if these same fans believe that their favorite team is investing in such initiatives or related environmental causes at the expense of fielding a competitive team. Staunch support from advocacy groups, among others, could serve to blunt fan criticism—if not grow the fan base—given the positive media attention and other marketing resources brought to bear. With this in mind, Major League Baseball currently partners with the National Resources Defense Council (NRDC), an environmental advocacy group based in New York, in an effort to assist its teams' green initiatives.

Facilities stressing environmental efficiencies also have an impact on municipalities and sponsors, each of which may be more inclined to invest in, or market through, the venue, its tenants, and special events. Municipalities are inclined to provide tax breaks or other incentives to venues delivering long-term, positive environmental impacts. In addition, the ability for sponsors to partner with green facilities adds a compelling dynamic to sponsors' existing business-to-business and business-to-consumer in-venue sports marketing strategies.

Accordingly, stakeholders that develop or provide the technology and related infrastructure necessary to implement green initiatives, such as architectural and design firms, as well as technology providers, must work closely to strike the proper balance between environmental and financial prudence.

VENUE TECHNOLOGY AND CONVERGENCE: FINAL THOUGHTS FROM COWBOYS STADIUM'S JACK HILL[52]

Jack Hill is the stadium general manager for Cowboys Stadium. Cowboys Stadium is home to the NFL's Dallas Cowboys and was named Sports Facility of the Year in 2010 by the SportsBusiness Journal, *in large part due to the diversity of events it held, including the NBA All-Star Game, which boasted the largest crowd to ever watch a basketball game, 108,713. Hill shared his perspective on convergence and venue technology with the SBI.*

SBI: How has venue technology changed the way the industry approaches the business of sports?

HILL: I believe there are three categories of technology: technology in general, technology with design, and technology with operations. Having been involved with all three phases, it has been interesting to watch how the three come together to change the way venues are constructed and marketed, and how related products and services are sold.

SBI: Can you provide an example that you have found particularly compelling over the years that features these elements?

HILL: Advancements in rendering have dramatically changed this industry. From a safety perspective, we can convey to fire marshals where smoke will travel, and how the heat will be distributed. From a sports perspective, we can accurately model the trajectory of a fly ball which, believe it or not, has serious ramifications for a venue and the teams that play there. We used this technology when I worked on the Texas Rangers ballpark in Arlington. We conducted a wind study which showed the temperature and how the wind would change under different conditions. Originally, the ballpark had a two-story building in center field. Bobby Valentine, the manager of the Rangers at the time, saw the model and mentioned that because of the wind current and the two-story building, players wouldn't be able to hit home runs at the stadium. We subsequently brought it to RWDI Labs to study it further using a wind tunnel, and it turned out he was right. We had to add a couple more stories and billboards to abate the wind in order to fix the problem.

SBI: Do you think fans, sponsors, or local governments appreciate the amount of work that goes into venue development? What do you think stands out to fans the most?

HILL: No, I don't think they appreciate or realize the amount of work that goes into these developments. With the Cowboys Stadium project, we surveyed the fans regarding their experience at the old Texas Stadium. Their responses indicated that the traffic experience was terrible because people tailgating took up multiple spaces in the parking lot where other people had passes to park. As a result, once fans arrived at the stadium, they were unable to park in the assigned lots for which they had already paid. We changed the policy to accommodate these fans but this affected the overall tailgating experience. Through our planning process for the new stadium we hired a consultant to help us assess parking. We currently have seventeen access points instead of the three that the old stadium had. Also, fans can now go online to dallascowboysmaps. com, type in their zip code, and find the best route to the stadium and their specific parking lot. The computer calculates everything, including congestion and road construction. This provides fans the quickest and easiest way to park, even if it sometimes seems counterintuitive to how they are accustomed to getting to their designated parking area. This benefits us because the fans have a better pre-game experience and can get into the stadium earlier. In addition to reducing the stress, it allows them to spend more time inside the stadium, likely spending money on concessions and team merchandise.

SBI: What other advancements have you seen with the new stadium?

HILL: Fans can watch one of over three thousand IP-based televisions throughout the stadium. We went out on a limb a bit with the IP TVs instead of co-ax-based television because the technology is very new. Cisco convinced us that this was the wave of the future because it allows the flexibility to literally put a different image on each monitor—and they were right because the team, our sponsors, and the fans really enjoy them.

SBI: Where have sponsors seen the biggest change with respect to technology?

HILL: Sponsors' ability to advertise and promote their products in the building is a huge benefit to all involved. The immersive experience of coming to the stadium and having any one of over three thousand monitors pitching their products is very attractive. Fans cannot stand in a concession line right now without seeing an ad that is dynamic instead of static. We can run a series of electronic ads for the sponsors and sell these by the minute instead of static signs and billboards that were once sold on a one-time basis for the entire season. This makes the whole process more auditable and flexible. Importantly, this has been accomplished without over-commercializing the venue, as we have always hoped to strike a balance between the quality and quantity of the marketing taking place.

SBI: Can you talk a bit about the stadium's high definition board and its impact on the fan experience?

HILL: We are still uncovering new ways to market and use the board which, at a height of 90 feet above the field with dimensions of 160 feet by 72 feet, is currently the largest HD board in the world. The stadium's design is such that it is built around arches that run through it which allowed us to hang the board, which weighs 1,200,000 pounds, over the middle of the field. It has enhanced the overall fan experience, particularly for those that are in the upper deck. The 6-foot, 5-inch player on the field is 65 feet tall and crystal clear on the HD board. Outside of football, we have had concerts and artists utilize the board during their performances. The board has become so popular that we have even had complaints when artists have chosen not to utilize it—even though we were not responsible for the decision. We have also constructed a mechanism that allows the board to be raised and lowered to the point where it can drop to as low as 25 feet above the field. In addition, we also maintain the capacity to hang other boards underneath the big board for events such as fights and basketball games, thereby giving us the flexibility to hold a variety of events.

SBI: What other technological elements stand out in the stadium?

HILL: The retractable roof. Because of its potential impact on game-day conditions and strategy, the NFL requires us to notify them ninety minutes before the game as to whether it will be open or closed.

SBI: What are the biggest challenges you face with venue technology?

HILL: We have to work with our fans about how best to utilize the technology that we have implemented stadium-wide. Fortunately, our fan base is technologically advanced, and this helps us deliver a great game-day experience to them. In addition to ensuring a great fan experience, the issue of "future proofing" venues is also a concern. As part of the program design, you have to make sure you have the space to accommodate new technology. Convincing stadium owners to leave free space is difficult because it can be used for revenue-generating purposes. But in order to maintain technological flexibility and scalability, reserving space is important.

SBI: What advice would you give those trying to monetize venue technology?

HILL: At the end of the day, you have to listen to your fans. You also have to look at everything and conduct a cost-benefit analysis. As the technology changes, you have to look at the cost implications and determine how much it enhances the fan experience. Ultimately, the goal is to have fans enjoy the building regardless of whether their team wins or loses. You also have to be conscientious about not resting on your laurels. We have a set of metrics that measure our results after every game and event. We know when the last car left the lot, how long it took a suite to have its food delivered, and how long the average concession line was. At the end of the season, it is easy to assess where we have succeeded and where room for improvement exists. Overall, and as a result of venue technology, we can continue to perfect the fan experience.

9 CORPORATE MARKETING

ESPN'S WIDE WORLD OF SPORTS

It was a clear and sunny day in Lake Buena Vista, Florida, on May 13, 2008. Ken Potrock eagerly watched as Disney executives announced the company's intention to rebrand the Wide World of Sports Complex. The facility would now incorporate myriad interactive elements and boast the ESPN name, known by fans everywhere as the "Worldwide Leader in Sports." The repositioning made perfect sense given Disney's ownership of ESPN and ESPN's current presence at the Walt Disney World Resort that included an ESPN Club restaurant and an annual "ESPN The Weekend" fan event at Disney's Hollywood Studio—both of which are routinely embraced by the sports enthusiasts visiting the Complex.

"Our involvement in the Disney sports complex will provide greater opportunities for us to connect directly with athletes, coaches, and fans in a highly immersive way," said George Bodenheimer, president of ESPN and ABC Sports. "Our involvement also provides us with a unique and exciting new media platform that will enable our advertisers and sponsors to reach new customers and bring their products and services to life."[1] Just months earlier, Potrock had been promoted to become senior vice president of Global Sports Enterprises, effectively placing him in charge of Disney's enormous athletic venue. In the previous decade, under the leadership of former Cincinnati Bengals linebacker Reggie Williams, Disney's Complex had evolved to become a thriving sports destination that brought hundreds of thousands of visitors annually to the Orlando area.

Williams had left the project for health reasons in late 2007, and Potrock was given the challenge of trying to find new ways to expand the facility's success and international stature and, in the process, increase revenue. While the Complex had worked extremely well for Disney in the past, given its ability to leverage its theme parks and hotels, it had never quite taken full advantage of the Disney brand and its considerable reach. Accordingly, Potrock and his fellow Disney executives decided a rebranding of the facility was in order.

In February 2010, following years of research and analysis, Disney unveiled the rebranded ESPN Wide World of Sports Complex. "Rebranding with ESPN is one of those, 'Why didn't we do this before?' ideas," Potrock said prior to the rebranding.[2] "If you're in the sports business and you happen to own a brand with the power of ESPN, why wouldn't you leverage that?"[3] Precisely how Potrock would leverage the ESPN brand to further position the facility as the nation's preeminent multisport venue would be his primary challenge in the months and years ahead.

Building the Wide World of Sports Complex

In 1971, the Walt Disney Company opened the Walt Disney World Resort just outside of Orlando, Florida, providing the company with the East Coast outpost it had been seeking for nearly a decade. Disney had enjoyed tremendous success with Disneyland in Anaheim, California, but realized that only 2 percent of its visitors came from east of the Mississippi River, where 75 percent of the country's population resided.[4]

Throughout the 1960s, and in an effort to control most of the business surrounding its planned theme park, Disney quietly purchased land in Orange and Osceola Counties in Central Florida. In 1965, just one year before his death, Walt Disney himself announced his vision for a new theme park, as well as EPCOT Center, both of which would become the major vacation destinations they remain today.

Over time, the Walt Disney World Resort added more attractions, culminating in the thirty-thousand-acre site that hosts four theme parks; two water parks; twenty-four Disney-owned hotels; five golf courses; and numerous shopping, dining, and recreation venues. The resort attracts in excess of sixteen million visitors each year.[5]

In 1995, Disney broke ground on the $100 million Complex, which opened two years later. The site would host the headquarters for the Amateur Athletic Union (AAU), as well as a 10,000-seat baseball stadium; a 5,500-seat fieldhouse that included six basketball courts; a tennis complex; and dozens of other soccer, football, lacrosse, baseball, and softball fields. The Complex also hosted the Atlanta Braves spring training camp, the Tampa Bay Buccaneers training camp, and the NBA Pre-Draft Camp, as well as a wide assortment of youth sporting events, including Pop Warner football and events featuring cheer and dance. At the time, Disney officials said the Complex was built for four reasons: to promote Walt Disney World, fill hotel rooms, attract sponsors, and enhance Walt Disney World Resort's image as a sports destination.[6]

Still, in its early years, the Complex struggled. Disney hosted the biggest events it possibly could, attracting a smorgasbord of athletic competitions to which it attempted to sell tickets. This included numerous Harlem Globetrotters games, international youth soccer tournaments, collegiate tournaments in several sports for the Atlantic Coast and Metro-Atlantic Athletic Conferences, a college football All-Star game, and U.S. and international events for sports such as wrestling, boxing, track and field, beach volleyball, and basketball.

While Orlando was a growing market, it was still only the twenty-seventh largest in the U.S., with a population of approximately two million, so it was uncommon that enough residents in the area would be willing and able to fill the venues each night. Therefore, Disney looked to expand the reach, scope, and overall allure of the Complex.

Disney sports executives became responsible for generating more value from the under-utilized complex. What they found was that attendance was not the sole determinant for success, and that by better aligning the Complex's association with Disney, it could become the world's premier multisport venue, increasing Disney shareholder value in the process.

"We weren't effectively leveraging Disney, and in particular Disney World," Potrock recalls. "There was a standoffishness that kept the sports business separate from the Walt Disney World business. In the early days there were questions about the credibility of Disney entering the sports world."[7]

A Sports Destination

Disney refocused the venue's efforts to leverage Disney World as a sports destination. Rather than stretch the staff to attract the biggest and best events possible, Disney instead worked to attract a large quantity of youth, amateur, and collegiate sporting events. Many of these youth teams came from around the world, lured by the added feature of a trip to Disney World while competing at a first-class sports venue.

The Complex worked with the theme parks and the on-site resort hotels to create a wide variety of vacation packages. The packages were not only for the youth teams, but also targeted "affiliated spectators," those demonstrating their support for the athletes such as parents, family, and friends. Disney created opportunities for the teams to be picked up at the Orlando airport by shuttle and then stay at a Disney hotel, compete in Disney sports facilities, attend several Disney theme parks, and shop and dine at Disney-owned establishments. It was not uncommon for an entire team and their supporters to spend an entire week at Disney World without ever leaving the premises.

Several sports associations were attracted to the Complex because of the comprehensive and enjoyable vacation packages that could accompany their events. Disney worked to make many of these packages affordable so that they would often be on par, price-wise, with other cities that bid to host youth sporting events. "You have to play to your strength, and here in Florida that's about hospitality. It's about 'destination,'" Potrock says. "People choose to come here from far away for a reason, whether it's for the theme parks, entertainment, vacation, or to the Wide World of Sports Complex for competition. I call it a 'double dip experience.' Many people are coming here for pre-eminent competition, but they're also having a good time while they're doing it."[8]

As a result, the Complex began to flourish. The Complex has attracted millions of athletes in total, and now averages nearly 300,000 athletes and 1.5 million spectators per year.[9] The AAU holds over forty different annual national championships at the Complex alone, and the venue itself holds nearly two hundred sporting events per year. Since opening, the Complex has attracted athletes from nearly seventy countries that have participated in sixty different sports.[10] Events such as the Disney Soccer Showcase, which was created in 2000, have now become the nation's top youth event for the sport. The U.S. Specialty Sports Association, which holds events for a wide variety of sports, uses the facility for six weekends a year, and its annual softball tournament brings in ten thousand athletes and thirty thousand people total.[11] It's estimated that roughly half of all people associated with these events stay in a Disney hotel, and the rest stay in nearby hotels that serve as a boon to the local Orlando and Kissimmee economies.[12]

The Complex has also become popular with many top coaches who wish to train athletes. Superstar athletes including Peyton Manning and Mia Hamm have competed at or hosted exhibitions or clinics at the Complex. It is also now home to a wide variety of endurance events, including the Walt Disney World Marathon and Princess Half Marathon.

Retail opportunities at these events were (and remain) plentiful. For every event held at the Complex, a separate line of merchandise was produced that was purchased by about 90 percent of attendees.[13] The merchandise arm of Disney found that nearly 40 percent of these event-related retail items were purchased by women, and thus made sure to have a variety of products available to suit their needs.[14]

The success of the Complex created sponsorship opportunities as well, particularly by brands that are associated with families. The Ballpark at Disney's Wide World of Sports Complex, which hosted Atlanta Braves spring training and later hosted several Tampa Bay Rays regular season games and inaugural World Baseball Classic games, was renamed Champion Stadium after Hanesbrands Inc. purchased the naming rights. Hewlett-Packard (HP) purchased the naming rights to the field house in 2010, and featured the HP brand, while the Complex's plethora of fields became Hess Sports Fields. Alamo Rent-A-Car, Josten's, Toro, and Sharpie also established significant marketing presences at the site. In addition, English Premier League soccer club Chelsea became the official soccer club of the Complex. The team became a presenting sponsor of the Disney Soccer Showcase, and would host coaching and player clinics at the Complex, along with occasionally training there. "These are all very strong and very solid brands," Potrock says. "But they're not just interested in hanging a sign. They want to activate with the athletes that are at our complex."[15]

The Complex engages with its partners in unique ways, and offers sponsors the free opportunity to use services from Creative Inc., a concepting division of Walt Disney World Marketing. This allows its corporate partners to best leverage their sponsorship of the Complex. "We ask all of our partners, 'Are there things you're trying to do with your brand that you can't do now, and how can we help?'" Potrock said. "We want a win-win situation for everyone."[16]

Disney believes that there is still more demand that the Complex can meet. In late 2008, it completed a new 70,000-square-foot fieldhouse called the Josten's Center; Josten's is a leading manufacturer of high school and college rings and yearbooks. The facility can accommodate twelve volleyball courts, six basketball courts, or two roller hockey rinks, and also host events for wrestling, martial arts, and the Special Olympics, among other sports. In 2010, the Complex further diversified its portfolio by hosting such events as Major League Gaming's regional championships and the National Archery in Schools Program. In 2012, Disney is expected to complete the building of a 160,000-square-foot one-hundred-lane bowling alley, which will be the largest in the U.S. It will host annual men's and women's opens of the U.S. Bowling Congress tournament that draws eighty thousand participants a year.[17]

The Next Chapter

Potrock replaced Williams in late 2007 and was immediately impressed by what he saw. "I was blown away by what was happening there," he said. "There were 740 soccer teams using the facilities, one hundred major college coaches watching them, college football athletes preparing for combines, the University of Florida football team training for a bowl game and, in the field house, 120 high school basketball teams competing."[18]

With a new partnership agreement with ESPN finalized, Potrock and his team had to continue to fill Disney and surrounding area hotels with athletes while also leveraging the ESPN brand. For ESPN, the new partnership provided greater efficiency and control over event broadcasts that it would produce at the Complex's new broadcast production facility. As part of the re-branding, ESPN said it would increase the number of events it broadcast from the Complex, already at twenty.[19] One of these events included a Thanksgiving weekend college basketball tournament called the Old Spice Classic. While there were open seats at the field house in 2008, the event featured as impressive a lineup of top-ranked NCAA schools as any early season basketball tournament, and it provided ESPN the opportunity to air some marquee matchups.

ESPN had already been investing heavily in youth and amateur sports with the 2005 launch of cable network ESPNU and the 2008 launch of ESPN RISE, a multimedia brand targeting fourteen- to eighteen-year-olds with high school sports content across ESPN's media platforms. In fact, in the summer of 2009 the Complex hosted the first ever RISE Games, sponsored by Target. In 2010, more than thirteen thousand student athletes competed at the event held in mid-July.[20]

Adding to the ESPN integration of the Complex, ESPN Innovation Lab was opened in late 2009. This state-of-the-art facility is used as a working research facility that is tasked with developing new tools for on-air coverage of events. Technology applications that have come out of the lab include Ball Track, which was utilized during the 2009 "MLB Home Run Derby"; ESPN Snap Zoom, which was included on ESPN's broadcast of *Monday Night Football*; and ESPN3D, which was featured throughout the 2010 World Cup. The ESPN Innovation Lab is open to visitors as well, thereby adding another point of contact with the ESPN brand.

With a commanding presence at the Complex, ESPN further enhances its brand with youth athletes and families. These athletes can compete in premier events at Disney's first-class facilities and potentially be broadcast as if they were on *SportsCenter* or find themselves on ESPN3. And later, between a visit to a theme park or water park, they can eat, play, or just relax at the new ESPN Wide World of Sports Grill and watch HD highlights of their own sports competitions recorded earlier in the day. Disney has labeled this the "ESPN effect," which essentially provides athletes visiting the Complex the experience of being on ESPN itself.[21]

"Now even my sons can feel as if they've made the big time. They're on ESPN," Potrock says. "And they know that win or lose, I'm taking them to Disney World."[22]

CORPORATE MARKETING: AN OVERVIEW

The combining of the ESPN and Disney brands to develop the Complex illustrates just one of the myriad ways corporations have gone about building brand equity through sports. Overall, corporations strive to achieve sustainable competitive advantages when utilizing sports marketing. This is particularly true when it comes to marketing their products and services at sports venues.

Although there are modern-day examples of at-venue corporate marketing dating back to the early part of the twentieth century, such as Nathan's "sponsorship" of the Coney Island Hot Dog Eating Contest beginning in 1916, the first truly comprehensive marketing alliances did not appear until the 1950s.

Anheuser-Busch's 1953 purchase of the St. Louis Cardinal's Sportsman's Park and the subsequent renaming of it to Busch Stadium is one of the first documented cases of venue-centric corporate branding in sports. Anheuser-Busch originally proposed to rename the stadium "Budweiser Stadium," after the iconic American lager, but MLB commissioner Ford Frick denied the request citing concerns over commercialization.[23]

Not long after being allowed to rename the stadium, Anheuser-Busch released "Busch Bavarian Beer," known to this day as Busch Beer. The successive purchase of the St. Louis Cardinals and their home field by Anheuser-Busch in 1953 was a distinct marketing play by August Busch Jr., then president of the company, as evidenced by Busch's comments in a board of directors meeting that the grounds for the purchase of the team was its promotional potential.[24] According to a Busch family biography, "The Cardinals were quickly transformed into a traveling billboard for the brewery."[25] History also suggests that August Busch Jr. informed his board of directors that the development of the Cardinals would have untold value for Anheuser-Busch, and that changing the stadium name to that of the company was one of the finest moves in the history of Anheuser-Busch.[26]

Venue-related sports marketing and corporate branding took permanent hold in the 1970s with the first sponsorship of a major sports series in the NASCAR Winston Cup Series, and the execution of the first naming rights deals for stadiums, most notably Schaefer Stadium and Rich Stadium.

Due to the passing of the Public Health Cigarette Smoking Act, R. J. Reynolds Tobacco Company was banned from advertising on television and radio beginning in 1971. Not only did this development force the reallocation of marketing dollars, it also required the company to be more creative and tactical when allocating marketing resources. Because R. J. Reynolds recognized the demographic fit with NASCAR fans, it negotiated to become the primary sponsor of NASCAR's premier racing division, ultimately renaming it the "NASCAR Winston Cup Series" after the company's cigarette brand, Winston.

The first naming rights deals for stadiums occurred at about the same time, when the Schaefer Brewing Company paid the New England Patriots $150,000 in 1971 for stadium naming rights through 1982, while in 1973 the Buffalo Bills sold the rights to name their new stadium to Rich Foods, Inc., which agreed to pay $1.5 million over twenty-five years.[27] Opportunity for branding and marketing awareness was not lost on either of these companies. The Schaefer Brewing Company's famous slogan "The one beer to have when you're having more than one" was fitting for the notoriously unruly Boston fans.

These early examples were the precursor to the extensive venue-centric corporate marketing deals that followed in the 1980s and continue today. In 1986, John Hancock Financial Services became the first corporation to sponsor a college football post-season bowl game when the company sponsored the Sun Bowl, which was, in the process, renamed the John Hancock Sun Bowl. This sponsorship was pertinent in meeting the company goal of reshaping its image from old-fashioned and conservative to modern and innovative, while also building brand recognition on the West Coast for a primarily East Coast–based business.

In the twenty years since Hancock's landmark sponsorship, at-venue sports marketing has continued to grow, with nearly every major sports facility not only carrying a corporate name but extensively weaving corporate marketing initiatives throughout. Beyond historic examples are contemporary ones that have taken the corporate presence at sporting events and facilities to previously unheard of levels, particularly ESPN's Wide World of Sports Complex; London's O_2 Dome; and Red Bull's marketing ubiquity, as witnessed at many of its own branded events.

THE O_2

The Millennium Dome, which opened on January 1, 2000, and cost $1.5 billion to construct, was a giant white tent-like structure reaching nearly 1,200 feet in diameter and standing 165 feet high. Built along London's River Thames and financed predominantly through public funding, the Millennium Dome immediately became one of the United Kingdom's most recognizable landmarks. Although it was Britain's largest tourist attraction in 2000 with 6.5 million visitors, it was labeled London's "great white elephant" for reaching only half of the original government-promised 12 million visitors.[28] With no apparent succession plan in place and recurring financial problems, the Millennium Dome closed its doors at the end of 2000.

The dome was purchased by Anschutz Entertainment Group (AEG) in 2002 and reopened in 2007 as The O_2, a $700 million redevelopment of the original. The O_2 was then showcased as the sports and entertainment centerpiece of a $3.6 billion regeneration of London's Greenwich Peninsula.[29] Beneath the dome are twenty acres that include a 20,000-seat sports arena and concert hall called The O_2 arena, an intimate 2,350-seat music venue called indigO_2, an eleven-screen cinema with one 750-seat theatre that displays Europe's largest movie screen, a seventy-thousand-square foot exhibition space, and numerous additional entertainment options including over twenty upscale bars, clubs, and restaurants.

AEG Europe CEO David Campbell believes the mix of sports and entertainment is vital, noting, "Music drives the business in Europe because it doesn't have the same professional sports structure as the United States."[30] In fact, The O_2 arena sold more than 1.3 million tickets prior to its opening and, in the first year, surpassed New York's Madison Square Garden as the busiest music venue in the world, selling 2.2 million tickets.[31] The arena has surpassed the record by hosting music legends such as Bon Jovi, the Rolling Stones, Led Zeppelin, and Elton John. The arena has also hosted a wide array of major sporting events including NBA preseason games, NHL regular season games, championship boxing and mixed martial arts bouts, the Artistic World Gymnastic Champion-ship, and the ATP World Tour Finals. Subsequently, the arena was designated as a 2012 Olympics venue for the gymnastics and basketball finals. Though music is the primary driver of the business, Campbell likens the venue to a chame-leon. "First and foremost The O_2 is a place for live entertainment—whether that happens to be sports, or whether that happens to be family shows, or whether that happens to be music—it doesn't really matter."[32]

Appreciating that The O_2 was mere minutes from central London and knowing that the venue's ownership and management group, AEG, was intent on developing innovative marketing platforms highlighting the at-venue con-vergence of sports, entertainment, and technology, twelve corporations became the venue's founding partners.[33] These partners, which each paid in excess of $1.5 million per year, included BMW, adidas, NEC, Credit Suisse, ADT, InBev, Nestlé, VISA, Natwest, Coke, Lastminute.co and, of course, O_2. Campbell believes that "[t]he primary key to making such partnerships work is a long-term commitment from both sides, and involvement from the sponsors in cre-ating the overall customer experience."[34]

Founding partner O_2, the world's largest telecommunications operator, signed a $12 million, fifteen-year deal to secure the complex's primary naming rights.[35] As part of the deal, O_2 prominently displays its name and logo at myriad sites within the tent, including The O_2 arena and indigO_2. In working with the venue, the company has gone beyond the strategic placement of its name and logo by creating more interactive marketing experiences, including those that deliver exclusive benefits for O_2 customers. These member-exclusive benefits include priority ticketing to music and major sporting events up to forty-eight hours prior to general release, priority parking, the option to upgrade seats at the venue, opportunities to jump the queues through fast-track queuing sys-tems, access to exclusive music content, and admission to the O_2 Blueroom—a VIP-only bar for O_2 customers decorated in corporate colors. Customers gain access to the O_2 Blueroom by texting a short code to then receive a bar-coded mobile ticket for entry. Once inside the bar, the customers can change the pho-tographic images on the screen at the back of the bar and request music on the jukebox—all through their mobile phones.[36] In addition, O_2 customers can access "refresh bubbles" where they can recharge their cell phones, experiment with new mobile entertainment services, and have a drink or massage.[37] The partnership proved to be a major success for O_2, with "brand love" rising 12 percent and "brand consideration" up 20 percent within the first year.[38]

Japanese computer giant NEC, like O_2, has utilized The O_2 to showcase cutting-edge technology that reinforces its brand status. NEC clientele experience the most advanced technology in the world in a small room within The O_2 arena. This room is protected by a locked glass cabinet and is used to display and market NEC's future technologies—including a robot called PaPeRo that is capable of identifying people through facial recognition software, showing its emotions through dancing, expressing itself through speech, and contributing with everyday tasks such as opening the curtains and entertaining children with riddles, quizzes, and other games. Also found within this exclusive room is a laptop with a screen so flexible that it can be wrung out as if it were a washcloth, and a device called Plume that allows for the scanning of handwritten documents into computer text.[39] After experiencing NEC's future technologies, the clients are taken upstairs to a sporting event or music show where they can experience NEC's current technology, including the large cinema projectors, network servers, biometric security systems, RFID attendance tracking systems, and storage that have been integrated throughout the venue.

Campbell believes the next step is to create that consumer experience outside of the venue. He says, "Although you can't replicate the live experience, sponsors are looking at how they can talk to the consumer before they arrive at the event, how they can talk to the consumer after they have left, and how they can build more of a relationship with the consumer beyond the two to three hours they are in the building."[40]

As a sports-anchored development, The O_2 has successfully relied on convergence to integrate the marketing wants and needs of its twelve founding partners. In doing so, founding sponsors have distinctively positioned and reinforced their brands with core target markets, resulting in The O_2 becoming a global leader in at-venue corporate marketing.

RED BULL

Throughout the past decade, Austrian-based Red Bull has grown dramatically and boasts worldwide annual sales in excess of $4 billion and a U.S. market share greater than 40 percent.[41] However, the maker of the world's most popular energy drink didn't always possess the cachet and brand reverence it has today. In 1984 the product was so badly panned by taste testers that it led a leading research team to remark, "No other product has ever failed this convincingly."[42]

Product refinement and aggressive marketing techniques, commonly involving novel approaches to sports marketing, have enabled the company to overcome this early challenge and post impressive annual growth rates, often in excess of 45 percent.[43] In fact, in its keen efforts to be authentically woven into the fabric of sports, Red Bull has invested nearly $500 million in sports marketing during the course of a single year, frequently bypassing traditional advertising and sponsorship in favor of team and event ownership.[44] According to Robert Hollander, managing director of Amalfi Ventures and CEO of the IBeam Group, LLC, this investment has enabled Red Bull to "be edgier, wilder, and more extreme than the other major players in the beverage industry, thus creating—and then extending—a particular lifestyle for its consumers."[45]

In 1995, Red Bull purchased SV Austria Salzburg, traditionally one of the strongest teams in Austria's Bundesliga, the highest-level soccer league in the country. Red Bull immediately rebranded the team by changing the name to FC Red Bull Salzburg and replacing the traditional purple and white uniforms with red, blue, and yellow colors in an effort to link the team's brand to that of the company's product. A small pair of wings now adorns the motif of the club crest on the uniforms in promotion of Red Bull's signature slogan "It gives you wings." From the onset, Red Bull endured the risks and challenges associated with rebranding a sports team, experiencing backlash due to the clear intention to sever ties with the "old" Austria Salzburg, alienating traditional fans in the process.[46] However, as Hollander states, "although there is a transition period, if the team ultimately wins, few care what they are called."[47]

This would serve as a precautionary reminder as to how Red Bull approached future branding efforts. In 2003, Red Bull opened Red Bull Arena in Salzburg to house the FC Red Bull Salzburg games. The dual franchise ownership and arena sponsorship is only one example of Red Bull's strategy to control and monetize the entire consumer marketing experience at venue. It also provided Red Bull the opportunity to capture more value from events such as the 2008 European Football Championship, which filled the 31,895-seat Red Bull Arena and subsequently extended the brand's reach. The company replicated this approach when purchasing the EC Salzburg hockey team in 2000 and renaming it EC Red Bull Salzburg while rebranding the team with Red Bull's colors and logo.

In 2005, Red Bull defied conventional wisdom by entering Formula 1 (F1) Racing with the purchase of the Jaguar team from Ford Motor Company for a reported $1 along with the guarantee to invest $400 million in the team over the following three seasons.[48] After renaming the recently acquired team Red Bull Racing, the company purchased a second team from Minardi and renamed it Toro Rosso Racing, which is Italian for Red Bull. Traditionally, F1 has been dominated by auto-manufacturer-owned teams such as Ferrari and Toyota that secure separate sponsorship deals. Dual ownership and sponsorship provided Red Bull full control of tis teams, its brand positioning, and its messaging. This is critically important when appreciating that each F1 race is viewed worldwide by in excess of a hundred million fans.

A year later, Red Bull entered NASCAR by acquiring and sponsoring not one but two racing teams. While Red Bull does not disclose its marketing budget, primary sponsors of a single stock car routinely spend between $15 million and $20 million annually for the type of exposure NASCAR provides.[49] The #83 flagship car is driven by Brian Vickers and is numbered after an 8.3-ounce Red Bull can. Marketing and brand presence is prevalent at the traveling trackside Red Bull merchandise trailer, where fans secure driver autographs and purchase branded apparel and souvenirs. Once again, Red Bull had penetrated a new market by devising a marketing paradigm that allowed it to deftly integrate the corporate brand into America's top racing league.

Red Bull also purchased the New York/New Jersey MetroStars of Major League Soccer (MLS) in 2006 from AEG for $100 million. The deal included ownership of the team as well as a 50 percent stake of a to-be-constructed stadium. The following year, and in an effort to have absolute control over both the team and the venue, Red Bull acquired the remaining 50 percent stake in the stadium. As with Red Bull's previous acquisitions, it renamed the MetroStars, to become the New York Red Bulls, and prominently displayed the Red Bull logo on the front of the uniforms. Though it is not uncommon to find soccer teams named after corporations internationally, Red Bull is one of the only professional sports teams that is currently owned and named after a corporation in the United States. In addition, the company announced that its new venue, which opened in 2010, would be named Red Bull Arena. Unlike many new venues, Red Bull Arena does not have founding corporate partners, choosing instead to maintain the primary focus on its own branding initiatives, including the subtle promotion of key Red Bull endorsers Shaun White and James "Bubba" Stewart, among others. This strategy was embraced by several corporations that later became "official sponsors" of the arena, namely Panasonic, Prudential, and Continental Airlines.

By controlling both the arena and the team, the company has the opportunity to market not only to soccer fans in attendance but also to those attending other events at the facility, further ensuring its tactical marketing reach to those that consume sports and entertainment in-venue. One way Red Bull takes full advantage of this opportunity is by requiring employees to attend Red Bull "classes," a unified training system to better acclimate Red Bull Arena staff to the company, its expectations, and, of course, the brand—a move that will certainly deliver a more cohesive marketing message to the fans.[50]

In line with Red Bull's tradition of owning events and teams rather than just sponsoring them, it has created a number of events over the past several years that ostensibly have allowed it to market to millions of spectators while building brand awareness and affinity. These events include Flugtag (pronounced floog-targ, this is German for "flying machine"), which began in Austria in the early 1990s but didn't come to the United States until 2001. Flugtag is an event in which participants compete to fly the furthest off of a platform over water in homemade flying machines. United States events were held in 2008 in Tampa Bay, Chicago, and Portland, Oregon, which drew a crowd of more than eighty thousand, nearly 15 percent of the city's population.[51] Red Bull continued staging these events in 2010 in the host cities of Miami, Minneapolis/St. Paul, Long Beach, and Philadelphia. Red Bull's marketing director, Anoushka Feiler, stated that by creating its own events, Red Bull has people step into its world and experience the brand.[52] In doing so, Red Bull transcends sports and event marketing by adding a lifestyle component to its product positioning, further solidifying and reinforcing its brand attributes.

As much as Red Bull is known for the highly caffeinated taste of its Red Bull energy drink, it has equally proven its ability to build and extend brand awareness utilizing non-traditional marketing strategies and tactics. According to Hollander, Red Bull is unique because "while it takes a big financial commitment and it is logistically difficult for corporate marketing of this sort, Red Bull has found a niche by showcasing extreme sports events and utilizing marketing partners to help further their brand."[53] Red Bull's approach to activating its sports marketing initiatives in an effort to drive sales and increase market share will be watched closely by the competition as they too seek to differentiate their brands by using sports and entertainment venues as seamless marketing vehicles.

CORPORATE MARKETING: THE BOTTOM LINE

ESPN's Wide World of Sports Complex, The O$_2$'s approach to sponsorship activation, and Red Bull's integrated marketing campaigns all signify the increasing sophistication of corporate sports marketing on a global basis. This sophistication requires not only subjective results, such as enhanced brand awareness, but quantifiable results as well. Tangible and intangible results are not measured—or obsessed over—by only the sponsoring corporation, venues, and sports franchises, but rather by all stakeholders having an impact on the flow of funds throughout the sports business, including the federal government. To this end, stakeholders must be sure to deliver appropriate levels of brand immersion. Those that partner with or otherwise link their brands to other corporate partners must be mindful that such marketing relationships must prove additive to be most effective. When successfully accomplished, these corporate marketing initiatives will engage patrons and, in the process, help them build and extend their brands, as well as increase shareholder value.

Vertical Brand Immersion

A fine line exists between tactical and appropriate levels of sports marketing and "over the top," borderline-offensive levels of immersion and activation. What may be deemed optimal by certain stakeholders may be deemed inappropriate by others. While this is certainly subjective on many levels, affected stakeholders—especially sponsors, sports franchises and leagues, and venue owners and operators—must be vigilant when striking the balance. Anything short of this may alienate sought-after fans and consumers and raise concerns among corporate shareholders.

Creating and owning one's own content or events may deliver a precise and controlled marketing environment, but this may not be desirable or feasible for some sponsors. Nonetheless, the lessons learned from Red Bull reinforce the benefits of brand immersion; benefits that can be achieved regardless of scale and absent complete vertical integration. Developing, extending, and reinforcing brand messaging, ranging from passive activities such as event signage to more hands-on opportunities such as test driving a sponsor's vehicle at a golf tournament, are vital. Disney has capitalized on this immersion by outfitting its twenty-seven thousand hotel rooms at Disney World with a channel that highlights its ESPN Complex.[54] Given the specific opportunity at hand, these branding initiatives must be supported by appropriate levels of business development conducive to driving sales; otherwise such marketing efforts will fall well short of intended results.

The extensive and authentic linking of a corporate brand to that of an event can reinforce the attributes of both. When a corporate marketer or brand is revered as part of the experience, and believed by consumers to be integral to the overall positioning and legitimacy of the event itself, the sponsor prospers. Examples of this have included the "Big Three" automakers' (General Motors, Ford, and Chrysler) presence in NASCAR. They have historically provided vehicles and technical expertise, as well as sponsored races and provided marketing dollars to race teams. This vertical presence has enabled them to live up to the adage "Win on Sunday, sell on Monday."

Sponsors must carefully balance their own need for revenue generation with the risk of becoming caricatures of themselves in the eyes of consumers when too extensive of a marketing presence exists. Should this occur, a negative return on investment is created because the amount of human and financial resources pledged to such marketing activities is overcome by consumer disdain.

While NASCAR fans and consumers have embraced the Big Three's presence for decades, this stance is not equally embraced by the federal government, which has provided the automotive manufacturing industry billions of dollars in order to remain operational. In short, the return on investment once required by corporate shareholders now extends to the federal government which, due to its investment, has become a major shareholder as well. Consequently, it is increasingly important not only to demonstrate the merits of sports marketing campaigns designed to strike a chord with consumers and help increase sales over time, but also to articulate the value created via business-to-business marketing campaigns—often to those with little or no sports marketing acumen.

Vertical brand immersion through sports marketing enables major companies to reach suppliers and vendors while simultaneously conducting business development with other (potential) strategic partners. These behind-the-scenes activities, which have fueled corporate sports marketing, now must be tracked and catalogued in much the same way other elements of a sponsorship are scored. Although they can be far more subtle and can take longer to germinate, business-to-business marketing relationships have been the primary reason many industries have maintained a strong connection to sports over the years. Given the results-driven environment now enveloping sports marketing at all levels, to include scrutiny by untraditional stakeholders, it is mandatory that marketers demonstrate the value of such brand immersion, whether undertaken in business-to-consumer or business-to-business capacities, or both.

Horizontal Brand Integration

Brand integration can also be accomplished through horizontal integration, as evidenced by the Hanesbrand (Champion and Hanes) partnership with ESPN's Wide World of Sports. From stadium naming rights and the sponsorship of key lacrosse events to co-sponsorship with Target of the inaugural RISE Games, the partnership between the Complex and Champion and Hanes has been strategically planned and implemented. Joining forces with complementary brands can simultaneously reinforce a brand's strengths to engaged consumers while enhancing the brand with those less familiar with the company or organization. Although substantial benefits exist for sponsors that horizontally align, selecting the wrong partner or otherwise having your brand compromised due to a partner's shortcoming can be devastating. Any ill-conceived marketing alliances may have a detrimental impact on myriad stakeholders seeking consistency and clarity of message.

As is the case with vertical brand immersion, horizontal brand integration involves subjectivity; subjectivity that can have a profound impact on numerous stakeholders, particularly sponsors, sports franchises and leagues, venue owners and operators, media partners, and even athletes.

Event organizers, as well as sports leagues and teams, must consider themselves de facto outsourced marketing departments charged with providing creative services and activation. They must advocate for their corporate partners by helping them develop, manage, and monetize opportunities. Increasingly, a failure to do so signals poor customer service and increases the likelihood that a corporate partner will not renew its marketing relationship. Inherent in this service philosophy is going beyond the basics of assisting the corporate partner to capture data about attendees, provide on-site trial usage of a product or service, or enjoy positive media coverage. Event organizers, leagues, and teams must also fend off increasingly sophisticated ambush marketing campaigns that occur when companies or organizations that are unaffiliated with the sporting event undertake advertising, promotional, and other marketing activities in and around venues.

Given the extraordinary importance of return on marketing investment, official, exclusive marketing relationships must take priority. At the same time, sponsors seek to craft marketing relationships that make ambush marketing more difficult. The All England Lawn Tennis Club's approach to addressing ambush marketing at its Wimbledon tournament, when coupled with the tournament sponsors' approach to integration, personifies this. Expressly stated on its website, Wimbledon organizers state as a key objective to "enhance the unique character and image of The (Wimbledon) Championships by keeping our courts and grounds relatively free of commercial sponsorship and product placement. Hence the lack of overt advertising around the Grounds. This helps to give the event and the Wimbledon brand a special resonance that TV and companies around the world wish to be associated with, and enables the Club to derive revenue which goes towards the funding of The Championships and British tennis."[55]

Wimbledon sponsors, including Polo Ralph Lauren and Rolex, welcome this approach. Polo Ralph Lauren outfits chair umpires and ball persons and has a unique presence in the Centre Court Gift Shop. Such a relationship differentiates the brand from those endorsed by superstars such as Roger Federer, who wears Nike. Similarly, Rolex, the tournament's official timekeeper since 1978, is able to feature its pristine presence even though Maria Sharapova endorses TAG Heuer. In such settings, official brands coexist, a matter of great importance to athletes who are directly and indirectly affected by the quantity and quality of competing brands, whether these brands are official partners or engaged in ambush marketing. The extent to which corporate marketing clutter exists and how it is addressed by governing bodies, including event organizers, plays a role when one is determining the value of endorsement contracts. Moreover, inappropriate levels of corporate marketing, whatever the reason or source, is of keen interest to sports leagues and unions, as any detrimental marketing activities will have an impact on the revenue generated and ultimately shared with athletes.

Engaging and Quantifiable Marketing Experiences

Successful sports marketers, such as those operating London's O_2, go well beyond developing and implementing vertical and horizontal marketing initiatives. They also deliver engaging, service-oriented experiences to consumers, whether these consumers are individuals, corporations, or both. No matter how compelling such engaging experiences may appear to be from marketing and branding perspectives, those that fail to unlock and deliver measurable economic return will falter. In an era in which perception can be reality, those that devise sports marketing campaigns are increasingly scrutinized by a growing list of stakeholders. Once limited to feedback from colleagues and pushback from consumers, sports marketers are now forced to take a more comprehensive approach when evaluating the extent to which engaging experiences are resonating with consumer groups, are implemented in a cost effective manner, and are seen as prudent from a public relations perspective. Stakeholders with a vested interest include sponsors, sports franchises and leagues, venue owners and operators, and, increasingly, the public sector at all levels.

Those that host events, whether they be amateur or professional sports leagues, or even smaller regional organizations managing local 10K races, must work with corporate partners to make compelling impacts on consumers, especially when these consumers are fans and participants. Consumers must be appropriately engaged from the moment they arrive so that a positive association with a corporate partner begins immediately.

For example, in Atlanta, those that arrive in a Lexus to watch Braves games at Turner Field have their own designated parking area—one that includes Lexus branding. Providing such touchpoints creates a positive consumer sentiment toward the teams and the affiliated corporate brand, as long as the customer service is commensurate with consumer expectation. Properly activated and serviced, it leaves a lasting impression because it serves as both the initial and final touchpoint between fans and the brands, while simultaneously stressing a commitment to customer service with precisely the targeted demographic the auto manufacturer is hoping to retain. By offering special benefits for consumers that purchase their products or services, corporate marketers accomplish the dual goals of rewarding loyalty and stoking interest, while creating a lasting effect in the process that transcends mere name recognition.

Any inability to qualify and quantify results produced by such business-to-consumer marketing initiatives, whether they are conducted within the venue or areas immediately surrounding it, may incur added scrutiny from constituents. The sports business industry and the stakeholders affected by it also remain concerned about the role of government oversight in corporate marketing, especially that attached to business-to-business sports marketing, particularly hospitality. Regardless of the extent to which government influence yielded during the economic downturn of 2008–2010 will remain, those marketing sports must be aggressive in communicating the benefits of sports marketing. Any inability to justify sports marketing expenditures will bring with it negative public and corporate relations, along with growing shareholder concern. Sports leagues, such as NASCAR, and sponsors, especially Bank of America, have been at the forefront, devising strategies and articulating the merits of corporate marketing attached to sports.

NASCAR understands that engaging experiences transcend event-day activities and activation. It founded the Fuel for Business Council, which comprises dozens of NASCAR's largest sponsors, including those that sponsor venues, teams, and drivers. Meeting quarterly, these business partners are dedicated to uncovering additional business-to-business opportunities between and among NASCAR's family of partners.

Former Bank of America CEO Kenneth Lewis, realizing the sensitivity involved in sports marketing, particularly for those in the financial services industry, in 2009 reminded the federal government, bank shareholders, and consumers of sports marketing's merits. "I was never inclined to pump big sums of money into sports marketing until I saw the facts and the numbers," he said. "In general terms, for every dollar we spend on sports marketing, we get $10 in revenue and $3 in earnings. This is not wasted money."[56]

CORPORATE MARKETING AND CONVERGENCE: FINAL THOUGHTS FROM THE LOS ANGELES ANGELS OF ANAHEIM'S ARTE MORENO[57]

Arte Moreno is the owner of Major League Baseball's Los Angeles Angels of Anaheim. The Angels, World Series champions in 2002, are one of MLB's perennially contending franchises. Moreno shared his perspective on convergence and corporate marketing with the SBI.

SBI: What are the most important factors surrounding the convergence of sports, entertainment, and corporate marketing?

MORENO: When we look at this convergence, the most important factor for us is the creation of a positive baseball experience. We place a high priority on taking care of our fans. Our fans are our customers, and the number one rule in sales and marketing is that the customer is always right. Next, we consider our product offering. We are in the entertainment business, and when I acquired the Angels, the team had just won a World Series championship. We had to match that positive excitement and continue to keep the energy that came with that success. That enthusiasm had to be sustained and built upon with fans, sponsors, and anyone else who came into contact with the organization. The classic quotation in sales is, "It's the sizzle, not the steak." In other words, how you are greeted when you walk in the door, your client relationships, the pricing, quality, and service, matters tremendously. However, so too do results. As our franchise continues to excel on the field, we believe we are providing those who conduct business with the Angels both the sizzle and the steak.

SBI: What did you focus on when building the Angels' brand?

MORENO: First and foremost, we turned to our fan base. As our primary customer we wanted to know what they required in order to enjoy the same experience they had when the team was winning the World Series. It is always necessary to set a high expectation in terms of customer service, and then deliver upon it. If you hope to sell advertisements to local and national advertisers, it is vital to tell them how many fans we are going to deliver. When we are selling to sponsors, they need to know that we will be giving them a return on their investment—and engaged, well-serviced fans help us demonstrate that. The advertisers seek to build awareness of their name and brand in order to increase business. We strive to provide a successful vehicle for them in their own client relationships. We become partners in the same cause.

SBI: Besides the return on investment, what are you trying to accomplish in order to elevate the team's brand?

MORENO: We need to remain affordable. As one example, we compare our baseball experience to the movie industry. If we are trying to attract families, we need to consider comparative analysis. For us, it is not consistent to offer a low-price ticket and yet charge $20 for parking. The fan may develop a negative attitude before walking in the door. If souvenirs are over-priced, a $20 hat for example, parents may not be able to afford anything for their children. When I came into the Angels organization, I made marketing to the kids a high priority. If these future customers have the opportunity to develop a strong loyalty now by wearing the team colors, then they become part of the Angels family. They have a team to call their own, they enjoy our stadium experience, and we strive to maintain that positive enthusiasm. That is what branding is all about.

SBI: How did you change the culture when you took over the franchise?

MORENO: When I first started with the Angels, everyone, including myself, wore white shirts and ties. Then we realized that we needed to promote the brand ourselves. So now we wear red shirts with the Angels' "A" on them. I want my customer to buy a shirt or product so I, along with my employees, promote the team by wearing the Angels logo. We cannot ever forget about our brand. We branded our team on the color red, the "A" logo, and the Angels name. Everything else exists to support that brand. Culturally, I believe we must lead by example.

SBI: How do you connect with your clients?

MORENO: It is of utmost importance to communicate with your clients and fans. We try to fill whatever needs our fans or sponsors have every time we see them or speak with them. We are always selling and providing service. Service is a high priority: we strive to show constant appreciation to those who invest in our Angels experience. I treat our stadium and our team as my business. If I see a cigarette butt or hot dog wrapper lying on the ground, I pick it up. People may say it's not my responsibility—but it's the concept of not being entitled to anything. We all must pitch in regardless of our position, and show pride for our team. The stadium is our home, and it represents our business to the customer. We cannot assume the customer will buy a ticket from us, but rather we have to market the tickets to them. Once we identify our customers, get them to the ballpark, buy them a hat and give them a coupon for food, we have now introduced our customer to the game. After the game has ended we now have people wearing our Angels logo, providing free advertising for us. This can then lead to word-of-mouth advertising, which is very valuable.

SBI: What are the important factors in marketing your team going forward?

MORENO: When you are in a tough economy, the magic word is *accountability*. We are accountable for people having an exciting baseball experience. We want families and kids to come to the ballpark—and we want them to receive great value when they do. Baseball is never going to be able to grow unless we keep introducing it to new customers. Therefore, we work very hard to attract the new generation of customer. We are always looking for the "hook" when we are attempting to build our fan base and create long-term customers. We believe the "hook" is the fan's interest in the game, and what it takes to keep them as a fan.

SBI: How did changing the name to the Los Angeles Angels of Anaheim come about?

MORENO: The original franchise was named the Los Angeles Angels. With the move of the team to Anaheim the name became the California Angels. However, we believe no one outside of the state could tell where in California the Angels were located. When Disney bought the team, they made the decision to change the name to the Anaheim Angels. Disney was thinking about building a regional sports and entertainment area while cross-branding the baseball team with the Anaheim Ducks NHL team and Disneyland. The change of the name to Anaheim caused the club to go from identifying with one of the biggest marketplaces, Los Angeles, with its estimated eighteen million people in the greater metropolitan area, to identifying with approximately three hundred thousand people in Anaheim. I looked at where the majority of our ticketholders were coming from and decided we needed to increase our audience. I wanted to reach the larger audience with the change of the name. This has broadened our approach locally, regionally, and nationally.

SBI: How did the name change affect your relationship with the sponsors?

MORENO: We told our sponsors they would receive more exposure on radio and television through the expanded market identity. The name change also helped with attracting sponsorship buys in bidding situations, because we now identify with the entire metro market. When trying to attract sponsors we compete with other teams. The name *Anaheim* did not bring the obvious connection to the Los Angeles region for those making the sports advertising buys for these sponsors. Regionally, the name change was emotional but outside the region, the move made business sense. It all comes back to accountability and telling our clients what they would be receiving for their investment. The quantitative measurement of positioning them properly and advertising their product to the entire Los Angeles market is the key.

SBI: How have convergence and branding affected your approach?

MORENO: We must continue to provide an affordable and enjoyable Angels baseball experience. This gives us the opportunity to sell and market our products not only to our fans but to our corporate sponsors. Identifying what the customer needs and then how you provide service to the customer is ultimately what makes the difference. We want every night to be a special event because a customer may only come to the ballpark one time. It is important to make every game the best baseball experience possible.

NOTES AND INDEX

NOTES

Introduction

1. "Juvenal," Encyclopedia Britannica Online, www.britannica.com/EBchecked/topic/308974/Juvenal (accessed June 14, 2009).

2. Leonard Koppett, *Baker Field: Birthplace of Sports Television*, Columbia University, Spring 1999.

3. Stefan Szymanski and Andrew S. Zimbalist, *National Pastime: How Americans Play Baseball and the Rest of the World Plays Soccer* (Washington, DC: Brookings Institution Press, 2005), p. 148.

4. Corporate Fact Sheet, ESPN Corporate Information, January 10, 2010.

5. Claudia La Rocca, "Rings of Power," *Financial History*, Spring 2004.

6. "TV by the Numbers," March 21, 2009, http://tvbythenumbers.com/2009/03/21/top-100-rated-tv-shows-of-all-time/14922.

7. "Super Bowl 2007: Advertising History—40 Years of Prices and Audiences," *Advertising Age*, http://blogs.loc.gov/inside_adams/2010/02/super-advertising-bowl (accessed June 7, 2010).

8. Aaron Kuriloff, "NFL, Electronic Arts to Release Wii Fitness Video Based on Football Drills," Bloomberg News, July 20, 2010.

9. Fantasy Sports Trade Association, www.FSTA.org (accessed May 6, 2010).

Part I

1. "Sponsors" and "advertisers" can be different. Sponsors tend to have extensive relationships with teams or leagues—they buy signage, frequently have a suite, and typically not only advertise to consumers during the events but also promote their close affiliation with the team or league via promotions and other marketing campaigns. Advertisers simply buy media time or otherwise purchase media packages (print, radio, online, tv, and so on). So, while virtually all sponsors are indeed advertisers, not all advertisers have more robust relationships beyond spending money on advertising and this distinction is intended throughout the book.

2. Bill Molzon, "Television's Sports Heritage: The Early Days of Sports TV," Ameri-

can Sportscasters Online, www.americansportscastersonline.com/waynesbergarticle.
html (accessed April 26, 2010).

Chapter 1

1. Pat Forde, "An Embodiment of the Olympic Ideal, Phelps Saved the Games,"
ESPN.com, August 17, 2008.

2. Alex Werpin, "Phelps Delivers Record-Setting Saturday for NBC," *Broadcasting &
Cable*, August 17, 2008.

3. Jay Weiner, "Getting Our Arms Around Olympic Gigantism," *Sports Business
Journal*, August 5, 2008.

4. Ibid.

5. Howard Schlossberg, *Sports Marketing* (Boston: Blackwell, 1996), page 89.

6. "Beijing Games Show Significant Increases in Ratings and Average Viewers," NBC
press release, August 25, 2008.

7. Rich Sandomir, "NBC's Run Is Extended to 2012 with $2 Billion Bid," *New York
Times*, June 7, 2003.

8. Ibid.

9. Weiner, "Getting Our Arms Around Olympic Gigantism."

10. Independent research conducted by Phil Wallace of the Sports Business Institute, n.d.

11. "Ebersol Says NBC Couldn't Regain Momentum Lost Early On," *Sports Business
Daily*, February 27, 2006.

12. Thomas Heath and Jon Maynard, "Ratings Aren't Winning NBC Any Medals,"
Washington Post, February 17, 2006.

13. "Ni Hao from Beijing—Introducing Daily Olympics 2008," MarketWatch.com.,
August 8, 2008.

14. Sports Business Institute (SBI) interview with David Neal, October 17, 2008.
Throughout the research process, representatives of the SBI had the opportunity to conduct personal interviews with numerous industry executives. Insight gained from these
interviews is included throughout the text.

15. SBI interview with David Neal.

16. Tripp Mickle and Jon Ourand, "NBC Brings It Home with Mix of Order, Adven-
ture," *Sports Business Journal*, August 18, 2008.

17. Weiner, "Getting Our Arms Around Olympic Gigantism"; Ben Grossman, "NBC
Hits $1B in Ad Sales," *Broadcasting & Cable*, August 7, 2008.

18. Tripp Mickle, "8 legacies from Beijing," *Sports Business Journal*, August 25, 2008.

19. Rob Cox, "Chinese Peacock," *Wall Street Journal*, August 26, 2008.

20. Rick Kissell, Rick, "Olympics Still a Big Winner for NBC," *Daily Variety*, August
20, 2008.

21. Ibid.

22. Bill Carter, "MSNBC, CNBC Enjoy Olympics Ratings Boost," New York Times News Service, August 14, 2008.

23. SBI interview with David Neal.

24. "NBC Delivers Record Victory Margins on Strength of Olympics," *Sports Business Daily*, August 20, 2008.

25. Kenneth Corbin, "NBC's Mixed Olympic Report Card," Internetnews.com, August 25, 2008.

26. Ben Stelter, "Web Audience for Games Soars for NBC and Yahoo," *New York Times*, August 24, 2008.

27. Emily Steel, "NBC Didn't Cash in on Olympics Video," *Wall Street Journal*, August 23, 2008.

28. SBI interview with David Neal.

29. Bill Briggs, "Olympic Triumph Gives MSNBC Well-Timed Boost," Msnbc.com, March 4, 2010.

30. Harlem Globetrotters International, Inc., Company History, http://www.harlemglobetrotters.com/history/timeline (accessed May 6, 2010).

31. Personal e-mail from Josh Krulewitz, ESPN, April 15, 2009.

32. Sports Business Institute interview with John Skipper, April 2, 2009.

33. Michael Hiestand, " 'GameDay' Flag Relay Is Worth a Salute," *USA Today*, October 30, 2008.

34. Nielsen Media Research, n.d.

35. Ibid.

36. SBI interview with John Skipper.

37. "ESPN'S College Gameday to Be Built by the Home Depot for Three More Years," The Home Depot press release, August 29, 2006.

38. Ibid.

39. "The Home Depot Builds a Solid Foundation for 2007 College Football Season by Receiving Over $1 Million of Broadcast Exposure," Front Row Marketing Services press release, September 4, 2007.

40. SBI interview with John Skipper.

41. Ibid.

42. Jon Show, "Tapped Out or Still Ready to Scrap?" *Sports Business Journal*, November 3, 2008.

43. Joel Stein, "The Ultimate Fighting Machines," *Business 2.0 Magazine*, November 8, 2006.

44. Sports Business Institute interview with Frank and Lorenzo Fertitta, March 12, 2009.

45. Ken Pishna, "Kimbo Propels TUF 10 to Record Ratings," *MMA Weekly*, December 8, 2009.

46. Ibid.

47. SBI interview with Frank and Lorenzo Fertitta.

48. Mike Chiappetta, "UFC-Spike Partnership Lands Entire Ultimate Fighter Library Online," MMAfighter.com, April 29, 2010.

49. Ivan Trembow, "UFC's Pay-Per-View Buys Explode in 2006," *MMA Weekly*, July 13, 2006.

50. Kevin Baxter and Lance Pugmire, "Boxing Still Has a Fighting Chance; Mixed Martial Arts Is Rapidly Growing, but the Money Generated by Top-Name Boxers Dwarfs Their Rival," *Los Angeles Times*, December 5, 2008.

51. L. Jon Wertheim, "The New Main Event," *Sports Illustrated*, May 28, 2007.

52. Associated Press, February 22, 2010.

53. SBI interview with Frank and Lorenzo Fertitta.

54. Matthew Miller, "Ultimate Cash Machine," *Forbes*, May 5, 2008.

55. SBI interview with Frank and Lorenzo Fertitta.

56. "'UFC 75' on Spike TV Is Most Watched Event in UFC History," UFC press release, September 11, 2007.

57. SBI interview with Frank and Lorenzo Fertitta.

58. Ibid.

59. Dave Meltzer, "Lesnar Blasts UFC Toward Record Year," *Yahoo! Sports*, December 12, 2008.

60. Ibid.; SBI interview with Frank and Lorenzo Fertitta.

61. Miller, "Ultimate Cash Machine."

62. Frank O'Neill, "TV Usage Report," *CBS-TV Research Report*, February 27, 2009.

63. Shoulder programming is supporting content that typically takes place immediately before or after the primary programming.

64. Nick Harris, "1,000,000,000: Beijing Sets World TV Record," *The Sunday Times*, May 10, 2009.

65. *The Home Technology Monitor™ Ownership and Trend Report* (Cranford, NJ: Knowledge Networks, 2004–2009).

66. *MultiMedia Mentor™ Scan Report* (Cranford, NJ: Knowledge Networks, 2004–2009).

67. Edward Baig, "ESPN to Launch 3D Network in June," *USA Today*, January 5, 2010.

68. Sports Business Institute interview with David Hill, September 28, 2009.

Chapter 2

1. Steven L. Kent, *The Ultimate History of Video Games: The Story Behind the Craze That Touched Our Lives and Changed the World* (New York City: Three Rivers Press, 2001), p. 211.

2. Hoovers Company History: Nintendo, n.d.

3. Online Slideshows, BusinessWeek.com, n.d.

4. Sony Computer Entertainment, "PlayStation 2 Breaks Record as the Fastest Computer Entertainment Platform to Reach Cumulative Shipment of 100 Million Units," press release, November 30, 2005.

5. Victoria Murphy, "Microsoft's Midlife Crisis," *Forbes*, September 13, 2005.

6. Consolidated Financial Statements, Nintendo, April 24, 2008, http://www.nintendo.co.jp/ir/en/index.html (accessed May 6, 2010).

7. Hilary Goldstein, "Sony Losing Almost $250 per Console: The High-Cost of a Next-Gen System Revealed," Internet Gaming Network, IGN.com, November 16, 2006.

8. Wolfgang Gruener, "PlayStation 3 Loses $2.0 Billion," TGDaily.com, May 16, 2007.

9. The Hub, "Hoo-Wii," March-April 2007, www.hubmagazine.com/archives/the_hub/2007/mar_apr/the_hub17_nintendo.pdf (accessed May 6, 2010); Seth Schiesle, "Nintendo, Once Down, Devises Its Comeback," *New York Times*, May 26, 2007.

10. Rhys Blakely, "Nintendo Chief Helps Group to Be a Big Fish in a Big, Blue Ocean," *The Times* (London), July 13, 2007.

11. Sports Business Institute (SBI) interview with Perrin Kaplan, April 28, 2009.

12. Jared Leone, "They Got Game Again," *St. Petersburg Times*, February 10, 2008.

13. Dan Childs and Lana Zack, "Is Wii Worthy of American Heart Association Accolade?" Abcnews.com, May 17, 2010.

14. SBI interview with Perrin Kaplan.

15. Ibid.

16. Nintendo Co., Ltd. "Consolidated Financial Highlights" Nintendo Co., Ltd., 2009, http://www.nintendo.co.jp/ir/pdf/2009/091029e.pdf#page=9 (accessed December 20, 2009).

17. Reuters, "Nintendo Is Japan's 2nd Most Valuable Active Stock," September 25, 2007.

18. James Brightman, "NPD: Nintendo Drives '08 Industry Sales Past $21 Billion," *Game Daily*, January 15, 2009.

19. Ben Fritz and Alex Pham, "At E3, Checking Vital Signs Is Key for Console Rivals," *Los Angeles Times*, June 3, 2009.

20. Ibid.

21. SBI interview with Perrin Kaplan.

22. "Atari 2600 History," *AtariAge,* http://www.atariage.com/2600/index.html?SystemID=2600 (accessed May 6, 2010).

23. Mark Potts, "Video Games Are Enjoying a Resurgence in Popularity; Industry Revives with Better Graphics and New Enthusiasts," *Washington Post*, June 21, 1987.

24. Douglass C. McGill, "NEC Tries to Zap Nintendo in the Video Game Market," *New York Times*, May 24, 1989.

25. "Football Giants, FIFA and PES, Brace for Play-Off," News.com.au, http://www.news.com.au/fifa-v-pes/story-e6frfq1i-1111114713388 (accessed May 6, 2010).

26. "WWE(R) SmackDown(R) vs. Raw(R) 2010 Prepares to Enter the Virtual Ring," press release, THQ, June 2, 2009.

27. Edward Iwata, "Executive Suite: Tony Hawk Leaps to Top of Financial Empire," *USA Today*, March 9, 2008.

28. "Business Overview," World Wide Wrestling Entertainment, Inc., http://corporate.wwe.com/company/overview.jsp (accessed May 6, 2010).

29. "WrestleMania 25 Sets One-Day Box Office Record," April 13, 2009, www.wrestlinginc.com/wi/news/2009/0413/wwewrestlemania.

30. Greg Barr, "WrestleMania Slam into Houston," *Houston Business Journal*, March 27, 2009.

31. Sports Business Institute interview with Brian Farrell, October 15, 2008.

32. "The Number One Fighting Videogame Franchise Returns to the Virtual Ring."

33. SBI interview with Brian Farrell.

34. Ibid.

35. Tobi Elkin, "Videogames: Movies Gain as Game Fodder," *Advertising Age*, June 24, 2002.

36. Devin Leonard, "Calling Master Chief: A News Corp.–backed Professional Video-Game League Is Getting a Run for Its Money from Two Former Ad Guys," *Fortune*, August 21, 2008.

37. Sports Business Institute interview with Michael Sepso, January 29, 2009.

38. Eric Fisher, "Major League Gaming Secures $7.5M Round of Financing," *Sports Business Daily*," June 6, 2009.

39. Mark Hefflinger, "Major League Gaming Acquires Tournament Site GameBattles.com," *Digital Media Wire*, October 11, 2006.

40. Ibid.

41. Eric Fisher, "Major League Gaming Opens Season with Record Numbers," *Sports Business Journal*, April 21, 2008.

42. SBI interview with Michael Sepso.

43. David Radd, "Major League Gaming's Marketing Appeal," *Business Week*, March 12, 2008.

44. Ibid.

45. "Major League Gaming Announces 2009 Sponsor Line Up," PR Newswire, March 18, 2009.

46. SBI interview with Michael Sepso.

47. Ibid.

48. Radd, "Major League Gaming's Marketing Appeal"; Eric Fisher, "Major League Gaming Expands Content/Distribution Deal with ESPN," *Sports Business Daily*, May 28, 2009.

49. "Dr Pepper Unveils Major League Gaming Themed Bottle and Promotion as Part of Expanded Sponsorship," *Dr. Pepper* press release, November 19, 2009.

50. Ibid.

51. SBI interview with Michael Sepso.

52. "Major League Gaming Launches Licensed Headwear Line with National Retailer LIDS," MLG press release, November 17, 2009.

53. Eric Fisher, "Major League Gaming, Doritos Launching Gaming Combine Tonight," *Sports Business Daily,* February 23, 2010.

54. PricewaterhouseCoopers, *2008 Global Entertainment and Media Outlook Report,* n.d.

55. Ibid.

56. Dean Takahashi, Dean, "The Top 12 Trends of the Videogame Industry," *Venture Beat,* May 19, 2009.

57. Christopher Lawton and Yukuri Iwatani Kane, "Free Sports Games Score with the Online Set," *Wall Street Journal,* May 20, 2009.

58. Ibid.

59. Sports Business Institute interview with Peter Moore, September 2, 2009.

Chapter 3

1. *Sportsbusinessdaily.com* (accessed July 25, 2007).

2. Bill Plaschke, "Start of Something Big," Los Angeles Times, July 22, 2007.

3. Jere Longman, "U.S. Soccer: Sport of 70's, 80's, and 90's Still Waits," *New York Times,* June 3, 2002.

4. Malcolm Beith, with Patrick Falby, "Off to the Graveyard: Footballing Genius David Beckham Is Headed Across the Atlantic. Is This a New Beginning—or Just the end?" *Newsweek,* January 22, 2007.

5. Dan Sabbagh, "Beckham's Image Is Still Football's Most Valuable," *The Times of London,* July 4, 2006.

6. Mark Simpson, "Meet the Metrosexual," Salon.com, July 22, 2002.

7. Tahira Yaqoob, "Why I Feel Honoured to Be a Gay Icon, by David Beckham, as He Admits He Lets Posh Choose His Clothes," *Daily Mail,* December 25, 2007.

8. Sports Business Institute (SBI) interview with Shawn Hunter, July 31, 2008.

9. Paul Maidmen, "Becks and Bucks," Forbes.com, July 8, 2007.

10. "Love Is in the Hair: Japan Trends It Like Beckham," *The Age* (Australia), June 18, 2003.

11. SBI interview with Shawn Hunter.

12. Chris Isidore, "Brand It Like Beckham," CNNMoney.com, July 6, 2007.

13. SBI interview with Shawn Hunter.

14. Susan Gunelius, "David Beckham Boosts MLS," *Brandcurve,* November 24, 2007.

15.   Curtis Eichelberger, "Beckham Sparks $13.3 Million in Sales for Galaxy, Covers Salary," *Bloomberg News*, April 19, 2007.

16.   SBI interview with Shawn Hunter.

17.   Robin Abcarian and Grahame L. Jones, " 'World Domination' About to Take Detour; David and Victoria Beckham Appear Set to Forsake LA for Milan," *Los Angeles Times*, February 24, 2009.

18.   "David Beckham's Impact on MLS Match Ratings on ESPN2," *Sports Business Daily*, February 12, 2009.

19.   "1.1 Million Viewers for MLS Cup," Sportsmediawatch.com, December 6, 2009.

20.   Ibid.

21.   "Beckham's Extended Stay in Italy Confirmed," *ESPN Soccernet*, March 8, 2009; Nick Szczepanik, "Beckham Hails His 'Dream' Deal," *The Times of London*, March 9, 2009.

22.   James Munro and Austin Simon, "Beckham Planning to Buy MLS Team," BBC Sport Online, March 9, 2009.

23.   "Adcracker brand definitions," http://www.adcracker.com/brand/3-0-8.htm (accessed May 9, 2010).

24.   Home page, http://www.primelicensing.com.br/home/home.asp (accessed May 12, 2010); Paul Crowder and John Dower, directors, "Once in a Lifetime," documentary (Passion Pictures, 2006).

25.   "Pelé Takes a New Shot After Failed Ventures," *Wall Street Journal Online*, December 22, 2009.

26.   The Death of a Daredevil: The Extraordinary, Magnificent Life of Evel Knievel," *The Independent*, December 2, 2007.

27.   Sports Business Institute interview with Will Kassoy, September 12, 2008.

28.   SBI Interview with Will Kassoy.

29.   Matt Barton and Bill Loguidice, "The History of Tony Hawk's Pro Skater," Gamasutra.com, March 10, 2009.

30.   SBI interview with Will Kassoy.

31.   "How Tony Hawk Stays Aloft," *Business Week*, November 13, 2006.

32.   "Yao Ming, Cultural Envoy Across the Sea," *People's Daily Online*, July 28, 2006.

33.   Craig Smith and Mike Wise, "Eying NBA, China Will Make Athletes Pay," *New York Times*, April 25, 2002.

34.   Mei Fong, "Yao Ming Gives Reebok an Assist in China," *New York Times,* September 28, 2007.

35.   "Yao Ming Leads *Forbes*' Chinese Celebrity List for 5th Year," *China Daily*, March 13, 2008.

36.   Sports Business Institute interview with Adam Silver, September 8, 2008.

37.   SBI interview with Adam Silver.

38.   Ibid.

39. Eddie Pells, "Injury Doesn't Diminish Yao Ming's Ability to Sell Products," *USA Today*, March 11, 2008.

40. Sports Business Institute interview with Sandy Montag, December 21, 2009.

Chapter 4

1. Maury Brown, "MLBAM: The Stealthy Money Machine," *The Hardball Times*, December 5, 2005.

2. Steven Levy, "Covering All the Online Bases," *Newsweek*, June 25, 2007.

3. Ibid.

4. Bill King, "MLB's Web CEO Transitions into Tradition," *Sports Business Journal*, November 27, 2000.

5. Eric Fisher, "MLBAM to Roll Out Enhanced Content," *Sports Business Journal*, March 24, 2008.

6. Sports Business Institute (SBI) interview with Bob Bowman, October 13, 2008.

7. SBI interview with Bob Bowman.

8. Ron Grover and Tom Lowry, "Extra Innings in the Digital Game," *Business Week*, November 26, 2007; "MLB.com Sets New Online Ticketing Mark for Eighth Straight Year," MLBAM press release, July 22, 2008.

9. Eric Fisher, "MLB Clubs Split Over StubHub Deal," *Sports Business Journal*, August 6, 2007.

10. SBI interview with Bob Bowman.

11. Levy, "Covering All the Online Bases," *Newsweek*, June 25, 2007.

12. Ibid.

13. Eric Fisher, "What's Holding Back Wireless?" *Sports Business Journal*, June 16, 2008.

14. Eric Fisher, Eric, "MLBAM Announces Live Game Streaming Available on At Bat App," *Sports Business Daily*, June 17, 2009.

15. "MLB Brings Live Ballgames to Apple Devices," *Wall Street Journal Online*, July 22, 2009.

16. Eric Fisher, "MLBAM Puts Wheels on Production Demands," *Sports Business Journal*, November 12, 2007.

17. Jorge L. Ortiz, "MLB's Advanced Media Arm Pulls in Profits," *USA Today*, December 5, 2007; Chris Isidore, "Baseball's Secret $uccess $tory," CNNMoney.com, December 23, 2005.

18. SBI interview with Bob Bowman.

19. King Kaufman, "King Kaufman's Sports Daily," Salon.com, August 9, 2006.

20. Ibid.

21. John Ourand and Eric Fisher, "ESPN Seeks Better MLBAM Terms," *Sports Business Journal*, January 21, 2008.

22. SBI interview with Bob Bowman.

23. Ron Grover and Tom Lowry, "Extra Innings in the Digital Game," *Business Week*, November 26, 2007.

24. "IMG World Congress of Sports," *Sports Business Daily*, March 29, 2009.

25. SBI interview with Bob Bowman.

26. "A Whole New Ballgame: MLBtv Arrives on Playstation 3," PRnewswire, April 22. 2010.

27. SBI Interview with Bowman.

28. Peter Lewis, "The Media Business; ESPN and Prodigy Offering Sports Information Service," *New York Times*, March 30, 1994.

29. Udayan Gupta, "Scoring with Content: SportsLine USA Rewrites the Rules for Success on the Internet," *InformationWeek*, June 15, 1998.

30. Nielsen.com, "Sports Websites," September 2008.

31. Paul Festa, "ESPN Tackles NFL Net Deal," CNET News, May 20, 1998.

32. Ibid.

33. Bernhard Warner, "Play Ball," *The Industry Standard*, April 4, 2000.

34. Ibid.

35. Rivals.com, "About Us," www.rivals.com/content.asp?CID=36178 (accessed April 26, 2010).

36. Ibid.

37. "Anatomy of Yahoo!'s Rivals.com Acquisition," punctuative.com, June 21, 2007.

38. Sports Business Institute interview with Dave Morgan, April 21, 2009.

39. "National Signing Day Generates Big Traffic, Ad Buys for Sites," *Sports Business Daily*, February 6, 2008.

40. Ibid.

41. Darren Rovell, "Yahoo Buys Rivals.com: Is the Deal Worth It?" CNBC.com., June 21, 2007.

42. Rovell, "Yahoo Buys Rivals.com."

43. "Anatomy of Yahoo!'s Rivals.com Acquisition."

44. SBI interview with Dave Morgan.

45. Ibid.

46. Rovell, "Yahoo Buys Rivals.com."

47. Rivals.com, "About Us."

48. SBI interview with Dave Morgan.

49. Ibid.

50. Eric Fisher, "MLBAM Signs Fantasy Games License with ProTrade," *Sports Business Daily*, April 3, 2006; Eric Fisher, "ProTrade to Expand Offerings to Become Year-Round Experience," *Sports Business Daily*, July 9, 2007.

51. Josh Friedman, "Football Gets Arbitraged," *Los Angeles Times*, January 1, 2006.

52. Eric Fisher, "ProTrade Adds Social Networking, Rebrands," *Sports Business Journal*, April 28, 2008.

53. Sports Business Institute interview with Jeff Moorad, November 21, 2008.

54. Fisher, "ProTrade Adds Social Networking, Rebrands."

55. Mike Musgrove, "It's First and 10 for Fantasy Football on Facebook," *Washington Post*, August 24, 2008.

56. Eric Fisher, "No Fantasy: Big Numbers Expected," *Sports Business Journal*, July 14, 2008.

57. SBI interview with Jeff Moorad.

58. Nando Di Fino, "Facebook and Fantasy Football Finally Intersect," *Wall Street Journal*, October 12, 2009.

59. Eric Fisher, "MLBAM Strikes Partnership with S.F.-Based Citizen Sports Network," *Sports Business Journal*, April 22, 2009.

60. Eric Fisher, "Citizen Sports Sees Quick Response to New EPL Fantasy Offering," *SportsBusiness Journal*, July 30, 2009.

61. "Huffpost Game Changers: Who Is the Ultimate Game Changer in Sports?" HuffingtonPost.com, November 18, 2009.

62. Eric Fisher, "Yahoo Continues Digital Growth with Citizen Sports Purchase," *Sports Business Daily*, March 7, 2010.

63. SBI interview with Jeff Moorad.

64. Jay Yarow, "MLB's Real Competitive Advantage: How Baseball Is Using Cutting-Edge Technology to Rake in Millions on the Internet," *Business Week*, August 29, 2008.

65. Sports Business Institute interview with George Bodenheimer, October 22, 2009.

Chapter 5

1. "Verizon Wireless Completes Purchase of Alltel; Creates Nation's Largest Wireless Carrier," Verizon press release, January 9, 2009.

2. Andy Bernstein and Eric Fisher, "10 Questions and Answers for Wireless," *Sports Business Journal*, January 16, 2006; Staci D. Kramer, "Big Hopes for a Tiny Screen," *Sports Business Journal*, November 7, 2005.

3. "Mobile ESPN to Relaunch Service Through Verizon Wireless," The Associated Press, February 8, 2007.

4. Bernstein and Fisher, "10 Questions and Answers for Wireless."

5. Ibid.

6. "Fanscape," *The Sporting News*, December 2, 2005.

7. Bernstein and Fisher, "10 Questions and Answers for Wireless"; Edward C. Baig, "Verizon Revives ESPN Offering," *USA Today*, May 24, 2007.

8. Michael Lev-Ram, "As Mobile ESPN Falls, a Helio Rises," *Business 2.0 Magazine*, October 19, 2006.

9. Anthony Crupi, "Merrill Lynch: Time to Pull Plug on Mobile ESPN," *Mediaweek*, July 19, 2006; Li Yuan, Amol Sharma, and Melissa Marr, "Cellphone Start-Ups Struggle as Media Services Fail to Catch On," *The Wall Street Journal*, June 20, 2006.

10. Sports Business Institute (SBI) interview with Terry Denson, June 23, 2009.

11. Ibid.

12. "Coming to a Verizon Wireless Phone This Fall: Live ESPN Mobile TV Game Coverage of College Football Games," RedOrbit.com, September 11, 2009.

13. Sports Business Institute interview with Terry Denson.

14. Ibid.

15. Ibid.

16. Ibid.

17. "comScore Reports 6.5 Million Americans Watched Mobile Video in August," comScore press release, October 31, 2008.

18. Ibid.

19. "comScore Study Reveals That Mobile TV Currently Most Popular Among Males and Younger Age Segments," comScore press release, April 23, 2007.

20. Ibid.

21. "Increasing Text Usage (2004–2008)," CTIA—The Wireless Association, 2008.

22. Raymond Boyle, Deirdre Kevin, and Peter Flood, *Sport and the Media: Recent Economic, Legal and Technological Developments* (Mahwah, NJ: Routledge, 2004), p. 76.

23. Sports Business Institute interview with Blake Krikorian, February 12, 2009.

24. Ibid.

25. Ibid.

26. Ibid.

27. "Sling Media Introduces Slingbox 700U for Television Service Providers," Sling Media press release, January 6, 2010.

28. Ibid.

29. Harvey Kraft, "The Nike+ iPod Marketing Strategy: Develop Unique Lifestyle Relationships," marketingprofs.com, June 20, 2006.

30. Sports Business Institute interview with Michael Tchao, February 12, 2009.

31. NIKE, Inc., FY07 Q2 Earnings Conference Call Transcript, December 20, 2006.

32. NIKE, Inc., FY07 Q1 Earnings Conference Call Transcript, September 21, 2006.

33. "22 Million Miles and Counting, Nikeplus.com Becomes the World's Largest Online Running Destination," nikebiz.com, July 26, 2007.

34. "A Worldwide Milestone with More to Come!" insidenikerunning.nike.com, November 4, 2008.

35. SBI interview with Michael Tchao.

36. Ibid.

37. Neil Hughes, "Nike+ Heart Rate Monitor for Apple iPod Coming June 1," *Apple Insider,* May 18, 2010.

38. Sports Business Institute interview with Larry Witherspoon, September 25, 2009.

Chapter 6

1. "Poque, Poker: Origin and Spread," Encyclopedia Britannica Online, http://www.britannica.com/EBchecked/topic/470511/Poque (accessed April 26, 2010).

2. Nolan Dalla, "WSOP History—From Moss to Gold: A Brief History of the WSOP," World Series of Poker, www.wsop.com/wsop/history.asp (accessed April 26, 2010).

3. Poker.com, "WSOP History: The History of the World Series of Poker," www.poker.com/worldseriesofpoker/history.htm (accessed April 26, 2010).

4. Richard Sandomir, "Poker's Popularity Doesn't Appear Ready to Fold," *New York Times*, July 12, 2005.

5. Michael Hiestand, "NBC's Trials Coverage to Go Beyond Action," *USA Today*, July 9, 2004.

6. Adam Smeltz, "Eastern Graduate Wins $590K in World Series of Poker," *Courier-Post* (southern New Jersey), July 17, 2008.

7. "A Big Deal: Poker," *The Economist*, December 22, 2007.

8. Ibid.

9. Daniel G. Habib,"Online and Obsessed," *Sports Illustrated*, May 30, 2005.

10. "A Big Deal: Poker."

11. Sandomir, "Poker's Popularity Doesn't Appear Ready to Fold"; David Carr, "Doubling Up on 'Tilt,'" *The New York Times*, January 16, 2005.

12. Elaine Chaivarlis, "2009 WSOP Ante Up for Africa Recap," *PokerNews*, August 12, 2009.

13. I. Nelson Rose, "The Unlawful Internet Gambling and Enforcement Act of 2006 Analyzed," Casino City Times, October 2, 2006, www.casinocitytimes.com/article/the-unlawful-internet-gambling-enforcement-act-of-2006-analyzed-30106.

14. Fiona Walsh, "PartyGaming Drops Out of FTSE 100," *The Guardian*, October 9, 2006.

15. "World Series of Poker Main Event Starts Thursday," Associated Press, July 2, 2008.

16. House of Representatives Committee on Financial Services, "Frank Introduces Internet Gambling Regulation and Enforcement Act of 2007," press release, April 26, 2007.

17. Dan Cypra, "WSOP on ESPN Ratings up 11% in 2009," *Poker News Daily*, October 12, 2009.

18. Howard Stutz, "World Series of Poker 2007: Your Ad Here," *Gaming News*, June 25, 2007.

19. Sports Business Institute (SBI) interview with Jeffrey Pollack, August 7, 2008.

20. Ibid.

21. Adam Goldman, "Harrah's, ESPN Create Poker Circuit," Associated Press, September 20, 2005.

22. SBI interview with Jeffrey Pollack.

23. Erik Swanson, "ESPN Sees Ratings Jump for WSOP Final Under New Format," *Sports Business Daily*, November 14, 2008.

24. Ibid.

25. "About the WSOP," WSOP.com (accessed May 9, 2009).

26. Howard Stutz, "World Series of Poker: Main Event Attracts Second Largest Field in History," *Las Vegas Review Journal,* July 9, 2010..

27. SBI interview with Jeffrey Pollack.

28. Ibid.

29. "Gambling," Microsoft Encarta Online Encyclopedia 2008.

30. Ibid.

31. Ibid.

32. "Fantasy Sports Industry Grows to $800 Million Industry with 29.9 Million Players," PRWeb press release, July 10, 2008.

33. Sports Business Institute interview with David Yu, November 7, 2008.

34. Silicon Alley Insider, "Betfair," http://www.businessinsider.com/companies/betfair (accessed March 28, 2008).

35. Joe Drape, "Web Site Puts Focus on Fix in Sports Bets," *New York Times*, May 25, 2008; SBI interview with David Yu.

36. Doug Robson, "Slam Aimed at Gambling: In Wake of Troubling Revelations, Tennis' Governing Bodies Team Up to Avert Scandal," *USA Today*, December 18, 2007.

37. SBI interview with David Yu.

38. Ibid.

39. Matt Richtel, "Gambling Sites Offering Ways to Let Any User Be the Bookie," *New York Times,* July 6, 2004.

40. "Davydenko Fine Appeal Successful," BBC Sport, November 13, 2007; Joe Drape, "Talk of Efforts to Fix Matches Rattles Pro Tennis," *New York Times*, November 25, 2007.

41. SBI interview with David Yu.

42. Sportsbusinessdaily.com (accessed January 28, 2009).

43. "2010 NCAA March Madness on Demand Reaches New Traffic Heights," NCAA news release, April 6, 2010.

44. Annalisa Burgos, "March Madness: You Betcha," CNBC.com, March 16, 2007.

45. Ibid.

46. Sports Business Institute interview with Terry Jicinsky, June 10, 2009.

47. Matt Villano, "Victory Never Smelled Worse," *New York Times*, March 25, 2007.

48. "2009 Las Vegas Year-to-Date Executive Summary," LVCVA.com, http://www.lvcva.com/getfile/ES-YTD2008.pdf?fileID=479 (accessed May 20, 2010).

49. Ibid.

50. Ibid.

51. SBI interview with Terry Jicinsky.

52. "Festival Hall," Hardrockhotel.com, http://www.hardrockhotel.com/las-vegas/meetingsevents/special-events/festival-hall (accessed April 26, 2010).

53. Burgos, "March Madness: You Betcha.'"

54. Ibid.

55. SBI interview with Terry Jicinsky.

56. "Global Casinos & Gaming: Industry Profile," *Datamonitor*, April 2009, p. 29. This value excludes online gambling and is calculated as the total amount waged by customers minus the total amount paid out to customers as winnings, but before the payment of any applicable taxes, disbursements to charitable or other causes by games established for those purposes, or other expenses.

57. Bob Hartman, "Internet Gambling Industry Growth to Reach $528 Billion by 2015," CasinoGamblingWeb.com; source Merrill Lynch, December, 12, 2006.

58. Sports Business Institute interview with Frank Fahrenkopf, December 10, 2009.

Chapter 7

1. Sports Business Institute (SBI) interview with Malcolm Thorpe, March 16, 2009.

2. Douglas Robson, "Going for the Gold in the Persian Gulf," *Business Week*, April 7, 2008.

3. Government of Dubai, Dubai Statistics Centre, http://www.dsc.gov.ae/en/Pages/Home.aspx (accessed May 8, 2010).

4. UN Population Division, *Trends in Total Migration Stock*, 2006.

5. "Oil Share Dips in Dubai GDP," *AME Info*, June 9, 2007.

6. Government of Dubai, Dubai Statistics Centre, http://dsc.gov.ae/EN/Themes/Pages/Reports.aspx?TopicId=10 (accessed February 21, 2010).

7. Robson, "Going for the Gold in the Persian Gulf."

8. Ibid.

9. SBI interview with Malcolm Thorpe.

10. "Foreign Direct Investment," *Financial Times*, August 1, 2008.

11. "BCCI Wants ICC Headquarters in Mumbai," *CricketNext*, December 28, 2009.

12. "Update: Dubai Sports City Newsletter," January 2008.

13. SBI interview with Malcolm Thorpe.

14. Ibid.

15. "Profile: Dubai Holding," Zawya.com, www.zawya.com/cm/profile.cfm/cid1002706 (accessed April 26, 2010).

16. Lorne Manly, "It's Not a Mirage: Dubai Is Building a Sports Oasis," *The New York Times*, May 9, 2006.

17. Ibid.

18. SBI interview with Malcolm Thorpe.

19. Ibid.

20. "Mobilityland Company Information: About Suzuka Circuit," http://www.mobilityland.co.jp/english/suzuka (accessed May 8, 2010).

21. Ibid.

22. Center for Applied Business and Economic Research, Towson University, *The Impact of Oriole Park at Camden Yards on Maryland's Economy, 2006*, April 2007.

23. Sydney Organising Committee for the Olympic Games, Olympic Co-Ordination Authority, *The Sydney 2000 Olympic and Paralympic Games: A Report on the Financial Contribution by the New South Wales Government to the Sydney 2000 Games,* March 31, 2002.

24. "Business and Economic Benefits of the Sydney 2000 Games—A Collation of Evidence," Pricewaterhouse Coopers, 2001.

25. Ibid.

26. Ibid.

27. Christopher Kieran, "San Diego Padres Ballpark/Petco Park," *Business Week*, November 28, 2007.

28. Ibid.

29. *San Diego Union Tribune* editorial, "The Petco Boom," July 15, 2010.

30. Urban Land Institute, "ULI Development Case Studies: Coors Field," 2008, http://casestudies.uli.org/Profile.aspx?j=8216&p=5&c=8 (accessed April 26, 2010); Tim Romani and Ray Baker, "The Insiders' View of the Business of Sports," PowerPoint presentation, date and location unknown.

31. Alexander Garvin, "The American City: What Works, What Doesn't," *McGraw Hill-Professional*, June 19, 2002.

32. Ibid.

33. Sports Business Institute interview with Ray Baker, August 3, 2009.

34. George Merritt, "Coors Field Has Brought Denver Long Way," *USA Today*, October 25, 2007.

35. Ibid.

36. Romani and Baker, "The Insiders' View of the Business of Sports."

37. Downtown Denver Partnership, "Downtown Denver Sports," Downtowndenver.com, July, 2007, http://www.downtowndenver.com/Economic/documents/Sports_Aug07.pdf.

38. Ibid.

39. SBI interview with Ray Baker.

40. Romani and Baker, "The Insiders' View of the Business of Sports."

41. "The Business of Baseball: #21 Colorado Rockies," Forbes.com, April 7, 2010, http:

//www.forbes.com/lists/2010/33/baseball-valuations-10_The-Business-Of-Baseball_Rank.
html.

42. SBI interview with Ray Baker.

43. AEG Worldwide, "About Us," Corporate, http://www.aegworldwide.com/08_
corporate/about_us.html (accessed May 8, 2010).

44. AEG Worldwide, "About Us," The Ultimate Fan Experience, 2005, http://www.
aegworldwide.com/01_venues/the02.php (accessed May 8, 2010).

45. Sports Business Institute interview with Tim Leiweke, January 23, 2009.

46. Nokia Theatre, L.A. LIVE, press kit, 2007; Dan Laidman and Rick Orlov, "AEG
Finds New Partner for Entertainment Complex Near Staples Center; 56-Story, 1,100-
Room Convention Center Hotel Back on Track," *Daily News*, January 13, 2006.

47. SBI interview with Tim Leiweke.

48. Mathew Garrahan, "Downtown Goes Upmarket," *Financial Times*, October 28,
2008.

49. Beth Harris, "NBA Awards 2011 All-Star Game to Los Angeles," Associated Press,
June 7, 2009.

50. SBI interview with Tim Leiweke.

51. Reed Johnson, "The Conga Room at L.A. Live Is Thinking Big," *Los Angeles
Times*, December 7, 2008.

52. Sports Business Institute interview with Matt Rossetti, September 21, 2009.

Chapter 8

1. Sports Business Institute (SBI) interview with Michael Bidwill, June 11, 2009.

2. Nadine M. Post, "Arizona Stadium Builders Perform Movable Feats in Desert,"
Engineering News-Record, March 28, 2005.

3. "Wonders of the World: Cardinals Stadium," *Business Week*, February 27, 2006.

4. SBI interview with Michael Bidwill.

5. Jeff Yoders, "Constructing a Convertible," *Building Construction and Design*,
December 1, 2006; Don Muret, "The Cardinals' Signature Stadium," *Sports Business Journal*, September 18, 2006.

6. "Statistics," UniversityofPhoenixStadium.com (accessed January 19, 2010); Sports
Business Institute interview with John Drum, Arizona Cardinals Vice President of Stadium Operations, May 19, 2009.

7. Don Muret, "No Mirage: NFL Teams Watch as Cards Build New Kind of stadium," *Sports Business Journal*, December 12, 2005.

8. SBI interview with John Drum.

9. SBI interview with Michael Bidwill.

10. Muret, "The Cardinals' Signature Stadium."

11. Ibid.

12. SBI interview with Michael Bidwill.

13. Ibid.

14. Ibid.

15. John Cox, "Super Bowl's Super-Stadium Offers State-of-the-Art Wireless," *Network World*, January 22, 2008.

16. "How the NFL Is Using Business Technology and Information Technology Together," Baselinemag.com, August 29, 2008.

17. Ibid.

18. Scott Wong, "Stadium Name Deal: $154.4 Mil Over 20 Years," *Arizona Republic*, September 26, 2006.

19. Muret, "No Mirage."

20. "NFL Team Valuations: Arizona Cardinals," Forbes.com, September 10, 2008.

21. John Davis, "The First Night Baseball Games: Early Major League Games Were Few and Far Between," June 20, 2008, http://baseballhistory.suite101.com/article.cfm/first_night_baseball_games (accessed May 7, 2010).

22. "U.S. Cellular Field History 1910–1990," Major League Baseball, http://www.ballparksofbaseball.com/past/ComiskeyPark.htm (accessed May 9, 2010).

23. Vince Staten, *Why Is the Foul Pole Fair? (Or, Answers to the Baseball Questions Your Dad Hoped You Wouldn't Ask)* (New York: Simon & Schuster, 2004), pp. 238–240.

24. Travis McGee, "Sports Audio Adventures," *Sound & Video Contractor*, May 1, 2007.

25. "Sony Technology Outfits Arsenal Stadium in U.K.," Sony Sports Articles and Case Studies, 2007, http://pro.sony.com/bbsc/ssr/mkt-sports/mkt-sportsbrcacc/resource.articles.bbsccms-assets-mkt-sports-articles-enews0807uk.shtml (accessed May 7, 2010).

26. Don Coble, "NASCAR Offering New View for Fans; Handheld Scanners Provide Video, Radio Access. Devices Rent for $50 to $70 at Tracks," *Florida Times-Union*, April 12, 2006.

27. "NASCAR Digital Entertainment to Test Kangaroo.TV; Unique Handheld Broadcasting Device to Be Deployed at Seven NASCAR Craftsman Truck Series Events This Season," *Business Wire*, August 30, 2004.

28. "FAQ," General FAQ, Kangaroo TV, 2009.

29. "NASCAR Digital Entertainment to Test Kangaroo.TV."

30. David Paddon, "Five-Year Contract Has Kangaroo Media Jumping for Joy: Worth $10 Million U.S. in First Year. Nextel Will License, Market Montreal Firm's Multimedia Devices at NASCAR Races," *Montreal Gazette*, August 10, 2005.

31. Sports Business Institute interview with JP Brocket, February 19, 2009.

32. SBI interview with JP Brocket.

33. "Kangaroo Media Inc. Announces Closing of Private Placement," *CNW Telbec*,

August 23, 2005; "Kangaroo Media Inc. Completes Its $20 Million Private Placement of Common Shares," *CNW Telbec*, March 22, 2006.

34. "The Best Inventions of 2006," *Time Magazine*, Canadian Edition, November 13, 2006, p. 66.

35. "Kangaroo TV Partners with NFL and DIRECTV on a Season-Long Trial of 'NFL Sunday Ticket(TM) In-Stadium'—Handheld Device Will Bring Games and Stats to Fans at Selected NFL Stadiums," *PR Newswire*, September 27, 2006.

36. Ibid.

37. "Kangaroo Media Inc. Announces Fourth Quarter and Full-Year 2007 Financial Results," *CNW Telbec*, March 26, 2008.

38. Ibid.

39. "Kangaroo TV Offers Replays in Your Seat," MyFoxDetroit.com, January 18, 2010; Daniel Kaplan, "Dolphins Owner Stephen Ross Offering Kangaroo TV to NFL Teams," *SportsBusiness Daily*, March 24, 2010.

40. *SportsBusiness Daily*, March 15, 2010.

41. SBI interview with JP Brocket.

42. "Transforming Sports and Entertainment: In the Stadium and Beyond," Cisco press release, September 2007.

43. "Cisco Technology Places Santiago Bernabéu Stadium at the Forefront of Next-Generation Sports Arenas," Cisco press release, November 20, 2006.

44. Sports Business Institute interview with Ron Ricci, March 26, 2009.

45. "Manchester City Kicks Off Innovative SmartCard Services and Sponsorships with Wireless, RF-Enabled Intelligent Stadium," Hewlett-Packard press release, February 2004.

46. Ibid.

47. SBI interview with Ron Ricci.

48. "High-Tech Puts One in the Back of Munich's New Net," *Wireless Security Focus Report*, 2006.

49. "Yankees, Cisco Announce Details of Their New Partnership," *Sports Business Daily*, November 12, 2008.

50. Ibid.

51. Wylie Wong, "Home Sweet Dome," *Biz Tech Magazine*, June 2009.

52. Sports Business Institute interview with Jack Hill, December 30, 2010.

Chapter 9

1. "Disney Complex to Become ESPN-Branded Immersive Sports Venue," Disney press release, May 13, 2008.

2. Mark Albright, "Disney Adds ESPN Cachet," *St. Petersburg Times*, September 25, 2008.

3. Scott Powers, "ESPN Wide World of Sports Renamed," *Orlando Sentinel*, September 24, 2008, blogs.orlandosentinel.com.

4. Richard E. Fogleson, *Married to the Mouse* (New Haven, CT: Yale University Press, 2003), pp. 274.

5. "Economics Research Associates' Attraction Attendance Report 2007," Themed Entertainment Association, May 2008.

6. Scott Powers, "Not Just Another Cinderella Story," *Orlando Sentinel*, October 30, 2006.

7. Sports Business Institute (SBI) interview with Ken Potrock, April 16, 2009.

8. SBI interview with Ken Potrock.

9. Albright, "Disney Adds ESPN Cachet"; SBI interview with Ken Potrock.

10. Doug Smith, "And They Will Come: Disney Builds Magical Facilities for Youth Sports—and Moves a Ton of 3-Day Tickets in the Bargain," *USA Today*, September 10, 2008.

11. Powers, "Not Just Another Cinderella Story."

12. Ibid.

13. Alan Byrd, "Disney Sports Rolls Out New Logo, Merchandise," *Orlando Business Journal*, June 25, 1999.

14. Ibid.

15. SBI interview with Ken Potrock.

16. Ibid.

17. Albright, "Disney Adds ESPN Cachet."

18. "Inside Out," *Sports Business Journal*, January 21, 2008.

19. Albright, "Disney Adds ESPN Cachet."

20. "ESPN Rise Games Presented by Target 2010," *ESPN Media Zone*, May 10, 2010, http://www.espnmediazone3.com/us/2010/05/espn-rise-games-presented-by-target-2010.

21. Jeff Kober, "ESPN Wide World of Sports Complex Relaunches," *Mouseplanet*, February 26, 2010.

22. SBI interview with Potrock.

23. Andrew Zimbalist, *Baseball and Billions: A Probing Look Inside the Big Business of Our National Pastime* (New York: Basic Books, 1994), p. 32.

24. Ibid.

25. Unnamed biography cited in Zimbalist, *Baseball and Billions*.

26. Dr. Larry M. McCarthy and Dr. Richard Irwin, "Names in Lights: Corporate Purchase of Sport Facility Naming Rights," *Cyber-Journal of Sports Marketing*, 1998.

27. Alan E. Foulds, "Boston's Ballparks & Arenas," University Press of New England, 2005, p. 104.

28. "Branding the O₂: Welcome to the New Dome of Entertainment," *The Independent*, June 18, 2007.

29. Ross Netherly, "AEG's Global Blueprint," *Sports Business Journal*, November 19, 2007; Richard Wray, "No Place Like Dome for Major New Venue," guardian.co.uk, May 26, 2005.

30. Sports Business Institute interview with David Campbell, February 6, 2009.

31. "Bon Jovi Opens the O_2 On Record Setting Night—UK's Newest Concert Venue Opens to Rave Reviews and Record Numbers," AEG press release, June 25, 2007; "A Sponsored Walk Round the Big Top," *The Independent*, November 17, 2008.

32. SBI interview with David Campbell.

33. "A Sponsored Walk Round the Big Top."

34. SBI interview with David Campbell.

35. Netherly, "AEG's Global Blueprint."

36. "A Sponsored Walk Round the Big Top."

37. "Inside the O_2," O_2 press release, http://www.o2.com/about/14252.asp (accessed April 26, 2010).

38. James Aitchison, "Panel Session: What Can Sponsorship Do for a Brand?—O_2 and the O_2 London Arena," *World Advertising Research Center*, May 23, 2008.

39. "A Sponsored Walk Round the Big Top."

40. SBI interview with David Campbell.

41. Jason Blevins, "Red Bull, 'King' of Energy Drinks, Lets Wild Approach Do the Hawking," *Denver Post*, October 21, 2008.

42. Ibid.

43. Ibid.

44. Eric Pfanner, "Red Bull Storms into France," *International Herald Tribune*, June, 9, 2008.

45. Sports Business Institute interview with Robert Hollander, June 23, 2009.

46. Ric Jensen, Ph. D., et al. "How Do Fans React When Sports Teams Are Named After Corporation?" *The Sports Journal*, Vol. 11, no. 1, 2008.

47. SBI interview with Robert Hollander.

48. "Red Bull Snaps Up Jaguar F1 Team," BBC Sport, November 15, 2004.

49. Melanie Ho, "For Red Bull, It's Here, There and Everywhere—Energy Drink Maker Corners the Marketing," *Washington Post*, August, 23 2006.

50. Tripp Mickle, "Red Bull to Drill Brand into Stadium Staff," *Sports Business Journal*, September 15, 2008.

51. Nicole Santa Cruz, "80,000 Flock to Downtown Portland to See Flugtag Fliers Take Plunge," *The Oregonian*, August 2, 2008.

52. Brent Hunsberger, "Playbooks and Profits Blog—Red Bull Flugtag the Height of Experiential Marketing," *The Oregonian*, August 3, 2008.

53. SBI interview with Robert Hollander.

54. Daniel Kaplan, "ESPN's 3-D Push Started with a Little Disney World Magic," *Sports Business Journal,* May 31, 2010.

55. Wimbledon: The Official Site, www.wimbledon.org; "About Wimbledon—Ambush Marketing," http://www.wimbledon.org/en_GB/about/guide/ambushmarketing.html (accessed May 7, 2010).

56. Ben Klayman, "Bank of America CEO Defends Sports Marketing Deals," *Reuters*, March 12, 2009.

57. Sports Business Institute interview with Arte Moreno, September 23, 2009.

INDEX

AAU, *see* Amateur Athletic Union

Abbott and Costello, 94

ABC (American Broadcasting Company): *Monday Night Football*, 4, 5; Olympic broadcasts, 20–21; soccer matches, 75; *Superstars*, 27; *Wide World of Sports*, 15, 20, 78

Abu Dhabi, 180, 185

AC Milan, 75–76

Action sports: skateboarding, 78–81; Warped Tour, 176

Activision|Blizzard, 53, 79, 80

Adams, Roger, 31

Adidas, 79, 238

Advertising: cigarette, 236; distinction from sponsorship, 255n; Internet, 8, 114, 116, 117, 166; by local businesses, 141, 142; on mobile devices, 139–40, 141, 142; platforms, 93; radio, 14; at stadiums, 226–27; television commercials, 6–7, 24, 25, 27, 39, 125; in video games, 55, 60

AEG, *see* Anschutz Entertainment Group

AEG Sports, 72

Affleck, Ben, 151

AGA, *see* American Gaming Association

Aikman, Troy, 112

Ali, Muhammad (Cassius Clay), 3, 15

Allianz Arena, 217–18

Al Maktoum, Sheik Mohammed bin Rashid, 181, 182, 185

Al Maktoum family, 180, 181, 185

Al-Zarooni, Abdul Rahim, 182, 185

Amateur Athletic Union (AAU), 230, 232

Amateur sports: marketing to athletes, 141–43; Rivals.com, 108–11; running, 135–38. *See also* College sports; Youth sports

American Gaming Association (AGA), 168

American Heart Association, 49

American Youth Sports Organization (AYSO), 69

Anheuser-Busch, 6, 35, 208, 235–36

Anschutz, Philip, 70

Anschutz Entertainment Group (AEG): holdings, 192; L.A. LIVE, 191–94; musical tours, 74; O₂ Dome, 192, 237–39; soccer teams, 68, 70, 73, 75–76, 241

Apple Computer: athlete endorsements, 84; iPad, 103, 139; iPod, 135–37, 138; television commercials, 6. *See also* iPhone

Arenas, *see* Sports-anchored development; Stadiums and arenas

Arguello, Martin Vassallo, 159

Arizona Cardinals, 205–6, 207–8, 210, 222

Arizona Sports and Tourism Authority, 205, 206, 208

Arizona State University, 169, 205

Arledge, Roone, 4, 20, 21

Arsenal Football Club, 199, 212

Arseneau, Marc, 213

Association of Tennis Professionals (ATP), 159, 182, 238

AT&T, 79, 96, 126, 129–30

AT&T Park, 175–76
Atari, 7, 16, 46, 51, 52
Athlete branding: challenges, 91, 92, 120;
    communicating brands, 86–88, 120;
    creating brands, 85–86; development, 3,
    15; examples, 68–69, 70–76, 77–84, 90–
    92; global stars, 72, 76; guidelines, 84–
    89; history, 77; images, 70–71; Internet
    revenues, 117, 120; merchandise, 35, 72,
    74; in mixed-martial-arts, 33; monitor-
    ing, 89; overview, 76–78; participants,
    85–86; poker players, 154; soccer play-
    ers, 68–69, 70–76; target audiences, 85;
    television broadcasts and, 39–40
Athletes: amateur, 141–43; appearance
    fees, 181–82; fan clubs, 106; managers, 3;
    players' associations, 104, 117, 141, 196;
    revenue sources, 140, 141, 196; training
    with, 142–43. See also Endorsements
At-home convergence: milestones, 13–17;
    stakeholders, 17. See also Athlete brand-
    ing; Internet; Televised sporting events;
    Video games
Atlanta Braves, 28, 117, 230, 233, 247
Atlantic City, 166
At-venue convergence, 173–78. See also
    Corporate marketing; Sports-anchored
    development; Venue technology
Audio systems, 212, 217
Austrian soccer teams, 240
Automobiles: manufacturers, 244; radios,
    94
Auto racing: in Dubai, 182; Formula
    One, 215, 241; Motopia, 187. See also
    NASCAR
Away-from-home convergence, 93–95. See
    also Fantasy sports leagues; Gambling;
    Internet; Mobile technology
AYSO, see American Youth Sports
    Organization

Baker, Ray, 177, 189, 190, 191
Baltimore Orioles, 175, 187
Baltimore Ravens, 20, 187
Bank of America, 247

Barkley, Charles, 30, 151
Baseball: college, 2, 15, 27; fantasy leagues,
    114; minor league, 103, 211; movies, 94;
    night games, 211; players' union, 104;
    radio broadcasts, 14, 94; stadiums, 175,
    187, 189–91, 195, 218, 225, 235–36; tele-
    vised games, 28, 36–37; video games, 51,
    52. See also Major League Baseball
Basketball: college, 31, 65, 155–56, 160–63,
    169, 210; Harlem Globetrotters, 27,
    231; video games, 52. See also National
    Basketball Association
Beckham, David, 68–69, 70–76
Beckham, Victoria, 70, 74
Beijing Olympics, 19–20, 22–27, 37, 82, 159
Bend It Like Beckham, 72
Berman, Eddie, 99
Berman, Tom, 99
Betfair.com, 157–60, 164
Betting, *see* Gambling
Bidwill, Michael, 177, 206, 207, 208
Big Ten, 38, 39
Binion, Benny, 148, 152
Binion's Horseshoe and Casino, 147–48,
    152
Black, Andrew, 157
"Black Sox" scandal, 155
Blogs, 104, 107, 119
Bodenheimer, George, 96, 121–24, 229
Boom Boom HuckJam Tour, 80
Boston Red Sox, 103
Bowling, 45, 234–35
Bowman, Bob, 96, 100–101, 102, 104, 105
Boxing: athlete branding, 3, 15; news
    reels, 94; radio broadcasts, 14; televised
    matches, 15, 27, 28, 34
Bradenton Prep, 183
Brands: affinity, 220; definition, 76; ESPN,
    230, 234; horizontal integration, 245–
    46; leveraging, 230, 235; vertical im-
    mersion, 243–45. See also Advertising;
    Athlete branding; Corporate marketing
Britain, *see* London
Brocket, JP, 177, 213–14
Brooklyn Dodgers, 94

Budweiser, 208. *See also* Anheuser-Busch

Buffalo Bills, 236

Bukhatir, Abdulrahman, 182, 185

Busch, August, Jr., 235–36

Busch Stadium, 235–36

Business-to-business marketing, 244–45, 247

Cable television: growth, 16; Olympics coverage, 21, 23–24; reality shows, 33; sports networks, 16, 28, 37; sports programming, 28, 39. *See also* ESPN

Cablevision, 21

Campbell, David, 178, 237, 238, 239

Canada, sports-anchored developments, 201

Casinos: Atlantic City, 166; history, 155; Las Vegas, 147–48, 152, 153, 160, 161–63, 164, 166, 168; marketing, 164, 166; online gambling and, 170–71; poker tournaments, 147–48, 150, 152–54; sports books, 160, 161–63, 168

Cavic, Milorad, 19

CBS Sports, 20, 26, 130, 149

CBSsportsline.com, 17, 106, 107

CCS, *see* Cisco Connected Sports

Celebrities: at poker tournaments, 151; in Super Bowl commercials, 6. *See also* Athletes

Cell phones, *see* Mobile technology

Chad, Norman, 148

Chambers, John, 218

Champion Stadium, 233, 245

Chan, Johnny, 154

Charlotte Bobcats, 28

Chelsea Football Club, 233

Chevrolet, 6

Chicago Cubs, 28, 117

Chicago White Sox, 155, 211

Chick-fil-A, 31

China: basketball, 81, 82, 83, 84; Beijing Olympics, 19–20, 22–27, 37, 82, 159

Chrysler Corporation, 244

Cisco Connected Sports (CCS), 216

Cisco Sports and Entertainment, 216–19

Cisco Systems, 208, 209, 212, 216, 220, 226

Citizens Sports Network (CSN), 107, 111–14

Clay, Cassius (Muhammad Ali), 3, 15

Coca-Cola, 5, 6, 82, 208, 238

College GameDay, 29–32, 41, 121, 123

College sports: baseball, 2, 15, 27; basketball, 31, 65, 155–56, 160–63, 169, 210; betting scandals, 155–56, 169; conferences, 39; football, 29, 94, 123; lower-profile, 39; Rivals.com, 108–11; stadiums, 174; televised events, 39. *See also* NCAA

Colorado Rockies, 189, 190

Columbia University baseball team, 2, 15, 27

Comcast, 22, 41

Commercials, *see* Television commercials

Commissioner.com, 8

Compton, Kevin, 111

Computer games, 16, 51. *See also* Video games

Computers: linking to televisions, 40–41, 134–35. *See also* Technology

ComScore, 25, 26

Conrad, Frank, 14

Consumer demand for mobile technology, 131, 132, 139–40, 144

Consumer touchpoints, 10, 247

Convergence: at-home, 13–17; at-venue, 173–78; away-from-home, 93–95; common points, 1; consumer touchpoints, 10; definition, 1; distinction from tactical marketing, 1–2; history, 2–9; importance, 9; locales, 10

Coors Brewing Company, 189

Coors Field, 189–91, 195

Corporate marketing: bowl games, 236; brand affinity, 220; business-to-business, 244–45, 247; challenges, 243, 244, 245–46, 247; engaging experiences, 247–48; events, 242; history, 5–6, 235–37; licensing, 5; naming rights, 175, 189, 210, 235–36, 245; at Olympics, 5–6; Red Bull, 239–43; return on invest-

ment, 246; stakeholders, 247. *See also* Advertising; Brands; Endorsements; Sponsorships
Corso, Lee, 29, 30, 31
Costas, Bob, 22, 24
Couture, Randy, 34
Cowboys Stadium, 207, 218–19, 224, 225–27
Creative Inc., 233
Cricket, 179, 180, 182
Cronkite, Walter, 20
CSN, *see* Citizens Sports Network
Curry, Devin, 45
Czech Republic, Strahov Stadium, 199

Dallas Cowboys, *see* Cowboys Stadium
Davie, Art, 32
Davie Brown Entertainment, 73
Davydenko, Nikolay, 159
Delaware, sports gambling, 156, 168
Deng Xiaoping, 23
Denson, Terry, 97, 128, 129, 130, 140
Denver: Coors Field, 189–91, 195, 200; INVESCO Field at Mile High Stadium, 191
Denver Metropolitan Major League Baseball Stadium District, 189
DiGiovanni, Sundance, 56
Digital video recording (DVR), 133
DiMaggio, Joe, 3
DIRECTV, 24, 101, 134, 214–15
Discovery Channel, 149
Dish Network, 135
Disney World, 229, 230, 231, 232, 233, 244. *See also* Walt Disney Co.
Donaghy, Tim, 171
Donovan, Landon, 73
Doritos Pro-Gaming, 58
Dr Pepper, 57, 58
DSC, *see* Dubai Sports City
Dubai: debt, 185; real estate development, 180–81, 184–85; tourism, 180, 181, 184, 185
Dubailand, 184–85
Dubai Sports City (DSC), 179–80, 182–86, 197

Dubai World Cup, 181
Duke, Annie, 151
Dupuy, Bob, 100
DVR, *see* Digital video recording

EA, *see* Electronic Arts
EA SPORTS, 49, 52, 53, 59, 63–67
Ebersol, Dick, 21, 22, 23
EchoStar, 134, 135
Edison, Thomas, 94
Edmonton, Alberta, 201
Ed Sullivan Show, 27
Eisenman, Peter, 206–7
Electronic Arts (EA), 7, 16, 58, 63, 90, 127. *See also* EA SPORTS
Electronic scoreboards, 211, 219, 227
Els, Ernie, 179, 181
Emirates Stadium, 212
Endorsements: conflicts with event sponsors, 246; partnerships of sponsors and athletes, 88–89; personal branding and, 3, 71, 77, 79, 82, 84, 91–92; of Red Bull, 242
Energy efficiency, 223–24
English Premier League (EPL), 68, 71, 114, 132, 199, 233
Entertainment, *see* Convergence; Game-day experiences
Environmental Protection Agency (EPA), 224
Environmental sustainability, 223–24
EPA, *see* Environmental Protection Agency
EPL, *see* English Premier League
ESPN (Entertainment and Sports Programming Network): brand, 230, 234; *College GameDay*, 29–32, 41, 121, 123; establishment, 4, 28; executives, 26; influence, 4, 28; Innovation Lab, 234–35; Los Angeles building, 194; MLBAM and, 104–5; mobile content, 127–29; new platforms, 121–22, 123–24, 127–29; programming, 4–5, 8, 58; radio broadcasts, 122, 129, 194; revenues, 123; satellite radio station, 131; soccer

matches, 68, 75; *SportsCenter*, 4, 121, 129, 194, 235; Sprint FanView and, 176; technology, 118, 124; 3D programming, 40; websites, 30, 106, 121–22, 123; World Series of Poker, 147, 148, 149, 150, 152, 153; X Games, 5, 79, 122

ESPN.com, 16, 17, 104, 106, 107, 114, 118, 123, 127

ESPN MVP, 125–26, 128–29

ESPN Radio College GameDay, 31

ESPN RISE, 234, 245

ESPNU, 39, 234

ESPN Wide World of Sports Complex, 183, 229–35, 244, 245

ESPN Zone restaurants, 5, 192, 194

Europe, *see* London; Soccer

European PGA Tour, 215

Extreme sports, *see* Ultimate Fighting Championship

Facebook, 111, 112, 113, 114

Fahrenkopf, Frank, 97, 168–71

Falaknaz, Abdul Rahman, 182, 185

Fans, *see* Consumer demand; Game-day experiences

Fantasy sports leagues: baseball, 114; football, 113–14, 171; gambling and, 156–57, 171; licensing of player statistics, 104; mobile content, 129; revenues, 157; soccer, 114; websites, 8, 107, 111–12, 156–57

Fantasy Sports Trade Association, 113

Farha, Sam, 147–48

Farrell, Brian, 18, 53, 54–55

FCC, *see* Federal Communications Commission

FC Red Bull Salzburg, 240

Federal Communications Commission (FCC), 40, 131

Federer, Roger, 181, 246

Feiler, Anoushka, 242

Feller, Mark, 209

Ferguson, Alex, 72

Ferguson, Chris, 154

Fertitta, Frank, 17, 32–33, 34, 35, 36

Fertitta, Lorenzo, 17, 32–33, 34, 35, 36

Field hockey, 183

FIFA, *see* Soccer

FIFA video games, 53, 65

FIH, *see* International Hockey Federation

Fils-Aime, Reggie, 48

Flugtag, 242

Football: bowl games, 236; college, 29, 94, 123; fantasy leagues, 113–14, 171; movies, 94; night games, 211; video games, 7; XFL, 28. *See also* National Football League; Soccer

Forbes magazine, 82

Ford Motor Company, 241, 244

Foreman, George, 15

Formula One Racing, 215, 241

Founder Group, 83

Fowler, Chris, 29, 30

Fox Interactive Media, 110

Fox Sports: baseball broadcasts, 41; differentiation, 42–43; football broadcasts, 41, 43, 204–5; March Madness, 162; poker programming, 150; radio, 131; sponsors, 43–44; Verizon V CAST and, 130; websites, 107

Frank, Barney, 169

Frick, Ford, 235

Frito-Lay, 6

Front Row Marketing Services, 31

Fuji, 5

Gaines, Rowdy, 20

Galvin Corporation, 94

Gambling: Betfair.com, 157–60; blackjack, 111; fantasy leagues and, 156–57, 171; future of, 163, 169; growth, 163, 165–66, 169; history, 155–56; integrity of events and, 155, 159–60, 165, 167, 168, 169, 171; laws, 151–52, 156, 159, 164, 168, 169, 170–71; on mobile devices, 95; online, 147, 150, 151–52, 156, 157–60, 163–65, 166, 167, 169–70; opponents, 155, 170; regulations, 165, 167, 170–71; revenues, 163, 166, 170; scandals, 155–56, 159, 169, 171; sports betting, 155–56, 157–63, 165–66,

167, 168–69; stakeholders, 93. *See also* Poker

Gamebattles.com, 56, 58

Game-day experiences: costs, 38; fan expectations, 173; at sports-anchored developments, 175–77, 195–96, 203; technology and, 212, 216, 219, 220–22, 228

Game Day Vision, 215

Games, video, *see* Computer games; Video games

Game Show Network, 150

Gehrig, Lou, 94

General Electric, 22, 24

General Motors, 244

German stadiums, 217–18

Gila River Indian Community, 208

Gillespie, Billy, 109

Gillette, 71, 74

Gillette Cavalcade of Sports, 15, 27

Gin Mill, 19–20, 24

Golf: in Dubai, 179, 181–83, 184–85; mobile technology and, 215; PGA Championships, 215, 216; video games, 65

Golfers, 3

Google, 60

Gracie, Rorion, 32

Greece, ancient, 173

Green building, 223–24

Greene, Joe, 6

Green Jarvis, 204

Guitar Hero, 60

Gullit, Ruud, 75

H2 Gaming Capital, 170

Hamm, Mia, 232

Hanesbrands Inc., 233, 245

Hansen, Brendan, 19–20

Hard Rock Hotel and Casino, 161–62

Harlem Globetrotters, 27, 231

Harley Davidson, 35

Harmon, Butch, 183

Harrah's, 152, 154, 170

Harrison, Rodney, 204

Hawk, Frank, 79

Hawk, Pat, 81

Hawk, Tony, 53, 78–81, 91

HBO, 16, 28, 34

Hellmuth, Phil, 154

Henin, Justine, 181

Hewlett-Packard (HP), 233

Herbstreit, Kirk, 29, 30

Hi5, 111, 112

Hicks, Dan, 20, 24

Higginbotham, William, 51

Highbury Stadium, 199

High school sports, 108–11, 234. *See also* Youth sports

Hill, David, 17, 41–44

Hill, Jack, 177, 225–28

Hockey, 241. *See also* National Hockey League

Hodges, Russ, 94

HOK+Sport, 206–7

Hollander, Robert, 178, 240, 242

Home Depot, 31, 123

Home Depot Center, 68, 192

Horse racing, 168, 181

Houston Rockets, 83

Howard, Desmond, 29, 30–31

Hulu, 41, 134

Hunt, Lamar, 70

Hunter, Shawn, 18, 71–72, 73, 74

ICC, *see* International Cricket Council

IMG, *see* International Management Group

Inchon, Korea, Sungui Arena Complex, 200, 201–2

Insight Enterprises, 208, 209

International Cricket Council (ICC), 180, 183

International Hockey Federation (FIH), 183

International Management Group (IMG), 3, 77, 89–92, 180

International Olympic Committee (IOC), 6, 22, 159

Internet: advertising, 8, 114, 116, 117, 166;

athlete brand marketing, 90–91; blogs, 104, 107, 119; convergence with television, 118–19; customized content, 117–19; fan sites, 107–8, 110, 111–14, 119–20; future directions, 115–20, 123–24; gambling, 147, 150, 151–52, 163–65, 166, 167; league websites, 101, 103, 107, 116; local content, 118; merchandise sales, 116; mobile access, 139; Olympics coverage, 23, 25–26; online games, 55, 56–58, 62–63, 64; podcasts, 122; Rivals.com, 107, 108–11, 119; social networking sites, 111, 112–14, 119–20; sports information, 8, 16–17, 106–7; sports websites, 106–8; subscription modes, 115–17; targeted marketing, 117; ticket sales, 102, 107, 116; video download sites, 41; video streaming, 99, 101–2, 105, 116, 117–18; website traffic, 25–26. See also Fantasy sports leagues

INVESCO Field at Mile High Stadium, 191

IOC, see International Olympic Committee

iPad, 103, 139

iPhone: competition, 129–30; CSN app, 114; ESPN Radio app, 122; games, 55, 60; MLB.com app, 103, 130, 139, 143, 144; Nike+, 138; Web access, 129–30

IP networks, 208, 226

iPod, 135–37, 138

Ivey, Phil, 154

Iwata, Satoru, 48, 51

Jackson, Shoeless Joe, 155

James, LeBron, 82, 83

Japan, Suzuka circuit, 186–87

Jicinsky, Terry, 97, 161, 163

Jobs, Steve, 135–36

John Hancock Financial Services, 236

John Madden Football, 7

Johns Hopkins University, 32

Johnson, Randy, 95

Jones, Brent, 111

Josten's, 233

JumboTrons, 211

Juvenal, 2

Kangaroo Media, 213, 215

Kangaroo TV, 212–16

Kaplan, Perrin, 18, 49–50, 51

Kassoy, Will, 18, 79, 80–81

KDKA, 14

Kerns, Mike, 111, 112, 114

Kim, W. Chan, 48

Kissinger, Henry, 77

Kitajima, Kosuke, 20

Kleiner Perkins, 111

Knievel, Robert Craig "Evel," 78

Knight, Bobby, 30, 162

Knute Rockne: All American, 94

Korea, Sungui Arena Complex, 200, 201–2

Kraft, Robert, 70

Krikorian, Blake, 97, 132–33, 134, 135

Krikorian, Jason, 132–33

L.A. LIVE, 191–94, 198

Landis, Kennesaw Mountain, 155

Las Vegas: casinos, 147–48, 152, 153, 160, 161–63, 164, 166, 168; sports betting, 160, 161–63, 168; tourism, 161–63, 166; World Series of Poker, 147–54, 170

Las Vegas Convention and Visitors Authority (LVCVA), 161, 166

LEED (Leadership in Energy & Environmental Design) certification, 223

Leiweke, Tim, 74, 177, 193, 194

Lewis, Kenneth, 247

Lexus, 247

Lezak, Jason, 19–20

Licensing: for Internet, 104–5; for mobile technology, 104–5; at Olympics, 5; for video games, 52, 53–55, 60, 62–63

Liddell, Chuck, 34

LIDS, 58

Lipscomb, Steven, 149

Lloyd, David, 183

London: Highbury Stadium, 199; O₂ Dome, 192, 237–39; Olympics, 238

Los Angeles: L.A. LIVE, 191–94, 198; Olympics, 5–6; tourism, 193
Los Angeles Angels, 247–52
Los Angeles Dodgers, 99
Los Angeles Galaxy, 68–69, 70, 73–74, 75, 76, 192
Los Angeles Olympic Organizing Committee, 5
Luxury suites, 175, 207, 209, 218
LVCVA, *see* Las Vegas Convention and Visitors Authority

M&T Bank Stadium, 20, 187
Ma, Jeff, 111, 112, 114
Madden, John, 7, 90, 91
Madden Football, 7, 16, 49, 52, 64, 90, 127
Major League Baseball (MLB): All-Star Games, 211; betting scandals, 155; environmental sustainability, 224; mobile applications, 130; satellite radio station, 131; season, 36; team merchandise, 103; television network, 104; ticket sales, 102; video game licenses, 52; websites, 107; World Series, 247, 248. *See also* Baseball
Major League Baseball Advanced Media (MLBAM): evolution, 100–104, 119; mobile applications, 139, 143, 144; on-line ads, 114; Tickets.com, 143–46; video streaming of games, 99, 101–2, 105, 116
Major League Gaming (MLG), 56–58, 63
Major League Soccer (MLS): attendance, 73, 74; Beckham in Los Angeles, 68–69, 73–75; establishment, 70; teams, 241–42; televised matches, 75; website, 103. *See also* Soccer
Manchester City Football Stadium, 216, 217
Manchester United, 71, 72, 183, 217
Manning, Eli, 90–92, 204
Manning, Peyton, 90–91, 232
March Madness, 26, 65, 160–63, 210
Marketing, *see* Advertising; Corporate marketing
Mastrov, Mark, 35

Mauborgne, Renee, 48
McCain, John, 32
McCormack, Mark, 3, 89–90
McCourt, Jamie, 105
McDonald's, 5, 84
McEnroe, John, 60
McMahon, Vince, 54
Media: new platforms, 121–22, 123–24, 138–43; traditional, 117, 118, 120, 140, 142. *See also* Mobile technology; Radio; Television
Menendez, Robert, 169
Miami Dolphins, 215
Microsoft, 123
Microsoft Xbox, 47, 48, 50, 51, 55, 64
Millennium Dome, 237
Minardi, 241
Mitsubishi, 46, 211
Mixed-martial-arts (MMA), *see* Ultimate Fighting Championship
MLB, *see* Major League Baseball
MLBAM, *see* Major League Baseball Advanced Media
MLBlogs, 104
MLB Network, 37
MLB.tv, 99, 101–2, 105
MLG, *see* Major League Gaming
MLS, *see* Major League Soccer
MMA (mixed-martial-arts), *see* Ultimate Fighting Championship
Mobile ESPN, 127–28
Mobile gaming, 55, 59, 60–61
Mobile technology: advertising, 139–40, 141, 142; alerts, 121; applications, 103, 114, 122, 130, 131, 139, 140, 143, 144; cameras, 204; changes, 129–32, 138; consumer demand, 131, 132, 139–40, 144; future of, 138–43, 144–46; gambling, 95; Kangaroo TV, 212–16; Nike+, 135–38; pagers, 131; privacy issues, 143; SlingBox, 105, 132–35; sponsors' use of, 145; sports content, 95, 103, 121–22; at sports venues, 175–76, 204–5, 209, 212, 216–17, 219; stakeholders, 93; text messaging, 132; 3G, 132; ticket sales, 141, 145,

146; Verizon V CAST, 125–27, 128–31, 139; video, 125–27, 130, 134, 141, 143. *See also* iPhone

Monday Night Football, 4, 5

Moneymaker, Chris, 147–48, 150

Montag, Sandy, 18, 89–92

Moorad, Jeff, 96, 111, 112–13, 114

Moore, Peter, 18, 63–67

Moore, Tom, 148

Moreno, Arturo "Arte," 178, 247–52

Morgan, Dave, 96, 108, 109

Moss, Johnny, 149

Motorola, 72, 76

Movies, sports,, 94–95

MTR Gaming, 152

Murdoch, Rupert, 43

MyLeaderboard, 216

MySpace, 111, 112

Nadal, Rafael, 181

NASCAR: Fuel for Business Council, 247; Kangaroo TV, 212–16; Red Bull teams, 241; satellite radio station, 131; sponsors, 247; Sprint FanView, 176, 214, 216; Sprint Nextel Series, 213; Winston Cup Series, 236

NASCAR Digital Entertainment, 213

Nascimento, Edson Arantes do, *see* Pelé

Nash, Steve, 112

NASL, *see* North American Soccer League

National Basketball Association (NBA): All-Star Games, 193, 225; betting scandals, 171; stars, 81–84; televised games, 134; television broadcasts, 28; video games, 65; websites, 101, 107. *See also* Basketball

National Collegiate Athletic Association, *see* NCAA

National Football League (NFL): broadcasting rights, 28; night games, 211; online video streaming, 101; pre-game shows, 43; Super Bowl, 6, 27, 160, 162, 204–5, 210, 215; televised games, 4, 5, 15, 28, 101, 134; websites, 107; wireless video, 127. *See also* Football

National Hockey League (NHL), 39, 127, 130, 134

National Resources Defense Council (NRDC), 224

National Skateboarding Association, 79

NBA, *see* National Basketball Association

NBA China, 83

NBA.com, 101

NBC: mobile video, 127; *Nightly News*, 25; Olympics coverage, 19–20, 21–22, 23–27, 37; radio stations, 14; sports programming, 15, 27; *Today Show*, 25; websites, 23, 25, 26, 41, 101; World Poker Tour, 150; XFL, 28

NBCOlympics.com, 23, 25, 26

NBCSports.com, 101

NCAA (National Collegiate Athletic Association): betting scandals, 155–56, 169; men's basketball tournament, 26, 65, 160–63, 210; regulations, 40, 110; video games, 65. *See also* College sports

Neal, David, 17, 23, 24, 25, 26

NEC, 238, 239

NES, *see* Nintendo Entertainment System

Nevada, sports gambling, 156, 168. *See also* Las Vegas

New England Patriots, 204–5, 236

News Corp., 41

New York Giants, 15, 94, 204–5

New York Red Bulls, 200, 241–42

New York Yankees, 28, 63, 94, 95, 103, 218

Nextel, 213

NFL, *see* National Football League

NFL.com, 101

NFL Sunday Ticket, 214–15

NHL, *see* National Hockey League

Nielsen, 25, 26, 113, 149

Nielsen IAG, 25

Nike, 79, 82, 109

Nike+, 135–38, 142, 246

Nintendo: competition, 47, 51; Game Boy, 46; games, 7, 16; history, 45–46; Wii, 45, 48–51, 55, 59, 60, 65; *Wii Fit*, 50–51, 59

Nintendo Entertainment System (NES), 16, 46, 52

North American Soccer League (NASL), 69, 77

NRDC, *see* National Resources Defense Council

NTT DoCoMo, 132

O₂ (company), 238–39

O₂ arena, 192, 237–38, 239

O₂ Dome, 192, 237–39

Oak Investment Partners, 56

Obrestad, Annette, 154

Olympic Games: ancient, 173; Atlanta (1996), 22, 25; Barcelona (1992), 21–22; Beijing (2008), 19–20, 22–27, 37, 82, 159; future, 26, 238; London (2012), 238; Los Angeles (1984), 5–6; sports-anchored development and, 187–88; stars, 19–20, 77; Sydney (2000), 187–88; television broadcasts, 19–27, 37; Vancouver (2010), 26

O'Neal, Shaquille, 106, 127

Online content, *see* Internet

Orange, 145

Oriole Park at Camden Yards, 175, 187

Packer, Billy, 162

Packer, Kerry Francis Bullmore, 43

Pagers, 131

Parker, Mark, 135–36, 137

PartyPoker.net, 150, 151

PASPA, *see* Professional and Amateur Sports Protection Act

Pawar, Sharad, 183

Pelé (Edson Arantes do Nascimento), 69, 77

Pelé Sports AG, 77

Pentagram, 207–8

Pepsi, 6, 74, 77

Pepsi Center (Denver), 191

Perisol, Aaron, 19–20

Personal brands, *see* Athlete branding

Personal computers, *see* Computers

PETCO Park, 188

PGA Championships, 215, 216

Phelps, Michael, 19–20, 24

Piracy, 115–16

Plaschke, Bill, 69

Podcasts, 122

Poker: boom in, 150–51; as game of skill, 169, 170; origins, 148; stars, 147, 154; on television, 149, 150, 152; websites, 150, 158–59; World Poker Tour, 149, 150; World Series of Poker, 147–54, 170

PokerChamps.com, 158–59

PokerStars.com, 147, 150, 151

Pollack, Jeffrey, 97, 152–53, 154

Polo Ralph Lauren, 246

Pong, 51

Populous, 206

Potrock, Ken, 178, 229, 230, 231, 232, 233, 234, 235

Powell, Boog, 187

Prague, Strahov Stadium, 199

PRIDE Fighting Championships, 35

The Pride of the Yankees, 94

Prime Licensing, 77

Princeton University baseball team, 2, 15, 27

Prodigy, 106

Professional and Amateur Sports Protection Act of 1992 (PASPA), 156, 168, 169, 171

ProTrade, 111–12

Public financing, 174, 189, 190, 193, 198, 205, 223

Puck, Wolfgang, 192

Qualcomm, 130

Radio: advertising, 14; car, 94; ESPN, 122, 129, 194; iPhone applications, 122; satellite, 131; sports broadcasts, 14, 31, 93–94

Radio frequency identification (RFID), 217, 218, 219

Rasmussen, Bill, 4

Rasmussen, Scott, 4

Raymer, Greg, 150

RCA, 14–15

Reagan, Ronald, 94

Real estate, *see* Sports-anchored development; Stadiums and arenas
Reality television shows, 32, 33
Real Madrid, 72, 73, 216
Red Bull, 152, 239–43
Red Bull Racing, 241
Reebok, 82
Reilly, Rick, 127
RFID, *see* Radio frequency identification
Ricci, Ron, 177, 217
Rich Foods, Inc., 236
Rivals.com, 107, 108–11, 119
R. J. Reynolds Tobacco Company, 236
Rolex, 246
Rome, ancient, 2, 173
Ross, Stephen, 215
Rossetti, 200–203
Rossetti, Matt, 177, 200–203
Rotisserie Leagues, 8. *See also* Fantasy sports leagues
Rozelle, Pete, 4, 100
Running shoes, Nike+, 135–38, 142, 246
Ruth, Babe, 14
RWDI Labs, 225

Sabol, Steve, 204
SAD, *see* Sports-anchored development
SAFE Port Act, 151
San Diego Padres, 99, 188
San Francisco Giants, 99, 132, 145, 175–76
Santiago Bernabéu Stadium, 216–17
Sarnoff, David, 14–15
Satellite radio, 131
Satellite television, 24, 37, 101, 134, 135, 214–15
Schaefer Brewing Company, 236
Scoreboards, electronic, 211, 219, 227
Scout.com, 108, 110
SEG, *see* Semaphore Entertainment Group
Sega, 16, 46
Selig, Allan H. "Bud," 100
Semaphore Entertainment Group (SEG), 32
Sepso, Michael, 18, 56, 57, 58

Shanghai Sharks, 81, 82, 84
Sharapova, Maria, 246
Short message service (SMS), 132
Showtime, 28
Silver, Adam, 18, 82, 83
Sirius XM, 131
Skateboarding, 78–81
Skipper, John, 17, 26, 29, 30, 31
SlingBox, 105, 132–35
SlingCatcher, 134–35
Sling Media, 132–35, 140, 141
Smart cards, 217, 218
SMS, *see* Short message service
Snyder, Jimmy "The Greek," 149
Soccer: Austrian teams, 240; in Dubai, 182; English Premier League, 68, 71, 114, 132, 199, 233; fantasy leagues, 114; schools, 183; stadiums, 70, 199, 206, 216–18, 240, 241–42; in United States, 69–70, 73, 77; video games, 53, 65; World Cup, 40, 70, 72, 76, 217; youth, 69, 72, 232, 233. *See also* Beckham, David; Major League Soccer
Social networking sites, 111, 112–14, 119–20
Softball, 103, 232
Softbank, 158
Sony Electronics, 211, 212
Sony Playstation, 7, 47, 48, 50, 51, 54, 55, 105
Spain, Santiago Bernabéu Stadium, 216–17
Speed Network, 176, 213
Spike TV, 33, 34, 35
Spitz, Mark, 19
Sponsorships: distinction from advertising, 255n; of ESPN *College GameDay*, 31; event organizers and, 245–46, 247; by gambling-related businesses, 166; mobile technology and, 145; at Olympics, 5; of online games, 57; partnerships with athletes, 88–89; at stadiums, 208, 223, 226–27; television, 44; of Ultimate Fighting Championship, 35; World Series of Poker, 152, 159
Sporting events. *See also* Gambling;

Game-day experiences; Televised sporting events; Ticket sales
Sportsalert.com, 132
Sports-anchored development (SAD): challenges, 197; Coors Field, 189–91, 195, 200; critical success factors, 202–3; designs, 175, 187, 189, 203; Dubai Sports City, 179–80, 182–86, 197; ESPN Wide World of Sports Complex, 183, 229–35, 244, 245; failures, 196, 197, 198; future of, 195, 198–99, 202–3; game-day experiences, 175–77, 195–96, 203; history of concept, 186–89; L.A. LIVE, 191–94, 198; local businesses, 188, 221–22; mixed-use developments, 200, 201–2, 203; O₂ Dome, 192, 237–39; for Olympics, 187–88; public financing, 189, 190, 193, 198; relations with surrounding areas, 196, 221–22; revenues, 196, 199; self-contained, 197–98
Sports and entertainment convergence, see Convergence
Sports business industry, 9
SportsCenter, 4, 121, 129, 194, 235
Sports Illustrated, 106, 113–14, 127
Sportsline.com, 8
Sportsline USA, 106
Sports medicine, 183
SportsPage Score Pager, 131
Sprint, 103, 127, 128, 129, 220
Sprint FanView, 176, 214, 216
Sprint Nextel Series, 213
Stadiums and arenas: adaptive reuse, 198–99; amenities, 175; college, 174; designs, 175, 187, 189, 206–8, 222; at Dubai Sports City, 182; environmental sustainability, 223–24; evolution, 173–76; fan experiences, 173, 175–77; flexible uses, 174, 177, 220, 222–23, 227; lighting, 211; luxury suites, 175, 207, 209, 218; naming rights, 175, 189, 210, 233, 235–36, 245; public financing, 174, 189, 190, 205, 223; revenue sources, 175; sports-entertainment mix, 173; ticket sales, 217; traffic and parking, 226; University of

Phoenix Stadium, 204–10, 222. *See also* Sports-anchored development; Venue technology
StadiumVision, 218, 219
Stakeholders: in at-home convergence, 17; in corporate marketing, 247; in gambling, 93; in mobile technology, 93; in sports business industry, 9
STAPLES Center, 191, 192, 193, 194
Starwave, 106
Station Casinos, 32
Steinberg & Moorad Sports Management, 111
Stern, David, 134, 193
Stewart, James "Bubba," 242
Str8 Rippin, 58
Strahov Stadium, 199
Strategic alliances, 9, 61, 118–19, 120, 166
StubHub, 102
Sun Bowl, 236
Sungui Arena Complex, 200, 201–2
Sun Life Stadium, 215
Super Bowl: betting, 160, 162; commercials, 6, 7, 27; games, 204–5, 210, 215
Superstars, 27
Supreme Court, 104
SV Austria Salzburg, 240
Swimmers, 19–20, 24

TAG Heuer, 246
Target, 234, 245
Tatweer, 185
Taylor, Tom "TSquared," 58
TBS, 28, 117
Tchao, Michael, 97, 136, 137–38
Techniland Company, 187
Technology: advances, 95; radio frequency identification, 217, 218, 219; television, 40–41. *See also* Computers; Mobile technology; Venue technology; Video games
Televised sporting events: audiences, 3, 4, 36, 37, 43–44, 118; broadcast rights, 28, 37, 44, 141; college baseball, 2, 15, 27; content control, 38–40; convergence

with entertainment, 15–16; demand, 24, 36–37; early, 2–3, 15, 27–29; future of, 122–23; Olympic Games, 19–27, 37; pay-per-view events, 21, 28, 32, 34, 35, 36, 54; in primetime, 3–5, 21–22; regulations, 40; variety shows, 15; year-round programming, 36–37. *See also* ESPN

Television: convergence with Internet, 118–19; development, 14–15; digital video recording, 133; high-definition, 24, 37, 123, 218; reality shows, 32, 33; satellite, 24, 37, 101, 134, 135, 214–15; SlingBox technology, 105, 132–35; technological change, 40–41; 3D, 40, 122–23. *See also* Cable television; *and individual networks*

Television commercials: during Olympics, 24, 25; during sporting events, 6–7; during Super Bowl, 6, 7, 27; targeted, 39; for Verizon V CAST, 125. *See also* Advertising

Tengen, 52

Tennis: betting scandals, 159; in Dubai, 181, 186; U.S. Open, 216; video games, 60; Wimbledon tournament, 3, 246

Terry, Shannon, 108

Texas Rangers, 225

Text messaging, 132

Thackery, Ted, Jr., 149

Thomson, Bobby, 94

Thorpe, Malcolm, 177, 179, 180, 184, 185–86

THQ, 35, 52, 53–56, 62

Ticketmaster, 144

Ticket sales: buy-backs, 217; with mobile technology, 141, 145, 146; online, 102, 107, 116

Tickets.com, 102, 143–46

Tillman, Pat, 208

Time magazine, 5

Time Warner Cable, 28

T-Mobile, 129

Toro Rosso Racing, 241

Torres, Dara, 19

Toshiba, 48

Trans World International (TWI), 3

Travel Channel, 149

TVG, 160

TWI, *see* Trans World International

Tyree, David, 204–5

UAE, *see* United Arab Emirates

Ueberroth, Peter, 5

UFC, *see* Ultimate Fighting Championship

UFC Gyms, 35

UFC Magazine, 35

Ultimate Fighter, 33

Ultimate Fighting Championship (UFC), 32–36, 62

United Arab Emirates (UAE), 180. *See also* Dubai

U.S. Open, 216

U.S. Specialty Sports Association, 232

Universal Sports, 103

University of Kentucky, 109

University of Michigan, 211

University of Nebraska, 29

University of Phoenix, 210

University of Phoenix Stadium, 204–10, 222

Unlawful Internet Gambling Enforcement Act of 2006, 151, 156, 159, 164

USA Today, 6

Valentine, Bobby, 225

Veeck, Bill, 211

Venues, *see* At-venue convergence; Sports-anchored development; Stadiums and arenas

Venue technology: audio, 212, 217; challenges, 221, 227; cost-benefit analysis, 228; electronic scoreboards, 211, 219, 227; future of, 220–21; history, 210–12; integration, 218; IP networks, 208, 226; Kangaroo TV, 212–16; lighting, 211; perceptions of, 221; return on investment, 202; role in game-day experiences, 212, 216, 219, 220–22, 228; security systems,

209, 217–18; smart cards, 217, 218; in sports-anchored developments, 202; at University of Phoenix Stadium, 208–9; Wi-Fi networks, 175–76, 204–5, 209, 212, 216–17, 219

Verizon, 90, 91–92, 109, 152; V CAST, 125–27, 128–31, 139

Versus, 34, 39

Viacom, 33

Vickers, Brian, 241

Video games: advertising in, 55, 60; future of, 59–63, 65–66; history, 16, 45–48, 51–53; *Madden Football*, 7, 16, 49, 52, 64, 90, 127; market, 48–50, 55, 59–60, 61; on mobile devices, 55, 59, 60–61; online, 55, 56–58, 62–63, 64; professional leagues, 56–58, 62, 63; single-athlete, 91; skateboarding, 79, 80; social, 59; subscriptions, 127; *Undisputed*, 35; Wii, 45, 48–50

Video scoreboards, 211, 219, 227

Vodafone, 72

Walsh, Pete, 219

Walt Disney Co., 41, 45–46, 127, 183, 229, 249. *See also* Disney World; ESPN Wide World of Sports Complex

Warped Tour, 176

Washington State University, 30

WCSN, *see* World Championship Sports Network

Websites, *see* Internet

WEC, *see* World Extreme Cagefighting

Weissmuller, Johnny, 77

Welles, Orson, 14

Wells, H. G., 14

WGN, 28, 117

White, Dana, 32, 33

White, Shaun, 242

Wide World of Sports, 15, 20, 78

Wii, 45, 48–51, 55, 59, 60, 65

Wii Fit, 50–51, 59

William Morris Endeavor, 77

Williams, Reggie, 229, 234

Williams, Venus, 181

Wireless technology, *see* Mobile technology

WiseDV, 215–16

Witherspoon, Larry, 97, 143–46

WMCA-AM, 94

Woods, Tiger, 16, 65, 85, 91, 106, 181, 184

World Championship Sports Network (WCSN), 103, 105

World Cup, 40, 70, 72, 76, 217

World Extreme Cagefighting (WEC), 34

World Poker Tour (WPT), 149, 150

World Series of Poker (WSOP), 147–54, 170; celebrities, 151; history, 148–49; sponsors, 152, 159; television broadcasts, 147, 148, 149, 150

World Wrestling Entertainment (WWE), 28, 34, 36, 52, 53–55, 62

WPT, *see* World Poker Tour

Wray, Edward, 157

WSOP, *see* World Series of Poker

WWE, *see* World Wrestling Entertainment

WWE Smackdown, 53, 54–55

Wynkoop Brewing Company, 190

XFL, 28

X Games, 5, 79, 122

Yahoo!, 109–10

Yahoo! Sports, 16, 26, 104, 106–7, 114

Yamauchi, Fusajiro, 45

Yankee Entertainment and Sports Network, 28

Yao Ming, 81–84

Yao Ming Foundation, 84

Youth sports: academies, 72, 180, 182–83, 184; high school, 108–11, 234; tourism, 183

Yu, David, 97, 158, 159–60

Zuffa, LLC, 32–33, 34, 35, 36